W9-ATU-133

Church of the Brethren: Yesterday and Today

Edited by
Donald F. Durnbaugh

Contributors: Carl F. Bowman, S. Loren Bowman, Dale W. Brown, Pamela Brubaker, Karen Spohr Carter, B. Merle Crouse, Allen C. Deeter, Donald F. Durnbaugh, David B. Eller, Dale R. Stoffer, and Edward K. Ziegler

BRETHREN PRESS
Elgin, Illinois

Copyright © 1986 by Brethren Press, 1451 Dundee Avenue, Elgin, IL 60120.

All rights reserved. No portion of this book may be reproduced in any form or by any process or technique without the written consent of the publisher, except for brief quotations embodied in critical articles or reviews.

Cover by Debbie Noffsinger.

Portions of this book were previously published in *Church of the Brethren: Past and Present* (Elgin, IL: Brethren Press, 1971).

Library of Congress Cataloging in Publication Data
    Church of the Brethren.

        Bibliography: p.
        Includes index.
        1. Church of the Brethren.   I. Bowman, Carl F.
    II. Durnbaugh, Donald F.
    BX7821.2C482   1986   286'.5   86-4168
    ISBN 0-87178-151-4

Manufactured in the United States of America

Contributors

Carl F. Bowman. Assistant Professor of Sociology, Bridgewater College; Bridgewater, VA

S. Loren Bowman. Former General Secretary, General Board, Church of the Brethren; La Verne, CA

Dale W. Brown. Professor of Christian Theology, Bethany Theological Seminary; Oak Brook, IL

Pamela Brubaker. Union Theological Seminary; New York, NY

Karen Spohr Carter. Ordained minister; former member, General Board, Church of the Brethren; Daleville, VA

B. Merle Crouse. Staff for New Church Development, Parish Ministries Commission, General Board, Church of the Brethren; St. Cloud, FL

Allen C. Deeter. Administrative Coordinator, Brethren Colleges Abroad; Professor of Religion and Philosophy, Manchester College; North Manchester, IN

Donald F. Durnbaugh. Former Professor of Church History, Bethany Theological Seminary; former Moderator of the Annual Conference, Church of the Brethren; Huntingdon, PA

David B. Eller. Editor, Glencoe Publishing; Elgin, IL

Dale R. Stoffer. Pastor; Adjunct Professor, Ashland Theological Seminary; Columbus, OH

Edward K. Ziegler was an author, editor and pastor.

Contents

Foreword

There is a bit of false advertising in the title of this book. It purports to be about the Church of the Brethren "yesterday and today." Having read it with care, let me propose that the subtitle is not quite accurate. This is a book about tomorrow, about the Church of the Brethren tomorrow. It is an expression of respect and concern, of some anxiety about the humans who make it up and of considerable faith in the Lord who pulls it into the future.

That a book with so much history in it should be about the future may seem like a strange notion to some. History, in many eyes, is about "old, unhappy, far-off things, and battles long ago." They think of historians as antique-shop keepers and of history as relics under glass, to be dusted off for the curious few. Historians and history can fit such images. They need not and should not and, in the case of this book, do not.

To say that history is about projects and projections, about futurers, is one thing. To show it is another. Suppose we argue that in order to act well one must know who one is. Amnesiacs are disoriented. People who lack identity are victims, often passive. Individuals can be cured of amnesia and can find their identity. All they need is a functioning memory and an ambition to locate themselves. Social movements, and the Church of the Brethren is one, have no memory beyond the lifetime of those who make it up individually. They need more. Their history gives this to them.

History and identity: how do we connect them? Here's one way. A graduate theological school asked its specialist students either to take courses or pass tests in a number of areas, one of them being history or, in this case, church history. No exemptions. An enterprising student thought he would try to be the first exception. He asked for an interview with the head of the Church History field. "Professor, I'd like to take neither the courses nor the exam." All right, make your case. "You see, professor, I am not interested in the past. It does nothing to me or for me and I do nothing for it. It does nothing to inform my work as a modern theologian; I deal with ideas, with abstractions, with logic—not with stories, with the concrete, with events." The professor was moved. "That's a very interesting notion. How did you come to be so historyless? Tell me." The student replied: "Aw, prof, you wouldn't want me to take up so much of your time. To tell you why history does nothing for me I would have to go way back; I would have to tell you who I am and where I came from and all that happened to me along the way. . . ." The professor interrupted "You just lost." The student was describing quite well what history does. It explains us. It helps give us identity. It locates us and gives us power. Knowledge of the past, of a particular past, helps teach limits and inspires action.

You win, you do not lose, if you follow through with that kind of notion in reading this book. Non-members of the Church of the Brethren who read it, and I hope many will, will help understand this element of the whole church and thus see their place better than before. I assume more readers than not—except for us church historians and the like—will be members, will be "in the tradition." Some reject tradition; they want to start from scratch to find Utopia, greet the Millennium, or progress into the future. That does not work. As Eugene Goodheart said to a collegiate generation, speaking about the Greco-Roman and the Jewish-and-Christian lineages: "You may not possess the tradition, but the tradition possesses you."

The Church of the Brethren tradition "possesses" its children, its new generation, just as it comes to in the case of converts—of which, one hopes, there will be more in the future! Professor Durnbaugh and his colleagues unpack that tradition. Readers will learn, against the background of decades and centuries, why "this is how we do things," or "that isn't done among us," or "this we believe" or "this we reject." They can become self-conscious about what makes their identity and to whom they belong. They can get a hold on the present by understanding the past. Then they can work toward reform. That was another notion of the classic historians: we study the past in order to overcome the past.

To overcome the past: there are some aspects of the heritage that haunt, that limit. This book can help new generations or newcomers decide what is worth saving, what is worth restoring, what can be lightly left behind and what might need to be faced with courage. I found that it shattered many stereotypes. The Church of the Brethren tradition is much richer, more diverse, more pluralist, than its traditionalists or the nostalgic minded will let it be. Each reader will find different elements of the heritage that deserve revisiting or revising, but few will walk away unmindful or the sacrifice, the steadfastness, the devotion of foreparents. Few will get up from this reading without being more prepared to face tomorrow.

Theodor Adorno says that because most of history is the story of suffering, to forget or to intend to forget is to harm humanity, to disrespect the people who deserve to be remembered. Yet, as the second half of this book clearly shows, there is no interest at all in antiquarianism here. We could not, even if we chose to, live in the past. "The past is a foreign country; they do things differently there." The past can be burdening. There is also something of a "dead hand of tradition" that needs lifting. The chapters on polity, doctrine, mission, women, and several others show the challenges of today. Fortunately, their authors know that they must reach to the past for models, just as historian Durnbaugh, up front, in setting the historical stage, knows and shows that he and they are, indeed, talking about the future.

Martin E. Marty
The University of Chicago

Preface

This book is a successor to *The Church of the Brethren: Past and Present* (1971). It is not simply a revision to update what has happened in the denomination in the 15 intervening years; it is, in fact, a new book. It contains a new foreword, six completely new chapters, one chapter with new content and a revised section, four revised and updated chapters, and a new bibliographical essay.

The previous book retains its value in many ways. Present readers are encouraged to read chapters in that book to secure additional information not included in this one. After three printings, it was allowed to go out of print, to be succeeded by this volume. It is, however, available in many church libraries, in public and college libraries, and in private hands.

The editor and contributors to *The Church of the Brethren: Past and Present* have been pleased with the broad use and acceptance of their earlier book. Widely used in membership classes, church schools, colleges, and seminaries, it was generally acknowledged as the most complete current introduction to the life and work of the Church of the Brethren. A companion book is Emmert F. Bittinger, *Heritage and Promise* (1970, revised edition in 1983). A helpful study guide was made available for these two books: Allen C. Deeter, *Heirs of a Promise* (1972).

The 1971 volume was prepared originally for translation into German for publication in the ecumenical series, *Die Kirchen der Welt*; the German title is *Die Kirche der Brüder: Vergangenheit und Gegenwart*. The publishers, Evangelisches Verlagswerk, Stuttgart, generously allowed the English edition to be published by the Brethren Press. Contributors to the present volume also desire that their essays will make a contribution to ecumenical as well as denominational understanding. They associate themselves with the wish expressed in the 1971 volume: "It is . . . hoped that the book will be of some interest to the broader Christian community in describing the pilgrimage of a company of followers of Jesus Christ. Both the success and the failures here recorded may be instructive to those of all traditions who attempt to be faithful witnesses to Christian truth."

Although this book is devoted to the history and development of the Church of the Brethren, it also provides some limited information on other Brethren bodies. The chapter on "Beliefs" was written by a minister of the Brethren Church (Ashland, OH), Dale R. Stoffer. Other chapters were written by members of the Church of the Brethren. Their interpretations are their own; readers should understand that the book does not present an official, authorized denominational statement. Those wishing a concise introduction to the five largest Brethren groups should consult *Meet the Brethren*, ed. Donald F. Durnbaugh (1984).

Donald F. Durnbaugh
Oak Brook, IL

1

Early History

Donald F. Durnbaugh

On an August morning in 1708, five men and three women gathered at the small Eder Brook near the village of Schwarzenau in central Germany. Their purpose: to obey the command of Jesus Christ as they understood it by accepting baptism. In so doing they covenanted with each other to form a congregation of committed believers. By this simple but daring act they began a religious movement which numbers in 1985 some half-million adherents around the world within several denominations. The largest is called the Church of the Brethren; others, ranked in decreasing order by size, are the Fellowship of Grace Brethren Churches, the Brethren Church, the Old German Baptist Brethren, and the Dunkard Brethren. Yet smaller divisions of these five largest Brethren bodies exist as well.[1]

Many other religious groups have taken the biblical term *Brethren* as their name or as part of a name. This causes considerable confusion. The term *Brethren* used here refers only to those churches with lineage from the Schwarzenau congregation. Actually, those who came together in 1708 were reluctant to name themselves and simply called their group the "brethren," a term that in German referred equally to men and women. They were designated by outsiders in Europe as the New Baptists (*Neue Täufer*) or Schwarzenau Baptists to distinguish them from the Mennonites (*Alte Täufer*) with whom they had so much in common. Though the Brethren have had contacts with the Moravian Brethren, the Brethren in Christ (River Brethren), and the United Brethren, they should be distinguished from each. There was no historical connection with the 19th century British group known as the Christian Brethren or Plymouth Brethren.

In 1836 the Brethren decided that they should be known on legal papers as *Fraternity of German Baptists*; this they changed in 1871 to *German Baptist Brethren*. The latter name relates them to the Baptist movement, which has its own logic because the most striking of the Brethren practices is the baptism of adult believers by immersion (although this is by a threefold, forward motion not a single, backward motion as employed by Baptists). The form of baptism gave rise to a common nickname for Brethren: *Dunkers* (derived from the German *tunken*, to immerse). The nickname is often corrupted to *Dunkards* (generally disliked by Brethren); it is by this name that they are still known in parts of the United States. Since 1908 the official denominational designation for the largest branch of the movement has been the *Church of the Brethren*. In recent years there has been some agitation for a change in nomenclature by those who consider the name to discriminate against women but no formal request has been presented or adopted.

The brief historical sketch here presented intends to provide a general framework of information for the more detailed discussions of specific topics which follow. It is a concise narrative of the origin and expansion of the Brethren, necessarily touching only briefly on matters described more thoroughly in succeeding chapters. This plan will result in some repetition but offers in brief compass an overview of the Brethren movement which should be helpful.

Although many books and articles have been published about Brethren history, there is currently no adequate general historical account. The most comprehensive source of information is *The Brethren Encyclopedia* (1983–1984) in three volumes. Several of the larger Brethren bodies have published histories of their own development, all of which include information of the shared early history. There is evidence of a certain maturity in historical understanding, which gives promise of more useful histories in the future.

For many years Brethren did not encourage record-keeping and historical writing; they understood such activities to tend toward vanity and self-serving. They refused to keep statistics, so that with the important exception of 1770 (when a Baptist historian noted their numbers) there are neither accurate general records of membership nor even lists of congregations until 1882. (Individual leaders of some congregations did keep lists of baptisms, hence of membership.) Brethren were generally opposed to higher education (although they appreciated literacy) and did relatively little in the way of publishing until the last half of the 19th century. They did publish hymnals and devotional books but did so without providing the names of authors. So far was the penchant for humility carried out that Brethren in the 18th century ordinarily allowed initials only to be placed on their gravestones, made from common fieldstones.

European Beginnings

Brethren find their beginnings at the confluence of three religious streams—Reformed Protestantism, Radical Pietism, and Evangelical Anabaptism. Most of those who became Brethren were originally members of German Reformed (Calvinist) Churches. Their early religious education was, therefore, one of mainline Protestantism. This explains why the Brethren have stood historically within the broad tradition of Protestant orthodoxy, accepting basic Protestant doctrines. Yet, the early Brethren had problems with the established status of the Reformed Church, which they held to have become sterile and over-institutionalized. They were part of a renewal movement known as Pietism.

Pietism as a reform movement within German Protestantism is a well-known fact and has been duly recorded in the annals of church history. Many studies have analyzed the Pietist attempts to renew the church, to recover the essence of the Reformation by breaking through a hardened and disputatious Protestant scholasticism. Pietists sought to reform life to complete the earlier reformation of doctrine. Less studied is the dissenting wing of Pietism best designated as Radical Pietism. This had many Pietist emphases but was further marked by dependence upon the mystical theology of Jakob Boehme (1575–1624) and a policy of separation from the state churches. The historical understanding of the Radical Pietists was shaped by the learned Gottfried Arnold (1666–1714), who convinced them of the necessity of looking to the early Christian church as their standard and also of the decadence of the institutional churches of their day.

Thus by its own self-understanding, Radical Pietism tended to be antagonistic to church structures but several movements did crystallize from it. One was the Community of True Inspiration, founded in 1714. Stemming originally from the Camisard movement among suppressed Huguenots in late 17th century France, the Inspired triggered a wordy war of books and pamphlets from the ranks of the theologians. This was because of their astonishing claim that their leaders—J. F. Rock (1687–1749) and E. L. Gruber (1665–1728), with others—had the gift of speaking under direct, divine inspiration. Such important figures as A. H. Francke (1663–1727) and Count N. L. von Zinzendorf (1700–1760) were impressed by the claims of these New Prophets, who traveled as far afield as the Netherlands and Switzerland. In 1843 their remaining members migrated to America where they formed communitarian colonies, first near Buffalo, New York, and then at Amana, Iowa.

Emerging from Radical Pietism at the same time, but of quite a different temper, was the Brethren movement. Although numerically larger than the Inspired, the early Brethren passed virtually without notice by the scholarly world. Scattered condemnations in synodical protocols, some documents in administrative archives, a few critical comments in the writings of the Radical Pietists—these are about all that researchers have discovered to date. Yet, unlike the Amana movement, which is currently quiescent, the Brethren are vital, if relatively small, Free Church with worldwide commitments and contacts.

There are reasons for the lack of notice of the Brethren at the time of their inception. First, the Brethren lived to themselves and bothered no one. They were the kind of people sometimes called the "Quiet Ones in the Land" (*Die Stillen im Lande*). They ordinarily only came to the attention of the authorities because their immersion baptisms caused public excitement or by their refusal to accept military service. The Brethren were indeed zealous in spreading their faith both in Europe and America, but over the years they have been a retiring, inoffensive, and unobstructive people. A historian in colonial America said of them: "They are meek and pious Christians, and have justly acquired the character of the *Harmless Tunkers*."[2]

Another reason for the lack of notice is that within twenty-five years of their start most of them had left the Continent for America. How they might have developed had they stayed in Europe is impossible to say. The fact is that they left, and their history has been primarily centered on North America.

Perhaps the most important reason for their obscurity in Europe is that as the Brethren formed themselves into a community (*Gemeinde*) they discarded many of the concepts and practices of Radical Pietism. These included Boehmism, communitarianism, celibacy, refusal to work, antisacramentalism, and vocal criticism of authority. The best way to understand the early Brethren is to see them as a Radical Pietist group which appropriated an Anabaptist view of the church. They held to a gathered church of believers, the discipline of church members, a nonresistant approach to the state, and a theology of discipleship. To be sure, they retained some characteristics of their Pietist background, yet they were almost indistinguishable by outsiders from the Mennonites. These descendants of the 16th-century Anabaptists had won for themselves a tenuous tolerance in the Palatinate as sturdy farmers and in other areas of Germany as skilled craftsman. Therefore, in most places where the Brethren came they were considered to be identical with the Mennonites and consequently enjoyed similar toleration.

As many of the Brethren came from the Palatinate, it is necessary to portray briefly the situation obtaining there at the start of the 18th century. The area had hardly recovered from the devastation of the Thirty Years' War (1616–1648) when repeated French invasions during the War of the League of Augsburg (1688–1697) caused renewed havoc. Added to this were the burdens of an unfeeling ruler, a profligate court, an oppressive bureaucracy, and several years of drought and crop failures. The result was widespread unrest. So many subjects left for other lands that the term *Palatine* became the generic term for all German immigrants in America.

In the religious sphere there was much turmoil. The Reformed Church was the official or established faith in the Palatinate. Under the *Simultaneum* (1698) those Palatines who had converted to Roman Catholicism during the French occupation were guaranteed protection. As there were also some Lutherans in the Electorate—which had repeatedly changed its official religion under the principle *cuius regio, eius religio* (as the price, so the religion)—there was continual strife among the three confessions. The Reformed consistory (church office) repeatedly called its clergy to task for unbecoming behavior such as drunkenness at funerals. By all accounts, church life was a low ebb. Many of the devout hungered for nourishing spiritual food.

This some of them found in the teaching of Ernest Christoph Hochmann von Hochenau (1670–1721), a Radical Pietist leader. Of noble birth, Hochmann studied at several universities and seemed destined to a promising career in law or diplomacy. But after his conversion under Francke at the University of Halle, he refused attractive positions in order to spend the rest of his life as an itinerant evangelist of radical persuasion. The noted writer J. H. Jung-Stilling (1740-1817) ranked him as one of the "mainsprings of enthusiasm, pietism, separatism, and along with it, of true Christianity in Germany." Hochmann devoted his life to his own conversions and to the "thorough awakening and conversion of his brethren in Christ." (M. Goebel). In doing so, he came into conflict with the authorities, especially when he taught that separation from "Babylon"—the state churches—was essential for true salvation. All contemporaries agree that he was a personable and winsome individual, who quickly found friends and supporters among the nobility and the humble alike.[3]

In 1706 Hochmann was invited to come to Schriesheim, a few miles north of Heidelberg. There he held meeting for bible study and prayer in a mill owned by Alexander Mack (1679–1735), a member of a substantial family of the Reformed faith. Mack became one of Hochmann's closest associates and accompanied him on some of his travels. The Pietists at Schriesheim preached to laborers coming home from the fields, and soon work of their activity reached the local government. Soldiers sent to seize them reported that the group had left the area, but Hochmann and some companions were seized in nearby Mannheim and placed at hard labor. Rather than cease participating in the illegal conventicles, Mack sold his property and left Schriesheim with wife and children.

Similar incidents took place in Strasbourg (France), in the Basel area (Switzerland), in Württemberg (Germany), and elsewhere in the Palatinate, with much the same result. Those unwilling to accept passively the state church dictates had to leave their homes, often suffering the confiscation of their personal and real property. In a few cases children were taken from Pietist families to be raised by others.

Hochmann had earlier lived in Wittgenstein and likely indicated to his sympathizers that relative religious freedom was available there. This isolated and modestly-sized county in the region between the Eder and Lahn rivers became notorious as a place of refuge for religious dissenters. They clustered at Schwarzenau/Eder, the site of a manor house belonging to the noble Sayn-Wittgenstein family. Count Henrich Albrecht (1658–1723) and his sisters shocked their peers by associating with these radical commoners on a familiar basis.

As might be expected, many among the several hundred refugees who gathered in Schwarzenau and the surrounding hills there were intense discussions about the true faith. Some became discouraged and returned to their homes and their former faiths. Others became religious hermits. A third grouping was unwilling to return to the state churches and also disliked the extreme individualism of most Radical Pietists. The issue which brought matters to head was baptism. As the Wittgenstein radicals studied the New Testament and the lives of the early Christians they were impressed by the biblical injunction to be baptized upon their faith as "an appeal to God for a clear conscience, through the resurrection of Jesus Christ" (1 Pet. 3:21). Some became convinced that a congregation was necessary if they were to be completely obedient to the New Testament teachings. A visit by two "foreign brethren" (who may have been Dutch Collegiants) brought these growing concerns into the open.

Some of the Schwarzenau residents decided to send an open letter to those of their acquaintance, particularly in the Palatinate, announcing their intention to proceed with baptism. (They had earlier written to Hochmann to ask his opinion; he replied that water baptism was commanded biblically but cautioned that they not become sectarian by demanding it of everyone.) The open letter stated, in part:

> Our inner joy increased and we were strengthened in the Lord not to be negligent, and to come together in the fear of the Lord. . . . As we found that we all agreed with one spirit in this high calling, we have decided to announce this to our beloved brethren and friends through an open letter. This is to see whether they also find themselves convinced in their hearts to help confirm this high calling to the pride and glory of our Savior Jesus Christ, and to follow the Creator and Fulfiller of Faith. . . . So, then, if more brethren wish to begin this high act of baptism with us out of brotherly unity according to the teachings of Christ and the apostles, we announce in humbleness that we are interceding together in prayer and fasting with God.[4]

In late summer 1708 eight persons accepted baptism in the Eder Brook and thus began the Brethren movement. An unnamed brother baptized Mack, their leader, who proceeded to baptize his baptizer and then the other men and women.

News of the event spread rapidly, although it had been performed privately. Criticism came from two sides: from the rulers of surrounding territories who saw in the Brethren a revival of the kingdom of Anabaptists at Münster (1534–1535) and from the Radical Pietists, including Hochmann, who looked upon the development as an unfortunate fall back into the institutionalized error which had they known in the state churches. Count Henrich Albrecht was able to ward off outside attacks and Mack wrote two treatises (*Basic Questions*, 1713; *Rights and Ordinances*, 1715) to answer the religious critics. Thus there was time for the group to develop and expand.

They immediately began to witness to their newfound faith and gained converts among the inhabitants of Wittgenstein. Meetings in Schwarzenau grew so large that no house there could hold them; they then held meetings on the lawn. They sent several ministers on journeys into Switzerland, the Palatinate, Hamburg-Altona, the Netherlands, and elsewhere to found new congregations. The most important of the daughter groups came into being in the Marienborn area near Büdingen, where there was also considerable religious toleration. This branch, however, was forced to leave in 1715 and made its way to Krefeld. Brethren became active in that area on the Lower Rhine, much to the dismay of the local Reformed clergy. One of the annoyed officials satirized the religious pluralism there (which he found so distasteful) in this verse:

> Lutheran and Mennonite,
> Catholic and Israelite,
> Calvinist and New Baptist,
> all in Krefeld now exist.[5]

Records of the early years of Brethren life are spotty; however, it is known that often missioners and their converts were imprisoned, fined and otherwise punished. The most noted incident involved six men of Solingen, members of the Reformed faith, who were baptized by Brethren in the Wupper River. They were seized and imprisoned until several theological faculties could be asked for appropriate penalties. The mildest punishment recommended was lifelong incarceration at hard labor, which sentence was imposed. The six were sent to the border fortress at Jülich, where they suffered for nearly four years until release through the intervention of some Dutch gentlemen. Another brother, Christian Liebe (1670–1757), was sentenced to the Sicilian galleys for preaching in Bern, Switzerland, but was also eventually released through Dutch and Swiss assistance.

The Krefeld congregation provided the first contingent to migrate, leaving for Pennsylvania in 1719. Some internal problems about church discipline contributed to the economic and religious pressures experienced by Brethren as motivations for migration. The first considerable party of Germans to go to Pennsylvania had left from Krefeld in 1683, and it is not surprising that the Brethren turned to the Quaker-directed colony in pursuit of religious freedom and economic independence. The Reformed clergy from the area reported the Brethren departure. The General Synod noted its satisfaction that they had left and cautioned the pastors "to be very much on guard lest similar enthusiasts should insinuate themselves in the future."[6]

The original Schwarzenau Brethren left Wittgenstein in 1720, but whether it was because of religious suppression or the lack of economic support is not clear. They went to West Friesland in the Netherlands, where they settled in a marsh colony called Surhuisterveen. Dutch Collegiants provided aid for the trip to Friesland, and some from this conventicle-type society soon became members. In 1729 Alexander Mack led a large party of Brethren to Pennsylvania, at the urging of the Krefeld group which had emigrated earlier. Others left Europe in the 1730's, so that by 1740 most of the Brethren had departed. There are some slight references in the 1740s to Brethren remaining in Europe, but the remnants seemed either to have relapsed into complete separatism or to have joined a like-minded body such as the Mennonites.

There are no definite figures on the size that the Brethren attained in Europe, but it could have been hardly more than several hundred. One list drawn up in 1899 totaled about 250. Be that as it may, the Brethren turned their backs on the inhospitable Old World and sought their future in the New.

Colonial America

Christmas Day, 1723, marked the reactivation of the Brethren movement on American soil. After the arrival of the first group of immigrants in 1719, the newcomers busied themselves with establishing livelihoods in and around Germantown (north of Philadelphia) and farther inland. Some were craftsmen, especially weavers, and many became farmers because of the cheap land available. In 1722 Peter Becker (1687–1758) and two others visited the scattered Brethren and informed them of the intention to begin regular meetings that fall. The initiative found immediate support and church meetings were held in Germantown until bad winter weather made travel too difficult. This renewed interest continued in 1723, and soon some of those attending asked to be received as members by baptism.

The Pennsylvanians wrote to Friesland to secure advice on what to do; the answer came back that they should choose some apt person as their minister and proceed with the baptism. Becker, noted for his piety and fervent prayers, was chosen as the first minister in America. The first baptism and accompanying love feast was then held on December 25, 1723. The events sparked a remarkable awakening, especially among the young people, of revival proportions. This took place shortly before the Great Awakening which swept through the American colonies with such lasting effects on the course of religion in North America. An informed observer writing later suggested that the Brethren activity represented the first of many waves of revivals affecting the German population in the colonies.

In the autumn of 1724 the entire male membership of the Germantown congregation set forth on an evangelistic tour in the wilds of "Penn's Woods." Their expedition led to the formation of two new congregations, at Coventry and at Conestoga. (Another settlement near the Indian Creek was linked to the mother congregation.) The future seemed bright for the expansion of the Brethren witness, but serious division was in store. One of those baptized at Conestoga was Conrad Beissel (1691–1768), who thought himself a religious genius, which in some ways he undoubtedly was. A native of Eberbach/Neckar in Germany, Beissel had come into contact with Pietism as a journeyman baker in the Palatinate and Wetteravia. He came to the American shores in 1720 in the hope of joining a religious community known as the "Woman in the Wilderness" (Rev. 12:6), only to find it had dispersed before his arrival. He spent a year as a weaving apprentice of Peter Becker before going into the forest with a companion to live as hermits.

Following Beissel's baptism, his evident gifts made him the obvious choice to lead the new Conestoga congregation. Unfortunately for the Brethren, Beissel was determined to go his own way. He immediately introduced such doctrines as direct revelation (held to be superior to the scripture) and the necessity of celibacy; he also contended for certain Jewish practices such as dietary requirements and the observance of Saturday as the day of worship. These innovations quickly caused friction with the Germantown Brethren and led finally to a split in 1728. Not even the reconciling efforts of Mack when he reached American in 1729 were successful in shaking Beissel from his purpose.

His new admirers followed him when he moved farther into the wilderness, into what is now Lancaster County. They built crude huts around his cabin, after the model of the early Egyptian monastic communities. By the late 1730s a full-fledged Protestant monastery had taken form, with large buildings and three orders (brothers, sisters, and "householders," that is, families who lived nearby and belonged to the congregation). Ephrata, as it was called, became famous not only for its monastic qualities but also because of its cultural achievements. Choral music, printing, illuminating of manuscripts (*Fraktur*)—all reached a high state of perfection. Ephrata's fame spread across the Atlantic and accounts of it were printed in ecclesiastical journals in Germany. At its height, Ephrata counted as many as 350 members. Beissel's death, the increasing inroads of civilization around the monastery, and the self-sacrificial service of the community in turning their institution into a military hospital during the Revolutionary War, all played a role in its decline. The last monastic members died in the 19th century; some of the buildings still stand today as a state-administered historic shrine.

Despite the serious defection caused by Beissel, the Brethren went on to plant other congregations in colonies. By 1770 there were fifteen in Pennsylvania and one in New Jersey. Many of the Brethren or their descendants left that area in search for better land, and seventeen other congregations were founded before 1770 in Maryland (the first in 1743), Virginia (1752), North Carolina (1742), South Carolina (1748), and possibly in Georgia. A careful census compiled by the Baptist historian Morgan Edwards (1722–1795) listed over 1,500 baptized members and 42 ministers. Edwards estimated that the number of individuals related to the Brethren was five times the number of members. (Recent research has located other Brethren settlements not in the 1770 list.) There were few meetinghouses, as they preferred to "meet from house to house in imitation of the primitive church." The first meetinghouse was that of Germantown, built in 1770 and still standing, although in altered form. The oldest unchanged structure is the meetinghouse at Pricetown, Pennsylvania, a severely plain stone building constructed in 1777.

Brethren and Mennonites often settled in the same areas and had much in common. Relationships were occasionally strained because of the tendency of some of the Mennonites to join the Brethren, a more evangelistic group. According to contemporary reports, they found more spiritual life among the pietistically-tinged Brethren; the practice of immersion baptism was also appealing to bible-loving Mennonites. The Quakers, as the proprietors of the colony where most of the Brethren lived, had great influence upon them, as can be seen in the style of dress, meetinghouse architecture, and in some parts of church polity (the phrases "Annual Meeting" and "query" for items of business brought before the meeting are cases in point).

The immediate cause of regular Annual Meetings was provided by the synods held in 1742–43 under the sponsorship of Count Zinzendorf. The Moravian leader had come to America with the plan of uniting all German denominations into what he called the Congregation of God in the Spirit. Brethren delegates did attend the initial sessions but eventually dropped out. Their reasons were: they found the domination by the count offensive, the use of the lot to decide all matters dubious, and the synod itself a convert attempt to make all of the German Christians into Moravians. When Zinzendorf baptized some Indian converts by sprinkling, the immersionist Brethren withdrew permanently. A few Brethren were drawn to the Morvaians, however. One, Andreas Frey (fl. 1728–1750), accompanied Count Zinzendorf back to Europe, but later returned to write an often reprinted exposé of the bizarre conduct of the Moravians during their so-called "Sifting Time."

Some of the Brethren publications of the 18th century were polemical in nature, invariably responses to attacks made upon them. Alexander Mack, Jr. (1712–1803), was the most prolific writer among the colonial Brethren; his *Apologie* (1788) has been called the best defense of Brethren practice and thought of that period. He was also noted for his hymns and poems, which he wrote in great numbers, as did indeed several others. Some of these compositions were printed in hymnals such as the *Davidische Psalterspiel* (*Davidic Psaltery*) of 1744, used as well by groups and individuals beyond the Brethren. Brethren had issued a hymnbook in Germany in 1720 (*Geistreiches Gesang-Buch* or *Spiritual Songbook*) but few copies reached America.

Historians have often counted the production of the press of J. Christopher Sauer (1695–1758) as Brethren publications, but this is wrong for two reasons. The press was a private enterprise and Sauer was never a member of the Brethren, although very sympathetic to their point of view. His like-named son (1721–1784) did become a Brethren elder and did continue his father's printing establishment, one of the most important in North America. The Sauers have to their credit the first successful German-language newspaper and almanac. They also produced the first Bibles in an European tongue, the first religious magazine, and the first type cast in the American colonies.

The younger Sauer became one of the wealthiest men in Pennsylvania but he lost all of his property in the Revolutionary War. He and the other Brethren were appreciative of the liberties afforded them under British and were not eager to see the political condition changed. More importantly, Brethren were nonresistants and could not make common cause with a violent revolution. Their position was not accepted by the rebels and much suffering resulted. The Brethren stance is best expressed in the petition they, along with Mennonite leaders, sent to the Pennsylvania Assembly in 1775:

> The [Assembly's] advice to those who do not find Freedom of Conscience to take up Arms, that they ought to be helpful to those who are in Need and distressed Circumstances, we received with Cheerfulness towards all Men of what Station they may be—it being our Principle to feed the Hungry and give the Thirsty Drink;—we have dedicated ourselves to serve all Men in every Thing that can be helpful to the Preservation of Men's Lives, but we find no Freedom in giving, or doing, or assisting in anything by which Men's Lives are destroyed or hurt.—We beg the Patience of all those who believe we err in this Point.[7]

The Brethren were willing to pay taxes but they also supported those whose conscience forbade paying taxes for war. They brought church discipline upon those members who allowed themselves to be forced in mustering or into taking the oath of loyalty to the new government. A few actively supported the British cause, and some Brethren left the country for Canada after 1783 to remain under British rule. Most, however, tried to maintain strict neutrality. Although the impact of the Revolution has been overplayed in some histories, there is no question that the treatment suffered by many Brethren reinforced their conviction that they should hold themselves aloof from worldly affairs.

Early 19th Century

Far from being the "Dark Ages" or the "Wilderness Period" of Brethren history as it has sometimes been called, the first half of the 19th century was a vital era in the life of the church. The first half-century of the National epoch saw the arrival of the first Brethren on the Pacific Coast, the first systematic theological statement of Brethren doctrines, extensive publishing activity, and the appearance of outstanding leaders. It was, indeed, a major achievement just to keep the church together despite its scattering across the continent; this period saw the consolidation of the Brethren in the format which they kept until close to the end of the century. Floyd E. Mallott rightly observed: "There has been a tendency to apologize for the period, and to regard the greater urbanity and sophistication of the grandchildren of the period as indications of an improvement. We are confronted by the fact that the foundations of the existent church were laid during that period. It was the congregations planted then that have increased by division and extension; the membership on that soil has multiplied. The church of 1950 rests upon foundations that were substantially laid by 1850!"[8]

The negative side of the consolidation was a certain reliance on legalism which threatened to equate sound faith with the avoidance of the "world." Many of the minutes of the Annual Meetings of the 19th century read like a catalog of prohibitions. Among things to be spurned were bells, carpets, life insurance, lightning rods, likenesses, liquor, musical instruments, salaried ministers, secret societies, shows and fairs, tobacco, and wallpaper. Although such prohibitions may be easily satirized, they represent attempts to live simply and decently as good stewards of material treasures. There is reason to believe that these Brethren led full lives, although more austerely than most would now consider necessary. Of key importance was keeping the unity of the church by mutual agreement.

Brethren expansion across the country followed, or on occasion even preceded, the general move westward. Some areas of Ohio, Indiana, and Illinois were first settled by Brethren. Members were in Kentucky, Tennessee and Missouri by 1800, Iowa by 1844, and as far as Oregon by 1850. Eight years later there was a congregation in California. Annual Meetings were held in Ohio by 1822, in Indiana by 1848, and in Illinois by 1856. There were two main routes taken by those moving west. One was through the Cumberland Gap into Kentucky, Ohio and Indiana. The most heavily traveled was through Pittsburgh, thence either by wagon westward or by flatboat down the Ohio River.

The story of the Wolfe family can stand for many. George Wolfe, Sr. (d. 1809), moved in 1787 over the Alleghenies to Fayette County, Pennsylvania. In 1800 he and his family built a flatboat and traveled down the Monongahela River to the Ohio, and from there to Logan County, Kentucky. George Wolfe, Jr. (1780–1865), with his brother Jacob explored the woods of Illinois and moved there, first to Union and then to Adams County. Wolfe, Jr., became an influential figure in Illinois affairs as well as a Dunker elder and played a role in keeping slavery from that part of the territory. A nephew of Wolfe, Jr., also named George Wolfe (1809–1887), reached the west coast by way of Panama in 1856.

Quite often groups of Brethren settlers moved as colonies, settling together in order to help one another. They immediately began meeting for worship in their homes, which were often constructed so that several small rooms could be converted into one large meeting room by folding or sliding back walls. The Brethren way was to gain adherents by living their faith, not by overt evangelism. Their neighbors saw their sincerity and piety and were sometimes impressed enough to join them.

Of course, much of the Brethren growth took place in the East, as families grew and most of the children became members. Usually young people waited with baptism until they were ready to marry and settle down. As congregations grew larger, they were divided so that the original gatherings had many daughter colonies. It had been common to build several meetinghouses within each congregation for ease of travel, so each new grouping could be assigned its own churchhouse. The Conestoga congregation has often been pointed out as an example of how growth could occur by this method. By 1915 there were 27 separate congregations which had emerged from this one mother church.

There was little Brethren presence in the cities. A congregation was planted in 1813 in Philadelphia as an offshoot from Germantown. Despite vigorous leadership by Peter Keyser, Jr. (1766–1849), and other able ministers, it flourished but modestly. Because of its adoption of patterns of worship current among other denominations, the Philadelphia members were repeatedly in trouble with the rest of the Brethren.

Baltimore received a congregation during Revolutionary War times but it faltered and later disbanded at mid-century.

It was at this time that clearer identification of church offices came about. These offices included deacons (and deaconesses), ministers, and elders (sometimes called bishops). Church leaders were elected by the entire membership, both women and men, in the presence of elders from adjoining congregations. This method usually produced the most able, or at least the most sincere leadership. Congregations appreciated but did not demand eloquence. As there were customarily several ministers in each congregation, different talents could come into play. Some ministers were known as excellent counselors and administrators of church affairs ("housekeepers"), while others were known for their preaching.

No salary was paid to ministers; although expenses might be reimbursed, they seldom were asked for. Church officers were chosen for life. Eldership entailed an extra sacrifice, for this involved much traveling to other congregations. Most of these men had limited schooling, but they applied themselves to bible study and used the books they owned to good advantage. They sometimes developed considerable polish of presentation and acquaintance with theology, to judge by the comments of visitors. Their moral exhortations were enhanced by their living with their flocks. They had no reluctance to speak a word of prophetic judgment, for they could not be relieved of nonexistent salary.

Ministry was ordinarily lodged among older male members who had demonstrated sincerity in faith, competence in vocational pursuit, discipline in guiding a family, and regularity in conduct. A flurry of objection hit the church when Sarah Righter Major (1808–1884), originally of Philadelphia and later of Ohio, felt the call to preach. Although never ordained, she was also never completely silenced either. There are many accounts of the aptness and power of her biblically-based sermons and prayers.

The widely dispersed Brethren were kept together as a denomination by two agencies—the traveling elders and the Annual Meeting. Visits were made upon the initiative of individual ministers or upon the invitation of the local church leaders. Ordinarily several congregations were visited in the course of a single journey. Elder Jacob Leatherman (1797–1863) walked more than 10,000 miles in performing his ministerial duties in Maryland. The most notable example of sacrificial service was John Kline (1797–1864) of Virginia, who covered more than 100,000 miles by horseback during his lifetime, 30,000 of which were on the back of his favorite mare Nell. As Elder Kline traveled to preach and conduct services, he also arranged business matters, healed the ill, and brought news. The story of his life can be gleamed from his published diary (1900), albeit in heavily-edited form.

The Annual Meeting, held at Pentecost, brought together most of the elders and many other members. It was a time of much preaching (not unlike the camp meetings of the time but without their emotional excesses). Usually a large number of non-Brethren also attended. All in attendance were given hospitality in food and lodging by the host congregation, which had to provide huge quantities of meat and staples to feed the thousands in attendance. Meetings were often held in barns, as the largest structures available, although sometimes special frame shelters were built or tents erected.

A committee of elders, which came to be called Standing Committee, prepared the business for presentation to the assembly, often by combining several queries. Decision was by unanimous consent. If there were differences of opinion, the matter was set back for a year. The meeting was chaired by a moderator who was chosen both for his strong voice and for the respect he enjoyed. In 1856 it was agreed that there should be district gatherings of five or more local congregations to decide matters of limited import, saving the time of Annual Meeting for substantive discussion.

More than anything else, this system of conferences shaped the identity of the Brethren. This was well expressed by Henry Kurtz (1796–1874), who came to the Brethren from the Lutheran ministry:

> This (our yearly) meeting was altogether a new thing to us, if we except our common council meetings, with which we had become acquainted previously. These, our common council meeting I had learnt to consider as practical schools of Christian Wisdom and Christian Morality, where the general principles of the Gospel were applied to individual cases; there every Christian virtue, such as love, humility, patience, forbearance, etc., was called into exercise and where every moral evil was to be set in its true light, in order to remove it. And such a school, I now found, was also the yearly meeting, only on a much larger and higher scale.[9]

Brethren worship services were informal and lengthy. Men and boys, women and girls, sat on different sides of the plain meeting-house, on low, backless wooden benches. Ministers faced them, seated behind a long trestle table that was on the same level as the congregation to demonstrate that there was no difference in virtue between ministry and laity. A deacon customarily began the service by announcing a hymn, which he proceeded to "line." This entailed the reading of the first line or two, after which the congregation sang them. Then he read the next lines, with song following, until the hymn was completed. The reason for this practice (also known in colonial New England) was originally the lack of hymnals but it persisted even after hymnals were readily available.

After the reading of scripture and a long prayer (always concluded with the shared Lord's Prayer), it was time for the sermon. The minister commonly extended the courtesy down their ranks (they were seated according to seniority in office) until someone rose to preach. It was felt that the Spirit provided an appropriate text and inspired appropriate remarks upon it. Sermons usually consisted of expository efforts and ethical applications. Following the conclusion of the lengthy sermon, other ministers commented on the same text, endeavoring to reemphasize the good points made by the first speaker or bringing other reflections of their own. The service was terminated by prayer and singing of a hymn. The absence of musical instruments did not hamper the strong and harmonious congregational singing, and if anything, enhanced it.

The love feast was the high point of the church year. It was always preceded by the annual visit of the deacons in each home. The following questions were asked: "Are you still in the faith of the Gospel, as you declared when you were baptized? Are you, as far as you know, in peace and union with the church? Will you still labor with the Brethren for an increase in holiness, both in yourself and others?"[10] If the visit brought any stress or disharmony to light, the love feast could be postponed until the problem was resolved. Typically elders from distant congregations were in attendance and led in preaching and administering of the ordinance.

Revivals or "protracted meetings" were not customary before the latter part of the century. Brethren believed that decisions made under emotional strain would not last when the pressure was removed. Joining the church was the most serious action a person took in a lifetime and should be soberly weighed. "Count the cost" (Luke 14:28–29) was a favorite text. This reservation caused the loss of quite a number of Brethren to revivalistic bodies, which included the Brethren in Christ, the Evangelical Association, and the Church of God (Winebrennarian).

There were other significant membership losses during the same period. Universalism, which was popular in the post-Revolutionary era, stressed the belief that a God of love could never condemn sinners to eternal punishment. The atonement of Christ was sufficient for all humankind. The more radical of their number denied the reality of either punishment or reward in the afterlife. As the Brethren had in their beginnings accepted a mild form of universalism (universal restoration), they were susceptible to the aggressive movement. Entire congregations in North and South Carolina went over to the Universalists. These families provided much of the leadership for the southern branch of Universalism. In Kentucky, Ohio, Indiana, and Missouri, it was the Disciples of Christ who made inroads among the Brethren. A theology which appealed to frontier residents, articulate leadership by Alexander Campbell (1788-1866) and Barton Stone (1772-1844), and an emphasis upon Christian unity were characteristics of the Disciples (Christians). Hundreds of Brethren, indeed the entire Kentucky membership, went over to them. An active leader in the process was Joseph Hostetler (1797-1870).

There were several small schisms in the church during the first decades of the 19th century. The most serious took place in Indiana in 1848 when Peter Eyman (1805?-1852) and some others formed the Church of God (New Dunkers) which persisted until 1962.

An early doctrinal treatise was written by Elder Benjamin Bowman (1754-1829); its title was *A Brief and Simple Exhibition from the Word of God* (1823). This was read by a Lutheran-bred, Methodist class leader named Peter Nead (1797-1877), who was so impressed that he looked up the Brethren in Virginia and was baptized by them. He was convinced that they followed the New Testament teachings more closely than any other church body. After becoming a minister he began to write on the Brethren doctrines and published several volumes. These were gathered together in one book called popularly *Nead's Theology* (1850). It was influential in codifying the beliefs of the church and was much used for indoctrination of new members.

With the coming of the Civil War the Brethren were hit hard, but the conflict did not result in rupture as was true of almost all other denominations that had members on both sides of the Mason and Dixon line. This was for two reasons: first, the Brethren had never allowed members to hold slaves; and second, great efforts were made by leaders to keep contacts alive across the battle lines. Elder John Kline did yeoman work in this regard. Often elected moderator during the war years, he made repeated trips from his home in Virginia to the Northern states. His journeys, although purely on church business, brought him under Confederate suspicion of being a spy for the Union. He did not conceal his anti-slavery views and continued his church duties despite pointed threats. He spent time in a Harrisonburg jail for his efforts in freeing Brethren and Mennonites from the military. Some hotheaded local Confederate irregulars waylaid and murdered him in 1864.

The Brethren in the South suffered more severely than did those in the North during the war. This was because of their lack of support for the war and because the Confederacy needed manpower more desperately than did the Union. Although both in North and South it was possible to be freed from military service by paying a commutation tax ($300–500), administration of the exemption was more erratic in the South. Some Brethren were forced into the Southern army and were maltreated for refusing to fire on the enemy. Others fled to the Northern states to escape this fate and some hid away from their homes for long periods of time. On both sides Brethren congregations pooled their resources to help wartime taxes for their poorer members. Some of the Southern Brethren lost their homes, barns, livestock, equipment, and crops when the Northern armies embarked on scorched-earth policies. Sums of money collected after the war in Northern congregations helped destitute Brethren in Southern states.

The important point was that the Brethren came through the bloody struggle as a united people, and remained consistently loyal to their nonresistant principles. There is no doubt that church growth was hampered by the troubled times. By 1865, it is estimated, there were 20,000 members in some 200 congregations across the country. Great changes were in store for the denomination in the second half of the 19th century.

Notes

1. David B. Barrett, ed., *World Christian Encyclopedia* (Nairobi: 1982), 825; the calculation (for 1970) includes those affiliated with the churches as well as members. Barrett's actual projection for 1985 approached 676,000.
2. Morgan Edwards, *Materials Towards a History of the American Baptists* (1770), quoted in D. F. Durnbaugh, ed., *Brethren in Colonial America* (Elgin, IL: 1967), 175.
3. J. H. Jung-Stilling, *Theobald, oder die Schwärmer* (Leipzig: 1784), 1:36; Max Goebel, *Geschichte des christlichen Lebens* (Coblenz: 1852), 2: 816; Heinz Renkewitz, *Hochmann von Hochenau* (Breslau: 1935).
4. D. F. Durnbaugh, *European Origins of the Brethren* (Elgin, IL: 1958), 115–120.
5. Durnbaugh, *European Origins* (1958), 216.
6. Durnbaugh, *European Origins* (1958), 283.

7. *A Short and Sincere Declaration* (1775), published in Durnbaugh, *Colonial America* (1967), 363–365.
8. Floyd E. Mallott, *Studies in Brethren History* (Elgin, IL: 1954), 133–134.
9. Henry Kurtz, "Our Late Yearly Meeting, & the Gospel-Visitor," *The Monthly Gospel-Visitor*, 3 (June, 1853): 11.
10. Otho Winger, *History and Doctrines of the Church of the Brethren* (Elgin, IL: 1919), 206.

2

Recent History

Donald F. Durnbaugh

The 19th century Brethren were known as a "peculiar people" and were not offended in being thus labeled. Their distinctive manner of dress ("the garb"), restricted way of life, and vigorously defended cultic practices helped to keep them separate from the world. Like the early Christians whom they took as patterns, they thought of themselves, as in this world but not of it, as sojourners on their way to a better land. In the terminology of the sociologists of religion, the Brethren were sectarian.

Ellsworth Faris (1874–1953), a pioneer investigator of the concept of religious sectarianism, used the Brethren to illustrate the sect *par excellence*. He urged his colleagues to turn their attention to an examination of these Dunkers: "The religious sect, and particularly the modern isolated sect, has many advantages which ethnography does not afford. . . . If sociologists cared to give the same careful and detailed study to the foot-washing of the Dunkers . . . as they do the totem dances of the Australians or the taboos of the Bantus the material would not only be found equally interesting but in all probability more fruitful."[1] Faris was unaware that at the time of his writing (1928) the Brethren had already changed remarkably from their earlier character, but his reference to the Brethren as a "modern isolated sect" is an apt description of them during the previous era.

A sociologist visiting the Church of the Brethren in the 1980s would find feetwashing practiced (although some congregations have dropped its use), but he would hardly find the isolated sect so intriguing to Faris. Contemporary members of the Church of the Brethren live, dress, and conduct themselves very much like other middle-class American Protestants, although still largely Germanic in ethnic background rather than Anglo-Saxon. (A significant number of ethnic minorities entered the denomination in the past two decades.) Closer observation would reveal some continuing characteristics of the sectarian heritage: emphasis on the historic peace witness, sermons on the "simple life," familial feeling in the denomination, resistance to creedal statements, and openness to social concerns; an articulate group of younger church members express appreciation for the usefulness of the traditional values in meeting current problems. The sociologist would find some limited geographical area (Eastern Pennsylvania, Maryland, and the Southeast) where older behavioral patterns still persist. Two smaller Brethren bodies, the Old German Baptist Brethren and the Dunkard Brethren, perpetuate these practices.

It is, nevertheless, obvious that a tremendous transformation has taken place within the Church of the Brethren in less than a century. Some observers have claimed that the Brethren have changed more in a shorter period of time than other comparable denominations. Whether this is true or not, even a cursory glance at the recent history of the Brethren reveals radical and rapid change. What were the influences that caused this shift?

Several sociologically oriented studies have been undertaken to analyze the social factors involved. The greater density of population, compulsory public schooling, marriage outside the church membership, the impact of informational media—these are said to be leveling agents in making separatist groups more at one with the society. The only religious communities, it is held, to retard successfully this process are the Hutterites and the Amish who have virtually withdrawn from the outside world.

Others speak of the effect of the "sect-cycle." As sectarian groups mature, they tend to adopt the postures and practices of the church establishments from which they sprang. They become more concerned with nurture than conversion, with trained ministry rather than lay ministers, with involvement in society rather than fleeing from it. Strict discipline brings economic prosperity; prosperity brings with it an advance in class standing; and changed class standing calls into question previously held church views.

Others have laid more emphasis upon economic factors. The impact of industrialization was the key to the change, they maintain. As the USA became industrialized during and after the Civil War, all segments of the population were affected. A predominantly agricultural population (and the Brethren were almost complete rural in the 19th century) moved to the growing cities. As mass production made goods more plentiful, the old ways of living (and church rules about them) seemed to be passe. "The Dunker elder bought an automobile and stepped on the gas; out of the window went his broadbrim, followed by his wife's bonnet, followed by his whiskers."[2]

Perhaps it is possible to draw these several explanation together under the rubric *acculturation*. The immigrant religious fraternity, kept apart by its language, its demanding ethic, its close-knit family ties, and its self-understanding as a "called-out" people, gradually came to feel at home in the American culture. It is generally accurate to say that all of the currents which swept through American religious and national life also affected the Brethren, but usually after a lag of several decades. As we come closer to the contemporary scene, the lag becomes smaller and smaller. This holds true for theological trends, architectural styles, liturgical developments, and social issues.

The Brethren missionary thrust of the late 19th century is a case in point. Brethren involvement in missions experienced the same tensions as other groups at the beginning of the 19th century. Of course, the ways in which the Brethren responded to these various influences were molded by their own distinctive background. In certain fields, especially social concerns, the Brethren have not only been followers, but have also on occasion been leaders for Protestantism. This is evidenced by the impression that most Protestants aware of the Brethren identify them by their contributions to social welfare activity.

A key to the process of acculturation was the transfer from predominant use of the German language in worship and in the home setting to the English language of their neighbors. This transition came rapidly and early in the few urban congregation of the Brethren, as in Germantown, Philadelphia, and Baltimore. Soon after 1800 church records in those places began to be kept in English. The switch came much more slowly in rural congregations. One way to follow the shift is to notice the language of often-used church publications such as hymnals. By mid-century it was common to have English and German hymnals published and bound together, for there would be in the same congregation some members who spoke only German and some only English, as well as those who were bilingual. In the "free ministry" (self-supporting) system of the time, some speakers would preach only in German, some only in English, and some were fluent in both languages. With the dwindling knowledge of German in the later 19th century, its use in public services diminished rapidly. This shift in dominant language eased the introduction of the ways and values of the surrounding society. It is noticeable that some of the sharpest criticism of the "Progressive Brethren" prior to the church divisions of 1881–1883 was leveled at the "ignorant" elders who could not correctly write and speak English. The language shift heightened tensions as it became a symbol for openness to new ideas or stubborn adherence to old traditions.

Second Half of the 19th Century

The westward movement of the Brethren, so prominent in the first half of the 19th century, continued strongly in the latter half. Broadly speaking, the development filled in the gaps left in the push to the West Coast. In 1856, the same year that a congregation was planted in Oregon, the first church was organized in Kansas. This state saw rapid church extension, especially in the years after 1883, when in six years the number of congregations increased fourfold. Nebraska had its first church in 1866/68, Colorado in 1874, Washington in 1876, and Idaho in 1878. During the 1870/80s come congregations were established in the Southwestern states, including Texas and Louisiana, but these have always remained isolated. North Dakota and Oklahoma were settled in the 1890s. By 1908 there were 298 congregations, 816 ministers, and some 15,500 adult members in 19 of the 22 states west of the Mississippi River. Much of this membership, however, represented a migration from Brethren congregations in the East and Midwest, rather than new converts.

A novel element was the role of the transcontinental railroads. Having successfully pushed their tracks across the continent, the companies were now eager to attract settlers. These newcomers provided business as they moved and became customers for shipping farm produce to markets. German religious groups were especially courted, for they tended to move in large numbers and had the reputation of being stable and efficient farmers. As for the church leaders, they were able to find spiritual motivation to buttress the economic appeals made by the railroad companies. Colonization in the West could be and was interpreted as a means of extending church witness; leaders also thought that islands of morality could be formed there to continue the narrow way of religious truth. The overpopulated East was full of distractions. When increasing criticisms of colonization schemes were made, the attitude of some Brethren leaders was revealed in an editorial in a church periodical (1906):

> The railroads, though soulless corporations, are being used wonderfully by the Lord for the spread of the church. Even though it be true that the

agents for the railroads have been active in urging people to go and see and believe and settle, from sinister motives, that does not keep God and His real children from taking advantage of these opportunities for the glory of His name. . . . Today these roads may be reaping rich returns financially for their aggressive work. Well and good. These arteries of our nation have made it possible for the hands of the church to operate where, had they not gone, the church could not be now.[3]

Another boom of the same period was the inauguration of schools of higher learning. Nearly 40 institutions of academy (high school) level or above were started by Brethren between 1852 and 1923, most of short duration. Of these initiatives, eight exist today. There were many reasons given for the development of Brethren-sponsored schools. Young people from Brethren homes were in fact attending schools run by other church bodies, and it was argued that they would be lost to the church if no institutions were available in which they could receive education in an atmosphere conducive to Brethren values. Interestingly enough, at first the Brethren were scrupulous in keeping religious education as such from the school curricula, for this was held to be alone the prerogative of church and home. Bible courses, it was held, would be the opening wedge for the creation of seminaries, and then the path to a "hireling" ministry would be open.

Another reason for the surge of school openings was that they provided an acceptable avenue for financial investment. Prosperous Brethren could participate in what was hoped to be a profitable undertaking and be doing good at the same time. In fact, very few of the schools flourished in any business sense and many supporters lost heavily. Chronicles of the schools recount the sacrifices of founders and faculty. They had been encouraged in these ventures by the desire of many small towns where Brethren lived to secure schools. Usually land and often buildings were made available for these purposes by the town fathers, who saw economic and cultural advantage in having institutions of higher learning in their vicinities.

Accompanying the development of education and usually involving the same people was the upsurge in publication of periodicals. Although started and continued as private business venture, these papers were published on behalf of the denomination and were subject to criticism and control. Henry Kurtz (1796–1874) was the pioneer Brethren publisher with his *Monthly Gospel Visitor* in 1851. Formerly a Lutheran pastor in Pennsylvania, the German-born and well-educated Kurtz moved to Northeastern Ohio in 1827. For Kurtz a church periodical was needed to safeguard the unity of a widely scattering fellowship. It also was a useful way to solve doctrinal and practical problems by providing a sounding board for insights and conclusions. Further, he saw in the paper a means to promote certain values and ideals he felt to be important. In this he had great success, for he was ordinarily tactful enough to avoid strong opposition. Scholars see the Kurtz press as a pivotal point in Brethren history. The causes of higher education, mission, theological literacy, polity reform, aid for needy Brethren in distant places, and a wider vision of church life all found their first advocacy in the columns of the *Gospel Visitor*.

Kurtz found an effective associate in his publishing venture in James Quinter (1816–1888), who succeeded Kurtz as owner/editor of the periodical and became the leading Brethren educator and church statesman. In that day public debates were a popular way of airing, if not always solving, controversial public issues, including religious doctrines. It was Quinter who, reluctantly, was the champion of the Brethren cause, traveling the country to debate the distinctive Brethren tenets and ordinances with churchmen of other persuasions. Stenographic records of these several-day debates were published in journals and often in separate books.

The *Gospel Visitor* was not long the only Brethren periodical. Many others were soon introduced. Nearly 60 different papers have been identified as Brethren publications between 1851 and 1900. A steady process of merger took place, however, so that the principal organ remained the Kurtz/Quinter publication; after several mergers it was titled the *Gospel Messenger* in 1883. In 1897 it came under direct church ownership and has continued as the official house publication; after 1965 it was called simply *Messenger*. Published in the late 19th century in Mount Morris, Illinois, it was relocated in 1899 in Elgin, Illinois for better shipping connections. Developing from this enterprise was the Brethren Publishing House (known later as the Brethren Press) and, eventually, the central offices of the Church of the Brethren.

A more crusading and innovative kind of journalism was introduced by a one-time Kurtz associate, Henry R. Holsinger (1833–1905). He published the weekly *Christian Family Companion* (1864), a paper for young people (1870),the first hymnal with musical notation (1872), and the first full reports of Annual Meeting discussions (1876). Holsinger had a more aggressive approach to his publishing enterprise than either Kurtz or Quinter. These men were eager to see the church move ahead but were willing to suggest ideas and patiently cultivate support. Holsinger wanted to push the Brethren into reform, and used polemics, satire, and personal critique in the pages of his papers. He focused his impatience on the dominance by aging leadership in the annual conferences. Holsinger therefore argued for a thoroughgoing congregationalism in church polity, to allow more rapid change. New methods for church work were needed, he insisted; these included revival meetings, salaried pastors, Sunday schools, higher education, and lively literature.

These advanced views alarmed a number of conservative elders, many of them residents of Southwestern Ohio, who decided they needed to organize for the preservation of the "old order" of church practice. They were led by Elder Peter Nead, the foremost theological writer of the mid-century, and by Nead's son-in-law, Samuel Kinsey (1832–1883), the editor of the conservative journal, the *Vindicator* (1870ff.). These "Old Orders," who were often called the Miami Valley Elders, were frankly concerned about their loss of leadership and control of the denomination. They sent repeated petitions to the Annual Meeting, calling for a halt to innovations. Although they met with early success, those on the other side, dubbed the "Progressives," remained active as well. The largest group, those in the middle referred to as the "Conservatives," attempted to placate the Old Order element while gradually accepting some of the proposals of the Progressives. In 1880, the Annual Meeting replied to a petition from the Miami Valley:

> [W]hile we declare ourselves conservative in maintaining unchanged what may justly be considered the principles and peculiarities of our Fraternity, we also believe in the propriety and necessity of so adapting our labor and our principles to the religious wants of the world as will render our labor and principles most efficient in promoting the reformation of the world, the edification of the church and the glory of God. *Hence while we are conservative, we are also progressive* [emphasis added].[4]

This was received as a provocation by the ultra-conservative party, so they sent a near-ultimatum to the next Annual Meeting; it was rejected on a technicality as not having come by the regular channels through a district meeting. The Old Order element numbering perhaps 4,000 withdrew, organizing in 1881 as the Old German Baptist Brethren. At this point *German Baptist Brethren* was the legal name of the denomination. Therefore, the name *Old* German Baptist Brethren signified their conviction that they represented the true continuation of the original Brethren movement. The schism brought with it anguished division within congregation and families and some contention over control of church property.[5]

The pain was to be compounded by a corresponding exodus from the Progressive side. Many in the center party had become exasperated by the prodding for reform by Holsinger and his friends; they called for a committee of elders to be sent by Annual Meeting to visit Holsinger in his home congregation in Berlin, Pennsylvania, for investigation and discipline. Because of a dispute over procedure, the committee never came to a discussion of the real issues with the congregation, but nevertheless announced in August, 1881, that Holsinger was to be disfellowshipped until the next conference could pass final judgment. The committee action was sharply attacked and also defended during the months before the 1882 Annual Meeting, which began in a state of high tension. Many voices called for patience and mercy in deciding the issue, pointing out the potential for more church division. Holsinger extended an apology but the mood of the majority was for censure. The Berlin committee was upheld and Holsinger's expulsion confirmed. He could be restored by admitting his error and promising obedience to church discipline.

Those who rallied to the Progressive leader at this meeting decided to organize a new branch, called the Brethren Church. They waited, however, until 1883, to see if reconciliation could be effected with the main body. This did not happen. Perhaps 5,000 members sided with Holsinger. Many of those wishing reform decided to stay with the larger central body, believing that change could be implemented within the church structure. They were reluctant to cause more disunity than had already happened. In fact, all of the changes for which Holsinger had contended were soon introduced in the main body. This suggests that the second schism could have been avoided, given more tact on the part of the Progressives and more patience on the part of the conference leadership.

The Brethren Church became over the years more conservative in theology than the Church of the Brethren, perhaps because it was more open to modern currents of theology, which included fundamentalism. Debates on these issues may be followed in the pages of the periodical of the denomination, the *Brethren Evangelist*, and in the chronicles of the church college and seminary at Ashland, Ohio. Between 1936 and 1939 a sharp doctrinal struggle took place which resulted in the separate formation of the Fellowship of Grace Brethren Churches, with headquarters at Winona Lake, Indiana. The fundamentalistic Grace

Brethren publish the *Brethren Missionary Harold*, sponsor Grace College and Seminary, and are active in home and foreign missions. Their membership in 1985 was about three times that of the Brethren Church (45,000 and 15,000).[6]

Despite the internal upheaval of the early 1880s, the parent body of German Baptist Brethren (after 1908 known as the Church of the Brethren) experienced remarkable growth after the schism. It can perhaps best be explained that as the ultra-conservative and the progressive extremes left, the fairly united group which remained was free to turn its energies outward. Evangelists such as I. J. Rosenberger (1842–1923), I. N. H. Beahm (1859–1950), and H. C. Early (1855–1941) were noted for many converts during this time.

Developments in foreign missions demonstrated this renewed vigor. Missions had repeatedly been raised earlier as a concern for the Brethren, but met with little response until 1876, when a Macedonian call came from Denmark. (Henry Kurtz had preached and baptized in Switzerland during a visit to Europe in 1839 but this was a personal initiative.) A Dane named Christian Hope (1844–1899), who had migrated to America for religious freedom, read about the Brethren, sought them out, and joined them. They represented in his view the closest he could find to apostolic Christianity. He wrote to friends in Denmark from his new home in Illinois and arranged for the publication in Danish of some Brethren tracts, which he sent to his friends. Those in Denmark asked that someone should come to baptize them and form a church. Hope took the challenge to the district, which ordained him as a minister and decided to send him, with two elders, to Denmark in 1876. This, however, was a district initiative and the wider denomination gave but little support to its call for financial aid.

Following 1884 the mission interests of the Brethren were reorganized and support increased. When this mission board began its work it had a sum of $8.69 with which to work. By 1913 the annual receipts were over $100,000 and the board's assets amounted to nearly $1,000,000. Missions as "the great first work of the church" became the slogan for the denomination. This was the title of a book by Wilbur B. Stover (1866–1930), an indefatigable promoter of missions and one of the first Brethren missionary team to India in 1894. As other mission fields opened, those who accepted the missionary call became the heros and heroines of the church; they were received with acclaim as they returned on furloughs. The 1919 Annual Conference of the Church of the Brethren received a collection of $150,000 for missions. D. L. Miller (1841–1921), a wealthy merchant, educator, and writer, was a stalwart in broadening the vision of the Brethren by his reports of his world travels and his leadership on the mission board. Several districts began urban ministries in the late 19th century with modest success.

The 20th Century

The 20th century brought yet more changes to the Brethren. Of more than symbolic significance was the "dress question;" by this is meant the controversy over the enforcement of the denominational style of plain dress. The matter had repeatedly raised, even after the three-way split of the 1880, where it had been one of the chief points of contention. A representative committee was asked to bring a "closer, concise restatement of our position on this vexed question" to the 1910 Annual Conference. Its carefully worded and closely reasoned statement was accepted by the conference; however, another committee was asked to prepare a supplementary report. The second report reiterated the strong recommendation for a uniform manner or dress set forth in the 1910 policy statement but failed to insist on a specific style of dress for all members and thus removed dress as a matter of church discipline. Congregations could decide to disregard previous conference rulings. This opened the way for the rapid replacement of the distinctive garb by modest secular fashion. Several hundred members led by B. E. Kesler (1861–1952) withdrew to form the Dunkard Brethren as a protest against this and other modernizing trends.

One of the arguments for discontinuing the peculiar dress code was to free the Brethren to concern themselves more with the needs of the world. There is a clear trend toward greater public participation in the first decades of the 20th century, centering first on support of such causes as temperance and international arbitration of disputes. Church leaders were eager to throw the influence of the membership behind those agencies and movements working for social uplift and moral improvements. Brethren were now urged to be good citizens and make their voice heard on public issues. Martin G. Brumbaugh (1862–1930), a Brethren minister, became governor of Pennsylvania in 1915.

This involvement complicated Brethren reaction to the demands brought by World War I. In previous wars the Brethren position had been clear-cut; members could pay taxes if levied by the government; they could even pay a commutation fee, if imposed upon them, to avoid military service; but they could not themselves enter the military. When the United States began conscription in 1917, some Brethren church leaders took the position that strict nonresistance was no longer tenable. They argued that as the Brethren were active as citizens and enjoyed the privileges of citizenship, they could not now completely refuse calls to serve the nation in wartime. They recommended that Brethren draftees enter the army as noncombatants, a category provided by the draft law for those religiously opposed to killing.

The federal government delayed for a year in determining what kinds of duty in the armed services were considered to be noncombatant. The final delineation included the medical corps, as expected, but also the quartermaster and engineering units. This was unacceptable to many conscientious objectors. During the period between the declaration of war (April 6, 1917) and the administrative ruling (March 20, 1918), many young Brethren men were called into the army. Most of them had to decide for themselves how far they could go in cooperating with the army, although efforts were made to send Brethren elders to military camps as visitors and advisors. Those Brethren who refused to wear uniform and to carry out military orders often underwent harsh treatment. Camp officers tried to break their wills by harassment and brutality, and sometimes met with success.

In the meantime, leaders called a special conference at Goshen, Indiana, on January 9, 1918. The purpose was to reach consensus on the Brethren attitude to the world conflict and the military demands. Those attending drew up a comprehensive statement, consisting of resolutions to be sent to the US president, a theological and biblical justification for the refusal to bear arms, and a procedure for an organization to represent the church in these matters. The Goshen statement was printed and distributed to the congregations. It soon found its way to the War Department in Washington, D.C. as draftees produced it to answer the question why they would not fight. The federal government threatened prosecution of the conference officers for treason, which caused church leaders to withdraw the statement from circulation. Trial and possible imprisonment of leading churchmen were thus averted, but at the price of a weakening of the peace witness.

Some of the young men who went through the problems of the war experience were determined to devote their lives to the cause of peace, beginning with the strengthening of the peace position among Brethren. Notable among them were Dan West (1893–1971) and Michael Robert Zigler (1891-1985). They involved themselves deeply in the life of the denomination. West was known for his work with youth; M. R. Zigler was an executive and peace activist. They enlisted many in peace and service programs. Owing to the efforts of these and other leaders, with the advent of World War II the Church of the Brethren was more clearly prepared and unified, even though not all of the constituency held to the strict pacifist line. It was, in fact, a minority of church members who held a consistent position of conscientious objection during World War II.

These peace leaders were liberal in their theology, as were others who held the key positions in the denomination during the interwar period. Many had secured advanced education at schools such as Crozer, Yale, Vanderbilt, and Chicago, and had caught the vision of a church engaged in social justice issues. This created counterpressures, both from conservative Brethren who wished to remain more withdrawn from society and from those who had been influenced by a resurgent fundamentalism.

Middle Pennsylvania became the center of this theological conservatism. Juniata College, under the presidency of Charles C. Ellis (1874–1950) set up its own seminary, of a more conservative tenor than Bethany Bible School in Chicago (later called Bethany Biblical Seminary and then Bethany Theological Seminary). Bethany was founded in 1905 by Albert Cassel Wieand (1871–1954) and Emanuel B. Hoff (1860–1928). A possible church division was avoided when the Chicago school was accepted in 1925 as the property of the denomination and the Pennsylvania seminary terminated. Under the leadership of Wieand and D. W. Kurtz (1879–1949) the seminary developed as a moderately liberal institution.

The fundamentalist issue came to a head in 1941, when the Church of the Brethren became a member of the Federal (National) Council of Churches by conference action upon the recommendation of the Council of Boards, a coordinating group of Brethren agencies. Approval was also given at that time for membership in the World Council of Churches, then in process of formation. Calls came for reconsideration of the decision, as it was felt in some quarters that the conference had approved the affiliation without sufficient study. Since that time a vocal minority has protested the conciliar affiliation, charging modernism and left-leaning policies among council leaders and staff. Two Pennsylvania congregations suffered serious division in the 1940s over fundamentalism, although the courts ruled that property should be kept in the hands of the parties loyal to the church. Four small congregations in North Carolina left the church in 1962 over the issue.

Since the Brethren became active in political affairs, most have tended to vote the Republican ticket. The throes of the Depression of the 1930s, however, brought some changes. A survey made in 1934 by Kirby Page (1890–1957) on questions on military, political, and economic nature, included a large sample from the Brethren. One-fifth (over 500) of Brethren ministers polled answered the questionnaire.

One-half of them called for a "drastically reformed capitalism" as the most effective way to achieve a cooperative commonwealth and fully one-fourth favored socialism. Brethren became more concerned about economic justice, although as late as 1941 the Annual Conference suggested that members should be cautious in their union activity.

This period saw great involvement of the Brethren in the Sunday school movement. Only reluctantly accepted in the 19th century, this form of Christian education came into its own following the creation in 1896 of the denominational Sunday School Advisory Board. By 1921 an enrollment of nearly 140,000 was reported for the church schools; this increased to a high of 168,000 in 1960. The *Brethren Teacher's Quarterly*, which began in 1899 and attained broad circulation, was based on the International Lessons. Cooperation with other denominations was earlier and stronger in this field than in any other. Congregations increasingly included all age groups in their school programs and continued throughout the year.

Another influential innovation in the life of the Brethren was the camping movement. The first Brethren camp was perhaps that held in Nebraska in 1916, although other camps in Indiana and Pennsylvania were among the early permanent sites. Soon most of the districts of the denomination sought to develop their own camps as a place for intensive education. Visiting leadership awakened many of the children and young people to the possibilities and challenges of church vocations. This seemed even more effective in changing values and forming commitments than the Christian education taking place in the home congregations. By 1939 there were 20 Brethren camps in 13 states and Canada and in 1980 the 24 districts owned 36 camps.

Mid-20th Century

The impact of World War II intensified the tendency of the Brethren to become more deeply involved in society. This can be seen in the lives of two Brethren who achieved national prominence, Kermit Eby and Andrew W. Cordier.

Kermit Eby (1903–1962) became well known as an educator, labor leader, and intellectual gadfly, and also as an articulate interpreter of the Brethren heritage. Born and bred in a rural area near Elkhart, Indiana, he attended Manchester College and the University of Chicago, before becoming a teacher in Ann Arbor, Michigan. There he grew acquainted with leaders of the Congress of Industrial Organization, which was unionizing the Michigan auto workers. He was called to Washington, D.C. in 1942 by the labor movement as national educational director but eventually came to feel that the unions were insensitive to the needs of the rank-and-file members. As a freewheeling member of the University of Chicago faculty after 1948, Eby was known as a voice of conscience speaking out on all the current issues. Everywhere he went he called for the introduction of the virtues of honesty, integrity, industry, and caring human relationships which he had been given by his Dunker background.

A personality with similar beginnings was Andrew W. Cordier (1901–1975), former president of Columbia University and long-time official of the United Nations. Born into a Brethren family in Ohio, Cordier attended Manchester College and the University of Chicago (PhD, 1926) before returning to Manchester as professor of history and political science for 20 years. During this period he became an expert on international relations and an advisor to the influential US Senator Arthur H. Vandenberg (1884–1951). Cordier was brought into the State Department as a planner for an international agency to promote peace after the end of World War II. When the United Nations was formed, Cordier entered its service as a senior American official. He became the executive assistant of the first two secretary-generals and the under-secretary for General Assembly affairs, and was thus the highest ranking US citizen in United Nations service. He was often sent to trouble spots around the world to direct the UN presence. Some Brethren felt that in this role he departed from the denominational peace witness, but Cordier himself held that he was practicing the doctrine of reconciliation learned at Brethren conferences and love feasts.

Even before World War II the Brethren had been associated with programs to alleviate suffering in the world. Following World War I Brethren donated $267,000 to help the Armenians. Civil war in Spain and the Japanese invasion of China brought forth Brethren aid to war-sufferers. There was close cooperation with the American Friends Service Committee on several of these projects; the Brethren seemed to be following in Quaker footsteps in broadening the arena of their activities.

It was, therefore, not surprising that when the Brethren organized their own agency for relief and rehabilitation, they took the name Brethren Service Committee (1939). The onset of World War II made impossible much work overseas, although preparations went forward. Major Brethren Service effort centered in the Civilian Public Service (CPS) program. This represented a cooperative program of the Historic Peace Churches (Brethren, Mennonite, and Quakers) and the federal government to provide civilian work "of national importance" for religious objectors. The peace churches had lobbied to get total exemption for all conscientious objectors, whose sincerity was to be established by civilian tribunals after the British example. They were unsuccessful in obtaining this, and therefore agreed to help run camps for this civilian service. Young men entering CPS were to serve as long as men in military units and their support was to be provided by the churches. The government undertook to provide work, largely in the Park Service and conservation agencies, and supervisory personnel.

The agreement represented a tremendous undertaking for the three small denominations, especially as they were expected to support all conscientious objectors, regardless of background. The Brethren alone expended more than $1,250,000 between 1942 and 1946 to administer the CPS program for 3,000 men, who worked more than 2,5000,000 man-hours. The difficult administration of the program was placed in the hands of a young pastor from West Virginia, W. Harold Row (1912–1971). There were many problems in the base camps but the initiation of "detached programs" of mental hospital attendants, dairy testers, control patients, which were mostly self-supporting and socially more meaningful. They also brought a generally favorable public response to the plan.

Following the end of hostilities, BSC took on new life as the church threw itself into supplying urgently needed clothing, medicines, and food for millions of war sufferers around the world. It is fair to say that the Brethren Service displaced missions as the chief focus of the denomination, although support still ran high for the latter. In 1948 the Brethren had work in Austria, China, Ecuador, England, Ethiopia, France, Germany, Italy, Japan, Poland, and several other countries. Young college graduates spent several years of voluntary service in these foreign countries, administering programs and representing the church people at home, the donors of the relief goods. Some Brethren-sponsored agencies won interdenominational support, and many Brethren personnel were seconded to ecumenical agencies as staff workers. New Windsor, Maryland, the site of a former Brethren college, became the center of a relief operation of vast proportions. The program continues to this day, although the areas of need have shifted from Europe to Africa and Asia.

The postwar period was also a time for reorganization and reform in polity and church administration. The pattern during the 1920s and 1930s had been the creation of independent boards, of which the General Mission Board was by far the most powerful, to carry on the work of the denomination. The areas of competence of these boards tended to conflict, and they sometimes found themselves competing for funds. There was thus interest in creating a unified plan to effect greater efficiency in operation and better use of church funds. A Committee of Fifteen developed a comprehensive report on church polity which was accepted by conference in 1946 and implemented in 1947. A General Brotherhood Board of 25 members was created, incorporating the former boards within its five commissions. The Board acted as the administrative arm of the church under policies set by the Annual Conference. Church employees were supervised by the Board, whose members were chosen among five geographical regions defined by the report. This introduced another level of polity in addition to the districts, created in the mid-19th century.

This organization prevailed until the summer of 1968, when a restructuring plan was adopted. The new scheme called for a General Board of 25 elected members, divided into three commissions—World Ministries, Parish Ministries, and General Services. Three associate general secretaries led these commissions, with overall coordination provided by a general secretary. Two underlying principles of the plan were that the work of the church officials should be on a team basis with the possibility of shifting assignments as problems change, and that the general offices of the church should be concerned with consulting with local congregations rather than developing programs for handing down to the local areas. The general offices were to provide resources to aid congregations in carrying out their missions locally. This organization has remained basically intact through 1985, through many internal realignments. A personnel office, the Office of Human Resources, has emerged on equal standing with the three commissions. Some decentralization was initiated, with a number of staff workers in New Windsor, Maryland.

The mid-20th century has been marked by virtually complete utilization of full-time pastors by all congregations able to afford such leadership. (A very few congregations prefer the older pattern of self-supported, plural leadership.) Intensive efforts have been made to provide these pastors with more adequate compensation, according to a salary scale recommended by the Annual Conference and periodically revised, and more professional status. A recent trend has been to the "yoked parish" system where two or three small congregations are served by one pastor. This has been used also to link a Brethren congregation with a congregation of other denominational identity, particularly with Baptists. In the 1970s and 1980s more women entered pastoral ministries, either as the sole pastor, as part of a husband-wife pastoral team, or as one of a multiple staff.

In the 1950s and 1960s observers noted increasing emphasis upon local concerns, with congregational needs supplanting earlier concentration on missions or relief activities. The introduction of the unified budget at the time of the reorganization in 1946–1947 was in part an effort to control the popular appeal of these two causes. Pastors played an increasingly large role in the determination of policies of the General Board. From the 1930s to the 1950s it had been predominantly educators who had been chosen as moderators of the denomination. After 1960 pastors dominated in this office, considered to be the highest at the disposal of the church.

With the increasing centrality of the role of the salaried pastor, there was a corresponding decline in the importance of the traditional elder's role. This function was accordingly called into question, and, after several years of study and debate, was jettisoned at the Annual Conference of 1967. Those men who had been ordained as elders for life retained that status.

Major denominational attention and support in the 1950s and 1960s were devoted to the relocation of both the General Offices and the seminary. The offices and publishing house moved to a modern new plant on the outskirts of Elgin, Illinois, in 1959. The seminary sought a more spacious locale for its campus in Chicago's western suburbs, moving into a handsome new site in Oak Brook, Illinois, in 1963. Some opposed the latter move as an evasion of the needs of the inner city (the former campus was located in what had become a ghetto on Chicago's west side), but the majority in the denomination followed the recommendation of the seminary board in upholding the wisdom and necessity of relocation.

Great emphasis was placed during these years on church development, with attempts to begin new congregations in growing metropolitan areas. A statement on church extension adopted in 1958 pledged the Brethren to cooperate on a comity basis with other denominations. In order to attract those of other church backgrounds to the Brethren, they should be received by transfer without request for rebaptism; Brethren congregations were also encouraged to provide Sunday morning communion services after the usual Protestant pattern. This marked a major step away from traditional Brethren practice and was accepted only on the basis that the action was permissive and would not be binding on all congregations.

Following World War II there was a boom in new church building construction. This often brought with it a change from the former pattern of the pulpit in the center of the chancel, which had in turn supplanted the old meetinghouse style of a preacher's table along the long axis of the house at the same level as congregational seating. The newer trend was for a divided chancel, with lectern on one side, pulpit on the other, and communion table as a worship center in the middle. Architects, borrowing from traditional Protestant usage, often fenced off the chancel. Little attention was given to architectural accommodation of the Brethren practice of the love feast, which was, therefore, often relegated to the basement, now usually called the "fellowship hall." Gleaming kitchens provided the facilities for meals for the entire congregation on social occasions. The outer appearance of the buildings ordinarily incorporated real or suggested steeples, reminiscent of New England Congregational church style. Worship patterns as well became more structured and formal

This change in architecture represented change as well in the self-understanding of the denomination, although it was more felt than articulated. To help clarify its position, the Church of the Brethren sponsored a series of carefully-planned theological conferences in 1960, 1964, 1969, and 1981. The theme for the first consultation was "The Nature and Function of the Church." It included position papers, outside speakers, and intensive discussions. The mood of this first conference might be summed up in the statement that the Brethren should be more clearly identified with a "transformationist strategy in relation to the world." The second conference, which set as its topic "The Meaning of Membership in the Body of Christ," was composed of a broadly representative group, which both furthered discussion and hampered satisfactory resolution of the problems which presented themselves. The report of the conference found no unifying theme which could encompass the diverse Brethren membership. A commentator spoke of an "identity crisis" as the Brethren recognized the extent of their change from an earlier sectarian posture without being able to achieve clarity on feasible future options. A third conference on "Faithfulness in Charge" also found great pluralism within the denomination but seemed to consider this less an embarrassment than the 1964 study. Finally, a "Biblical/Theological Quest" held in two stages in 1981 was devoted more to encouraging wider theological discussion than plotting any denominational direction.

A test of Brethren pluralism took on sharp contours in 1965–1966 when Brethren were invited to enter as full participants into the Consultation on Church Union. This consultation, known as COCU, represented the most serious effort of the 20th century to unite major Protestant bodies in a church "truly reformed, truly catholic, and truly evangelical." From 1963 on Brethren attended annual COCU meetings as "observer-consultants." After a year of intense discussion in congregations, districts, and periodicals, delegates of the Annual Conference of 1966 voted decisively to abstain from full participation. At the same time the conference strongly reaffirmed its attachment to the ecumenical principle as practiced in concilar relationships and cooperation among Christian churches. In 1968 the conference decided against reopening the question.

During this period diversity began to take on organized forms. A conservative element founded the Brethren Revival Fellowship (BRF) in 1959. This largely Eastern group has continued to urge the Brethren through literature, periodic meetings, and classes to place more emphasis upon evangelism, scriptural authority, and doctrine, and less on social witness and action. Membership in the National and World Council of Churches and liberalism in denominational publications and curriculum materials have been heavily criticized by BRF members. The Fellowship supports a part-time staff worker and engages in informal pastoral placement. The charismatic movement, active in American churches since 1960, affected the Brethren. Since 1974 annual Holy Spirit conferences, at times on a regional basis, have brought together several hundred charismatic members of the Church of the Brethren.

Of quite different temper were the Brethren Action Movement and Brethren Peace Fellowship which coalesced around 1967. They desired more vigorous action in peace education and antiwar projects and formed loosely-linked fellowships across the country to accomplish these goals, with special attention to reaching Brethren students. The Brethren Action Movement was short-lived, ceasing activity in 1975 with the close of the war in Vietnam.

The On Earth Peace Assembly (OEPA) had similar peace motivation. Founded in 1974 by veteran peace activist M. R. Zigler, it is based in New Windsor, Maryland. OEPA gives major attention to monthly peace academies for Brethren young people, discussions on peace by vocational groupings, and several publishing efforts. Although of independent origin and support, it has sought to be closely related to the Church of the Brethren and in 1985 was still working out a plan of alignment with the denominational program.

A venture with ties to the On Earth Peace group is the Brethren Encyclopedia, Incorporated. It emerged from a series of meeting of historians from the five largest Brethren bodies—the Brethren Church, the Church of the Brethren, the Dunkard Brethren, the Fellowship of Grace Brethren Churches, and the Old German Baptist Brethren. In 1977 individual members of these five groups incorporated to produce a three-volume encyclopedia with Donald F. Durnbaugh as editor. Substantial financial support and much voluntary labor made possible the publication of the comprehensive reference work in 1983–1984. The cooperative effort resulted also in better feeling between the five Brethren bodies and proposals for continued joint projects.[7]

During the period from 1960 through 1985 the Church of the Brethren moved toward greater activity in peace and justice issues. Several denominational programs had this as their objective. They included Mission One (1965–1970) and a Fund for the Americas (1969ff.) which funded outreach projects of minority groups in the USA. A corollary in the area of missions was the creation of the *Misión Mutua en las Américas* program, designed after 1975 to link the Brethren with a church in the Latin America. Although attended by many difficulties, a connection was established in 1980 with a Pentecostal church in Cuba; the relationship continues on a low-key basis in 1985.

At the same time there was interest in the development of persons within the church. Many of the techniques of group dynamics were used in workshops, "group life laboratories," and retreats. The Mission Twelve program (1962ff.) brought together small groups from several congregations in a retreat setting over period of three weekends for intensive training interpersonal relationships. The plan was for these teams to return to their local churches where they could serve as resources for greater congregational vitality. The plan was supplanted in the 1980s by the People of the Covenant program, designed to advance congregational renewal through bible study. This decade also saw the design and implementation of other well-organized denominational programs in the areas of leadership training and stewardship.

Women came to play a greater role in the church after 1958 when full ordination was approved by conference action. Earlier women ministers had been given permanent licenses for preaching. The best-known female leader was Anna Beahm Mow (1893–1985), a missionary and educator noted for writing many helpful books. She was widely sought as a speaker and spiritual counsellor. A women's caucus was organized in 1973 to promote feminist causes. In the 1970s and 1980s women were elected to leadership positions in the church, on congregational, district, and national levels. These developments were celebrated in the First International Women's Conference on August 1–4, 1985, marking the centennial of organized women's activity in the Church of the Brethren.

A matter of great concern in the Church of the Brethren was the decline of church membership after 1963. The only real area of numerical growth came in Nigeria, where years of patient missionary work since 1922 were repaid by a flood of Africans seeking membership in the church. By 1973 the Nigerian church had become fully independent. Other former mission churches joined ecumenical bodies in their countries, including the United Evangelical Church of Ecuador (1965) and the Church of North India (1970). The number of Brethren missionaries in foreign countries diminished rapidly.

Some reasons for the decline in numbers in the USA were: conference actions that encouraged the removal of names of inactive members from church rolls, the increased involvement of the church in controversial areas of civil rights and peace, the greater mobility of families, the migration from rural areas to the city, and the overall lessening of religious interest in the United States. In 1981 the Annual Conference adopted a paper which studied the problems of diminishing membership. This was followed by a policy statement of the General Board (1984) to guide increased efforts in church growth and evangelism. A goal of 15 new congregations set in 1980 was surpassed before the target date of 1984 and replaced by a more ambitious goal.

The 1985 Annual Conference held in Phoenix, Arizona, recognized 18 fellowships and congregations which had been organized since 1980. Some of them were from minority ethnic groups. This represented a new development in Brethren church life, as Hispanics, Cambodians, Koreans, Filipinos, and Haitians joined with Blacks to enrich the cultural mix of the denomination. They seemed to find attractive the Brethren blend of biblical concern and social activism, congregational freedom and denominational connection, faithful traditionalism and openness to new forms.

Thus in 1985 the Church of the Brethren found itself at a turning point, seemingly poised for a resurgence in the number of members and continued eagerness to meet human needs in the world setting.

Notes

1. Ellsworth Faris, "The Sect and the Sectarian," *American Journal of Sociology*, 40 (May,1979): 75–89; originally published in 1928.
2. Quoted in Floyd E. Mallott, *Studies in Brethren History* (Elgin, IL: 1954), 264.
3. *The Missionary Visitor* (February, 1906): 97.
4. *Minutes of the Annual Meeting of the Church of the Brethren* (Elgin, IL: 1909), 382.
5. For a brief description of the history of the Old German Baptist Brethren after 1881 see John M. Kimmel, *Chronicles of the Brethren* (Covington, OH: 1951), 254–324.; see also Fred W. Benedict,

A Concise Presentation of the History, Belief, and Practice of the Dunkers (The Old German Baptist Brethren) (Covington, OH: 1960).

6. For histories of the two branches of the Progressive Brethren movement see Homer A. Kent, Sr., *Conquering Frontiers*, 2nd ed. (Winona Lake, IN: 1972) and Albert T. Ronk, *History of the Brethren Church* (Ashland, OH: 1968).

7. The genesis of the encyclopedia project is described in a special issue of *Brethren Life and Thought*, 30 (Summer, 1985); for brief descriptions of the five Brethren bodies (taken from articles in *The Brethren Encyclopedia*), see Donald F. Durnbaugh, ed., *Meet the Brethren* (Elgin, IL: 1984).

3

Beliefs

Dale R. Stoffer

From their inception the Brethren have had a twofold concern which has given shape to their beliefs. This dual concern was well expressed by Kermit Eby, a prominent educator and writer, as he reflected upon his Brethren roots: the Brethren "turned to the New Testament as their source of truth, and then looked out into the world."[1] The Brethren have ever been a people of the *Word* who sought to translate that Word into *life*. This biblical-existential approach will dictate the organization of this chapter. The doctrinal convictions that have characterized the Brethren throughout much of their history will first be considered and then the ways in which Brethren beliefs have ben reshaped in the desire to speak to a world that is constantly changing will be investigated.

Brethren Doctrine

Brethren cannot boast about their doctrinal creativity. They have historically accepted the great body of evangelical truths common to Protestantism. What can be said, however, is that the Brethren are unique in the way they have ordered these truths. Just as a quilt's special character depends upon the overall design created by the combination of various pieces of cloth, so also Brethren faith. Although Brethren share many emphases with other churches, it is how they have "quilted" together the various parts of the faith that created the unique design known as Brethren.

The Brethren pattern of belief was principally influenced by two movements: Radical Pietism and Anabaptism. From Radical Pietism the Brethren inherited such characteristics as devotional warmth, evangelistic zeal, and concern for individual salvation and piety. Anabaptism bequeathed to the Brethren its view of the church, notably the organization of the church, the theology of the ordinances, a concern for discipline, and a strong corporate identity, Whereas Radical Pietism gave Brethren faith its inner, spiritual, individual character, Anabaptism provided the outward, formal, corporate substance. One of the unique aspects of Brethren thought has been the desire to maintain a creative balance between these inner and outer aspects of the faith.

Sources of Authority: It must be realized that no matter how much Protestant churches affirm *sola scriptura* (scripture as sole authority), every Protestant group has certain presuppositions or sources of authority through which it filters its reading of Scripture. For example, scriptural interpretation is greatly influenced by the assumptions that one has concerning the character of God (Is holiness or love primary?), the work of Christ (Should the historical Jesus or the Christ of faith be stressed?), the ministry of the Holy Spirit (Is the Spirit still manifested through signs and wonders?), and the role of the church (Is the church coextensive with the state?).

The traditional Brethren approach to Scripture was governed by six sources of authority, all of which can be traced back to Anabaptism and/or Radical Pietism: God, Christ, Scripture, the Holy Spirit, the early church (primitivism), and the gathered church. The assumptions concerning these authorities remained fairly constant until the late 19th century, when modifications began to appear as the church struggled to discover its place in the modern world.

Alexander Mack, Sr., the earliest leader and doctrinal writer of the Brethren, maintained that the church owes its existence to God. God is the "Householder" (*Haus-Vater*), the source of all the commandments and ordinances to be kept in God's household. God alone has the prerogative to establish the church. This conviction caused Mack to offer a twofold apologetic for the formation of the Brethren. Their assurance of God's sovereign calling rested on the certainty of having been inwardly directed by God (a Radical Pietist criterion) and on the outward confirmation found in their commitment to follow the teachings of Christ (an Anabaptist touchstone).

In Brethren writings no other source of authority has been emphasized so strongly as Jesus Christ. A unique feature of the Brethren view of Christ's work is that they have given as much weight to the life of Jesus (the Jesus of history) as to his death and resurrection and the faith founded thereon (the Christ of faith). Thus Jesus by his death and resurrection, has made available to us salvation in his name. The believers' response is to have faith, a confident trust in God to bring about new life in those who turn to God. But Jesus has also revealed in his life and teachings all that God wills for God's people. The believers' response is obedience—not a slavish following of the minutiae of the law but joyful acceptance of God's will as an expression of love for what God has done for them. This latter emphasis explains why the Sermon on the Mount has played such a significant role in Brethren thought. Likewise, the above balance suggests why the Brethren have always maintained that saving faith will be known by obedience.

The other sources of authority gain their significance from their testimony to Christ. For example, the Brethren view of Scripture is christologically determined. Because the New Testament is the fullest revelation of God's will in Christ, it has priority over the Old. The Old Testament prefigures the New; the New Testament fulfills the Old. But the discontinuity between the testaments must not be overemphasized. The Brethren have also seen a definite continuity between the testaments based primarily on the conviction that there is a continuous line from the Old Testament people of God to the New (Mack followed Anabaptist thought that Israel is the church of the Old Testament).

The Brethren historically have seen Scripture as the church's objective authority, having priority over Christian tradition, human reason, private mystical experiences, and theological systems. They have generally accepted Scripture in an uncritical manner (the 20th century has brought interest in critical scholarship). Taking what they read in a simple, humble, obedient way, Brethren have also demonstrated a harmonizing hermeneutic (method of interpretation). Rather than seeing inherent conflicts between different writers, they have sought to synthesize the insights of various authors into a logical whole. This is best seen in the threefold communion service which combines the accounts of the Last Supper in the synoptic gospels with that of John.

Following the lead of the Anabaptists, the early Brethren sought a balance between the roles of Scripture and the Holy Spirit. Whereas Scripture is the outer Work, declaring God's will in an objective manner, the Holy Spirit is the inner Word, dwelling within the heart of the believer and serving as an internal law for the Christian. A necessary reciprocity exists between the two. Scripture can be understood spiritually only by the internal witness of the Holy Spirit, who, indeed, inspired all of Scripture, but Scripture limits and tests any questionable expressions of the Spirit.

The early Brethren showed a great deal of interest in the church of the first two centuries, combing available histories in order to discover as much as they could about the lifestyle of the early Christians. This interest derives from their primitivism: the Anabaptists stressed the importance of following the example and pattern of Christ and the apostles, while the influential Radical Pietist historian, Gottfried Arnold, held that the church of the first two centuries was the purest representation of true Christianity. On the basis of these sources, Brethren adopted a number of rites which had fallen into general disuse: the holy kiss, anointing with oil, the love feast, feetwashing, and threefold immersion baptism.

Throughout their history the Brethren have viewed the gathered church as the proving ground for the development of Christian character. God directs all believers to the church, God's household, as the place where they are to grow and mature into greater Christlikeness.

In looking at these foundational suppositions, it can be seen that the primary focus of Brethren thought is the creation of God-like character and life in a people committed to their Creator. Though necessarily beginning individually, this new character and life can be attained fully only in community. This observation leads to the two main areas of theology in which most of the beliefs that are unique to the Brethren are to be found: the views of salvation and the church.

The Doctrine of Salvation: The Brethren understanding of salvation again shows affinities to both Anabaptism and Radical Pietism. Formulations of the initial aspects of the salvation process (what is usually called conversion) prior to this century were generally quite simple: illumination, repentance, faith, baptism, forgiveness of sins, and the gift of the Holy Spirit. Other elements—adoption, justification, regeneration (this last term found mainly in the 19th century)—were at times mentioned but not developed as thoroughly as the preceding ones. Though illumination or enlightenment is not discussed much today, Brethren writers throughout the 18th and 19th centuries used this term to stress that salvation is a gift of God. God is the initiator, not only in providing salvation through Christ's work of redemption but also in making possible the appropriation of salvation. Here the Brethren followed the Reformation conviction that human rebellion against God necessitates God's work of illuminating minds and hearts concerning human spiritual need. This illumination occurs through the joint working of the Word of God in showing believers this need and of the Holy Spirit in bringing conviction of that truth.

God's initiative in illumination must be followed by the human responses of repentance and faith if conversion is to occur. The Brethren have historically given special emphasis to repentance. Peter Nead, a leading Brethren doctrinal writer of the 19th century, noted three essential aspects of repentance: 1) heartfelt sorrow for and bitter hatred of sins committed against God; 2) confession of sin to God; 3) amendment or reformation of life.[2] Nead, as well as other Brethren, underscored the point that repentance must go beyond mere sorrow. It must lead to a desire to reform one's life according to the will of God.

Whereas repentance might be called the negative side of conversion, faith may be called the positive side: they belong together. From the start, Brethren have insisted that faith must include two essential elements: 1) knowledge and 2) faithfulness or obedience. One must have a basic understanding of God and God's gracious work in Christ to receive salvation. If one is to live the Christian life, one must understand what it involves; one must be able to "count the cost." It was for this reason that the Brethren of the 18th and 19th centuries generally did not baptize members before their young adult years. But the Brethren emphasize even more forcefully that faith involves faithfulness and commitment to the teachings of Christ and the apostles. Saving faith will always be recognized by works of obedience.

The first act of this obedient faith was held to be baptism. It is for this reason, as an act of obedience to the command of Christ in Matthew 28:19, that baptism has played such a central role in the Brethren view of salvation. It is true that during the nineteenth century, Brethren apologetics for baptism bordered on baptismal regeneration, but earlier formulations of the significance of baptism rejected any *ex opere operato* view (the sacramental view that grace is conveyed through the rite simply by its performance). The "active ingredient" in baptism is not the act itself but the faith and obedience brought to the act. As Alexander Mack, Sr., expressed it, "Salvation is not dependent upon the water, but only upon the faith, which must be proved by love."[3] Because the Brethren rites are testimonies to faith and obedience and are visible portrayals of belief, Brethren have generally avoided the term "sacrament" in referring to them. They have preferred to call them "ordinances," indicating thereby that these acts have been ordained by Christ or the apostles.

God's promise of forgiveness of sins and the gift of the Holy Spirit (Acts 2:38) is fulfilled in the lives of those who respond in obedient, repentant faith. While forgiveness of sins *prepares* believers for the new life with God by breaking the power of sin and providing right standing before God, it is the Holy Spirit who *enables* believers to live the new life.

All the elements of salvation discussed so far deal only with that initial part of salvation called "conversion." While many groups influenced by revivalism and fundamentalism have tended to emphasize this side of salvation by making "being saved" all-important, this has not been true of the Brethren. As foundational as these elements are, they are not the end of the salvation experience. Nearly every element of the Brethren view of conversion points beyond itself to the necessity of living the new life in Christ. Thus repentance includes the resolve to reform one's life according to God's will; the faith that saves will be a faith that obeys and works; baptism is a pledge before God and the community of the individual's desire to live in faithfulness to Christ; the forgiveness of sins and the gift of the Holy Spirit both enable the believer to live the Christ-like life, the former by breaking the power of sin, the latter by giving the power and knowledge needed to grow in Christian maturity.

In addition, Brethren have understood salvation as both an event and a process. As an event, salvation is that point at which believers commit their lives to Christ as Lord and Savior and receive God's gracious gifts of forgiveness and the Holy Spirit. As a process, salvation involves that lifelong spiritual growth which is brought to completion only at the believers' glorification with Christ. Such a view is consistent with Scripture which can talk of salvation in the past, present, and future tenses.

Following the lead of the Pietists, the Brethren have insisted that the new birth must proceed into the new life. Interestingly, Brethren have not generally described the Christian life by the 19th century catchword—holiness—nor by the more theological term current in this century—sanctification. Rather they have preferred to portray the new life in Christ in Anabaptist and Pietist terms. It is described positively as humility, love for God and neighbor, and obedience and discipleship to Christ, negatively as self-denial and nonconformity to the world.

The same indebtedness to the Anabaptists and Pietists can be seen in the Brethren understanding of the believer's security or assurance. The latter term is the one Brethren seem to prefer. The Brethren have based assurance on both inward and outward qualities. Inwardly, the believer can have certainty about acceptance by God on the basis of the witness of the indwelling Spirit. Outwardly, assurance rests on the believer's growth in faith, love, and obedience, which are the fruit of the Spirit's inward work.

The Doctrine of the Church: The concept of the church has played an indispensable role in Brethren thought from the beginning. In fact, one of the main reasons why the early Brethren moved away from Radical Pietism and toward Anabaptism was because of their convictions about the church. They felt that total obedience to Christ (which the Radical Pietists stressed) required the existence of an organized body of believers. The spiritualized concept of the church held by Radical Pietists made impossible the observance of practices that were felt to be clearly ordained by Christ and the apostles: baptism, communion, and discipline. In looking for a contemporary model for the church which most mirrored that of the early church, Mack and his fellow Brethren were drawn to the Anabaptists.

It must be stressed that there is an indissoluble link between the doctrines of salvation and the church in Brethren thought. Many of the initial aspects of salvation point the individual to the church as the place in which the new life is to be lived out. This is true of baptism, which incorporates the repentant believer into God's people; forgiveness, which removes the barriers to fellowship not only with God but also with God's people; and the gift of the Holy Spirit, who unites the new believer with others who share a common confession. Brethren held that the Pietist insistence on the new life could be fully realized only in community. Here follow some of the characteristics that have typified the Brethren view of the church.

Church as Gemeinschaft: The foremost characteristic of the church for the Brethren is best expressed by the German word, *Gemeinschaft*. Referring to the intimate sense of unity which exists among people who share deep commitments, this term focuses attention on the "peoplehood" of the church rather than its institutional character. It is with good reason that the name *Brethren* became attached to the church. The Spiritual bonds and kinship that gave rise to the address "brother" and "sister" among the Radical Pietists and Anabaptists were carried over into Brethren circles. For all three groups, the cement which formed these bonds was the shared commitment to Jesus Christ and the new life which they had received in Him.

Several important Brethren characteristics derive from this *Gemeinschaft*. Notable is the practice of communion consisting of the three rites of feetwashing, love feast, and eucharist. Communion has been the time at which the community celebrates in existential fashion the full measure of what it means to be God's people. The community of faith reminds itself that the spiritual fellowship shared with Christ and one another is rooted in Christ's sacrificial death in the past, is continuing because of his spiritual presence in his people in the present, and will be fulfilled when God's dwelling place is with God's people (Rev.21:3). The church likewise recommits itself to that service to an love for one another which are the blessed "ties that bind."

Gemeinschaft has also exhibited itself in a deep sense of being "family" with one another. Mack's use of the New Testament imagery of the "household of God" to refer to the church is an expression of this family feeling. This sense of being brothers and sisters stretches beyond the confines of the local congregation to include all who share a common commitment to the church. Nothing exemplifies this better than the Annual Conference, which has the aura of a large family reunion.

A further expression of *Gemeinschaft* has been the involvement of the Church of the Brethren in the ecumenical movement. The Brethren were charter members of both the World and National Council of Churches and have supplied personnel for ecumenical concerns at a rate which is proportionately higher than that for most other denominations. They also introduced the practice of open communion and transfer of membership by affirmation of faith ahead of some other denominations of a similar type. Generally speaking, Brethren have sought to practice an open rather than a closed *Gemeinschaft*.

Church as Visible Community: Historically, the Brethren have maintained that the church is to be a visible representation of its Lord. This view is in conflict with the concept of the invisible church that conceives of the church as a mixed group, some committed Christians, some Christians in name only. This latter view holds that it is not the church's responsibility to weed out the good from the bad, for God will do that on the day of judgment.

The Brethren, however, have held that God's people are to be not only God's image-bearers but also God's character-bearers. Christians are to be God's *ekklesia*—the called-out ones—who are to show visibly by words, actions, and character that they follow God's way rather than the world's. Integral to this viewpoint has been the conception of baptism. Baptism has been understood as a pledge or covenant made by the individual before God and the community that he or she will live in faithfulness to Jesus Christ and to his word. Every individual is therefore accountable to God and the church to live the Christ-like life. These convictions led the early Brethren to adopt three practices that have come to be associated with the Brethren: nonconformity, nonresistance, and nonswearing.

Nonconformity is the principle that in all situations believers must obey God rather than men. Radical obedience to the teachings of Christ and the apostles is the hallmark of the Christian faith. Nonconformity has had a checkered history among the Brethren. During the early and mid-19th century, the church followed the Mennonites in adopting a lifestyle that caused them to be labeled the "Quiet Ones in the Lord" (*Die Stillen im Lande*). There was a tendency to withdraw from the world in order to protect the peculiar lifestyle and piety that had arisen among them. Coincident with this development was an attempt to "hedge the church in" by the adoption of casuistic rulings against possessions and practices ranging from lightning rods to likenesses (photographs). Reaction against such a legalistic interpretation of nonconformity has caused modern Brethren to be tempted in the opposite direction. There has been such a desire to "turn to the world" that the concept of nonconformity has been dismissed by some segments of the church as an anachronistic relic. However, renewed interest in the historic position of the church and in the doctrine of the "simple life" may bode well for a contemporary reconsideration of this doctrine.

The Brethren doctrine of nonresistance originally derived from their radical obedience to the words of Jesus (Matt. 5:39). From its inception the Church of the Brethren has maintained an opposition to violence as well as to militarism and welfare. Although there has been a decline in the commitment of the general membership to the peace position in the 20th century owing to the two world wars and acculturation, the official counsel of the church has been against noncombatant as well as combatant participation in the military. Many have felt it important to distinguish nonresistance from pacifism. As one Brethren writer noted, pacifism denotes "a societal technique prudentially calculated to resolve conflict situations and enable one to achieve his chosen social goals; it becomes a means of manipulating society—toward good ends, it goes without saying."[4] Nonresistance, however, refers more broadly to a lifestyle of defenseless love in the face of evil (whether manifested in individuals, groups, or nations) which is rooted in Jesus' own teachings and example.

The Brethren practice of the nonswearing of oaths is another expression of their obedience to the teachings of Jesus (Matt. 5:34–37). Like the preceding two doctrines, nonswearing needs to be viewed in a broader context. It assumes a lifestyle of honesty, integrity, and forthrightness, which makes the taking of oaths unnecessary. Indicative of the degree to which the Brethren of the last century lived these qualities was the slogan that arose in many communities populated by Brethren: "A Dunker's word is as good as his bond."

In striving to make visible God's character in their own, Brethren also developed a kind of realized eschatology (doctrine of last things). God's kingdom, God's rule, was not merely some future hope of the community. It had already begun to be experienced where God's people were truly following Christ in faithful obedience. Even though the

Brethren prior to the 20th century generally held a historic premillennial view of Christ's return, they tended to focus more upon the believer's conduct and character in this life. They were optimistic about God's ability to transform people's lives through the power of the Holy Spirit. Where people truly desired to live the Christ-like life, a community of God's presence and power could be realized.

Church as Disciplined Community: It follows from the above that there would be a great deal of concern for maintaining the purity of the community through discipline. In this conviction the Brethren followed the Anabaptists. Here again baptism played an integral role. Part of the baptismal vows was the pledge to give and receive counsel and discipline according to Matthew 18:15–17. This pledge was indicative of a willingness to yield oneself to the will of God through mutual submission and the renunciation of selfish pride. The motivation for discipline was twofold; maintenance of the purity of the church and concern for the spiritual welfare of every believer. Ideally (though not always practically) discipline was an expression of love.

Though the Brethren did practice the greater ban (avoidance) through the 19th century, the more frequent practice came to be the lesser ban (exclusion from the holy kiss, the church council, and the love feast). During this century, however, discipline in the formal sense has become almost nonexistent. No doubt this development is partially due to occasional legalistic, unloving applications of discipline in the past, but it is also the product of a more individualized, "enlightened" philosophy which has undercut the traditional Brethren values of mutual accountability and corporate unity and purity. This is another area, however, where there has been some recent reevaluation in the light of Brethren heritage.

Church as Hermeneutical Community: Brethren have adopted an unique approach to discerning truth. It balances two convictions, one derived from Pietism and the other from Anabaptism. From Pietism came the conviction that believers have the right and responsibility to study Scripture on their own without the interpretive constraints of papal dogma or theological and credal systems. It was felt that only in this way could the Holy Spirit be free to shed new light upon God's Word. For this reason Brethren have been noncredal. While the Brethren have not been averse to developing statements of belief, these have generally not been viewed as authoritative pronouncements of the church in the sense of being used as tests of fellowship.

From Anabaptism came the conviction that the community of faith should at all times strive to be one in mind as one in spirit. This concern led the Brethren to stress the importance of submission to mutual correction in the interpretation of Scripture and in matters of everyday practice. The phrase "mind of Christ" came to represent a method of mutual discernment, prayer, and sensitivity to Scripture, the goal of which was a Spirit-led consensus on any issue.

There have been occasions in Brethren history when one or the other of these convictions has been taken to an extreme. The individual's right to study and interpret Scripture led in some Brethren groups to the elevation of individual conscience over corporate consensus and to the extolling of congregational autonomy (a corporate expression of this view). At times the striving for unity has led to the formulation of various external rules and to their enforcement by making uniformity mandatory. When a proper tension is maintained between these two convictions, however, the church remains open to the insights of individuals and minority groups but still desires to arrive at the "mind of Christ" through frank discussion and mutual love and submission.

Church as Priesthood of All Believers: Given their Anabaptist and Radical Pietist roots, it is to be expected that the Brethren would accept this doctrine. Brethren have accepted both its individual and corporate implications. Thus, because each believer is a priest for his or her own soul, all are ultimately responsible for their own spiritual growth and development. Throughout their history Brethren have therefore placed special prominence upon individual and family Bible study and devotions. But because they are members intimately joined in the body of Christ, each has a priestly office to perform for others. All are to be concerned about the spiritual welfare of brothers and sisters in the faith.

This doctrine also had other expressions, especially in the area of polity. Prior to the impact of mainstream Christianity upon the Brethren in this century, the church had developed a system of unsalaried, "free" ministers and elders who were set apart by a nonsacramental ordination. Brethren held that the authority for calling ministers and elders, as well as deacons, rested in the local congregation with the concurrence of adjoining elders. Relying on the guidance of the Holy Spirit in prayer, the gathered body sought to select its leaders on the basis of evident character qualities and leadership potential. Even with the emergence of a salaried and educated ministry, the absence of a sacramental view of the ordinances has prevented the development of a sacerdotal concept of ministry (where clergy control the access to grace). Likewise, even though the distinction between laity and clergy has widened during the development of Brethren history, the Brethren have generally maintained an equality of status for the two groups. This quality is especially borne out in the church council meetings in which ministers have no more authority in deciding matters of business that do the laity.

Church as Mutual Aid Community Brethren have been concerned not only about the spiritual needs of one another within the body but also the material and physical needs. The love and mutual support befitting those who share a common allegiance to Jesus Christ has expressed itself during the course of Brethren history in such ways as the deacons' fund for the relief of the poor, self-insuring programs, barn-raisings, retirement facilities, tending the farm of a sick neighbor, or taking meals to a needy family.

Brethren have also understood that love for one's neighbor directs one out of the community of faith into the world. Until the 20th century, most relief efforts were carried on unofficially by individuals and local congregations. More extensive relief activities began with work by missionaries in India and China at the turn of the century in response to needs brought about by drought, famine, and war. Increasingly since the late 1930s, the Church of the Brethren has played a prominent role in relief and social service programs, both nationally and internationally. Through involvement in such agencies and programs as Brethren Volunteer Service, the Heifer Project, Church World Service, CROP, and the Brethren Disaster Network, Brethren have aided their neighbors throughout the United States and in some one hundred foreign nations.

Brethren Response to the World

As noted at the outset, Brethren thought can be understood best when it is recognized in its two-dimensional character: a desire to remain faithful to the Word (which tends to be Anabaptist) and a desire to come to terms with the contemporary world (which tends to be Pietist). The remainder of this chapter will address the latter desire, using a historical approach.

Until the Revolutionary War, Brethren maintained a healthy, creative balance between the two desires. Anabaptists that they were, the early Brethren showed a firm commitment to maintaining those beliefs and practices which they had derived from Scripture. In fact, their commitment to nonresistance and their unwillingness to renounce their pledge to honor the king of England was the source of much anguish for the Brethren during the Revolutionary War. The Brethren commitment to seek unity in thought and practice led them to begin the gatherings that came to be know as the Annual Meetings. In polity and lifestyle the Brethren emulated the Mennonites, around whose communities Brethren frequently settled.

Pietists that they were, the early Brethren showed a deep sense of piety, which evidenced itself in a rich and abundant hymnody and in numerous devotional writings. They manifested an evangelistic zeal that caused them to grow rapidly in Germany and then in America after their mass immigration. They exhibited a willingness to change their practice even of such an important rite as communion when they received new light on Scripture. There was a vibrancy to their faith that attracted many Mennonites to join them.

As with most new organizations, the Brethren experienced a period of consolidation and stricter definition of thought and practice after the leaders of the first two generations had died. Contributing to this process, which had begun by the late 1700s, was the insulation of the Brethren from the impact of American society. Three factors tended toward this cultural isolation: the retention of their German language and subculture; the tendency of the predominantly agrarian brethren to migrate westward (frequently in groups) in search of better and cheaper land; and the strong religious principles of simplicity and nonconformity to the world.

The period of consolidation, which lasted until the 1860s, had a number of significant expressions. In polity, Annual Meeting, through the decisions made at each gathering, gained increasing power as the church sought to conserve the "order of the Brethren" and to "fence out" the influence of American culture. In lifestyle, Brethren gave formal definition to their distinctive dress. Likewise, one's degree of Christianity came to be judged by outward marks—nonconformity to the world, nonresistance, faithfulness to the order if the church.

In thought, there was a clear shift in the direction of stricter definition, greater emphasis upon forms, and preservation of the "received tradition." Thus, Peter Nead helped to standardize the Brethren order of salvation as repentance, faith, and baptism, to which acts were promised the forgiveness of sins and the gift of the Holy Spirit. This more objective approach to salvation may have been partially a response to the more subjective, emotional approach taken by revivalist groups. In a concomitant development, the Brethren laid far more stress on the outward rites of communion and baptism. Doctrinal discussions frequently centered on a defense of these two practices.

Even more significant, baptism became a "means of grace" during this period. (The early Brethren would probably have followed Menno Simons in holding that Jesus Christ is the only means of grace.) Use of this term, which first appeared in Brethren literature in 1817, made the act of baptism necessary for the reception of the graces that follow—forgiveness, the gift of the Spirit adoption, etc. The early Brethren had argued for the necessity of Baptism by insisting that it was the response of a preceding obedient faith. In the new formulation the inward no longer led to the outward as was formerly the case, but the outward must precede the inward.

This period also witnessed a decline in the more creative expressions of piety—hymns and poetry—though much devotional literature continued to appear. Brethren also adopted a more passive approach to evangelism, waiting for prospective members to indicate their intentions to the church. All of these developments attest that the inner-outer dialectic, which had been so creatively maintained during the first two generations, had now shifted in the direction of outwardness. The Brethren tended to be far more concerned with defending and conserving the traditional forms than they were with ministering to the world outside their own subculture.

By the mid-19th century several socio-economic developments occurred, which were to have far-reaching effects on the Brethren. By the 1840s English had become the predominant language among them and their enclaves were increasingly being surrounded by American culture. Brethren were no longer able to hide behind some of the artificial fences they had erected. They were forced to come to terms with the society of the New World. During the 1850s, some of the leading figures in the church—Henry Kurtz, James Quinter, John Kline—began to advocate the use of such modern practices as periodical literature, Sunday schools, higher education, and evangelism. They believed that some of what modern culture offered could be used by the church to make it more effective in its mission.

During the 1860s and 1970s three distinct positions gradually evolved in response to this acculturating process. The left wing, known as the "Progressives," sought to "keep pace with the times." Led by H. R. Holsinger, this group advocated the use of any practice that would contribute to the mission of the church. The right wing, known as the "Old Orders," saw these innovations as entirely worldly and a departure from biblical Christianity. Guided by Peter Nead and his son-in-law, Samuel Kinsey, the Old Order Brethren sought to uphold the traditional order of the Brethren. The largest group, the Conservatives (the present Church of the Brethren) sought a middle ground. They were willing to see change, but it had to be gradual. For men such as R. H. Miller, Sr., James Quinter, and J. H. Moore, the unity of the main part of the church was more important than either progression or the old order.

Illuminating for this discussion are the positions of each of the groups on three questions: polity, the authorities used for determining faith and practice, and the attitude toward adaption to the world. It is interesting that the Old Order Brethren were disenchanted with the growing institutionalization of the church. Even though they desired that Annual Meeting decisions on doctrine and practice be uniformly observed in all local congregations, they sought greater simplicity in the organization of Annual Meeting. The Progressives shared the desire for greater simplicity in denominational government. They felt, however, that Annual Meeting decisions for which there was no gospel precept should be considered advisory only. Though in matters of doctrine there should be unity in the church, local congregations should be free to decide questions of government and custom. The Conservatives increasingly moved in the direction of making the decisions of Annual Meeting mandatory, especially as a response to the congregationalism of the Progressives. They held that the unity in faith and practice of the total community must have precedence over the liberty of the individual member or church.

As regards the authorities for determining faith and practice, the Old Order Brethren felt that the gospel as *interpreted* by the "ancient order of the Brethren" should be the primary authority in guiding the church. Annual Meeting should therefore serve primarily as the conservator of the established order. The Progressives were in agreement that matters explicitly described in the gospel must be observed and even felt that the "ancient customs" of the church should be respected, but they insisted that no tradition, including their own, could be elevated to a position equal with Scripture. Individual conscience could not be bound by externals for which there was no gospel authority. The Conservatives sought a middle way between these two positions. They combined belief in the priority of Scripture with a high regard for, yet a willingness to change, the received order.

On the issue of acculturation, the Old Order showed rigid opposition to all of the innovations and sought to preserve the order of the church as they knew it. The Progressives were the most open to the outside secular and religious world, earning themselves the label "the fast element" for their support of higher education, Sunday schools, revival meetings, a paid and educated ministry, and greater freedom in dress. The Conservatives again sought to steer a middle course between the two groups. They were open to change but it could not occur at the expense of the unity of the church.

The differences which culminated in a three-way division between 1881 and 1883 were more a matter of emphasis than essence. Each of the groups, while upholding certain aspects of the Brethren heritage, were in danger of minimizing others. The Old Orders, who assumed the name Old German Baptist Brethren, properly maintained the principles of community, nonconformity, and a simple, self-denying lifestyle. Yet the danger of their position was the legalizing of specific forms in which these principles were cast. The mission of the church became self-preservation rather than outreach to a needy world.

The Progressives, who took the designation the Brethren Church, were correct in criticizing the externalization of the order of the other two positions, which, they felt, was hampering the church's freedom to develop new means for meeting the spiritual needs of society. The very real danger of the Progressive position was that the strong emphasis on individual freedom and adaption to the world would serve to undermine the unity of the church and introduce influences which would dilute the Brethren heritage.

The error of the Conservatives was their abuse of their position of power at the Annual Meeting. They were so willing to be rid of the problems posed by the two groups that they relied on procedural technicalities to cut short the deliberative process with each.

The Conservatives emerged from the period of the division as a body which was more unified and had a more deliberate sense of its mission. They followed through with an agenda of gradual progression so that by 1900 they had adopted nearly all of the reforms which the Progressives had sought. Ironically, they even "out-progressed" the Progressives during the course of the 20th century. Indicative of this progressive spirit was the adoption of the name Church of the Brethren in 1908 and the gradual discarding of the distinctive dress after the 1911 Annual Meeting.

Even more significant for the direction of the church during this century was the education of many future denominational leaders during the interwar years in some of the leading liberal universities in America. They have been instrumental in guiding the church into some of its distinctive characteristics of this century: involvement in domestic and foreign social and relief programs, active participation in the ecumenical movement, and a strong peace witness.

These developments have not been without controversy, however. In 1926 a group known as the Dunkard Brethren withdrew from the church, sharply criticizing the "worldward drift" of the church. Since

the 1920s, individuals and congregations influenced by fundamentalism have voiced their opposition to these trends and some have withdrawn from the denomination. In 1959 a conservative,
non-fundamental group, the Brethren Revival Fellowship, was organized with the purpose of calling the church back to traditional Brethren values and practices. It has sought to carry out its reform program
within the denomination.

Because of the desire to enfold even these voices of criticism and
more recent advocates of the feminist and charismatic movement, the
Church of the Brethren has adopted a more pluralistic conception of its
life and witness. Although it has lost not only its sectarian identity but
also some of its sense of community as it turned outward in this century, the church has gained new visions of ministry and service. As one
might suspect, this transformation has been accompanied by a loss of
theological stability. But since the mid-1950s the church has engaged in
a variety of discussions in order to regain a sense of its identity and
mission. Thus the Puidoux conferences, the Believers' Church Conferences, and the Brethren Historians and Writers Conferences have
helped the church develop a deepening awareness of its historical and
theological heritage, and it is to be hoped, a clearer vision for the
future.

Concluding Observation

Two impulses have shaped Brethren thought: commitment to the
Word and commitment to reflecting the Word in this world (this latter
commitment has expressed itself both in world-denying and world-
affirming ways during the historical development of the Brethren). The
uniqueness of Brethren thought is therefore found in its being both
doctrinal (in the biblical theological sense) and *practical*. This insight
again brings forth the realization that Brethren thought has at its foundation a tension or dialectic between the inner life of the Spirit and its
outer, formal expression. Here follow some of the dialectical elements
in Brethren thought:

Pietism	*Anabaptism*
Inner Word (Spirit)	Outer Word (Scripture)
Freedom of Conscience	Uniformity
Individualism, congregational-ism	Community
Adaptation	Separation

Openness to new truth	Corporate consensus
Individual spiritual growth	Corporate purity

As the Brethren have tended to work with a harmonizing hermeneutic, it is in the midpoint of these two columns that their genius is to be found. The new life must begin as an individual experience of God's saving grace, but its ultimate fulfillment is attained only in community. It is always the inner life of the Spirit that gives life and vitality to the Christian life (thus the necessity of the devotional life) but the Spirit will always be manifested in visible, concrete forms (thus the significance of the ordinances and deeds of service). To overemphasize either side of the dialectic will lead to problems. Those concerned only with their own spiritual life will not have a deep sense of their responsibility to the church or to the world. Those concerned only with conserving past forms or serving the world run the danger of losing the vivifying and, at times, unsettling work of the Spirit.

In proper balance, Brethren thought will be both conservative and progressive. Its conservatism is based upon its unreserved commitment to Scripture as God's Word. Its progressivism is rooted in the realization that believers must be open to the Spirit's leading if their faith is to address the vital issues of the contemporary setting. Brethren must never be so conservative that they fail to address God's Word to the culture in forms that will speak to this age. Brethren must never be so progressive that they blunt the radicalness of God's truth by adopting the world's ways. It is within this that their heritage challenges Brethren to live.

Notes

1. Kenneth I. Morse, "Brethren Have a Plumb Line" (sidebar with "Kermit Eby" article), *The Brethren Encyclopedia* (1983–1984), 420.

2. Peter Nead, *The Wisdom and Power of God as Displaced in Creation and Redemption* (Cincinnati: 1866), 224–227.

3. Alexander Mack, Sr., "Basic Questions," in Donald F. Durnbaugh, ed., *European Origins of the Brethren* (Elgin, IL: 1958), 335.

4. Vernard Eller, "Beliefs," in Donald F. Durnbaugh, ed., *The Church of the Brethren: Past and Present* (Elgin, IL: 1971), 47–48.

4

Worship

Dale W. Brown

Brethren views of worship are similar to the meanings of the Greek word for liturgy embraced by the apostolic writers. In the New Testament, liturgy denotes not only the style of worship of the Christian community but also encompasses good works and acts of charity (2 Cor. 9:12; Phil. 2:30). The meaning is properly expressed by those who name the gathering for worship a church service and by Quakers who are fond of reminding Brethren that the service begins when the meeting ends.

The sacramental life includes the daily walk. The true mystery (sacrament) is the presence of the Spirit of Jesus Christ in the total life of his people. Symbols, ordinances, and practices are celebrated both inside and outside of church buildings. For example, the rite of baptism takes place indoors, for the most part. However, the earlier practice of baptizing in rivers, creeks, and lakes is being revived in many places. The anointing service takes place in homes or hospitals. The refusal to swear an oath becomes visible in relationship to civil government.

Today edifices for worship and fellowship are called *churches*. When earlier generations moved from homes to simple buildings, they called them *meetinghouses*. They avoided the terms *church* and *sanctuary* because they wished to reserve these words to designate the activity and location of the people of God. The people of God do not *go* to church; they *are* the church. Their beliefs about the meetinghouse pointed to the affirmation that all of celebrating this truth. They met together to celebrate that all of life is a sanctuary, a holy place.

Brethren were slow to adopt the pattern of the Christian year. For them every day was sacred. Like the Puritans, they did not observe special holy days. Such a focus can suggest that other days are not holy. As Lent, for example, is the time when all are called to live sacrificially, something like *Mardi Gras* is deemed necessary in traditional perspective for engaging in revelry and debauchery while it is still possible. Instead of accepting a time to sin and a time to be holy, Pietists declared that all days should be graced with Christian joy and holiness. As a result the Brethren did not keep the Sabbath as inviolate as many thought they should.

It was inevitable, however, that as even the Puritans created a special holy day (Thanksgiving), there evolved special times and days among the Brethren. One of these was the gathering for dealing with differences by means of queries, the Big (Annual) Meeting—a large church-family reunion and inspirational time for singing and preaching. A liturgical ingredient obviously crept in when the old Brethren appropriately fixed the date at Pentecost, a time which is only kept today by the Old Order branch of the movement. Today most Brethren observe holy days and many congregations adhere to the church year in the hope that special occasions can celebrate God's grace in such a way as to enhance loving relationships in the days that follow.

It has been conjectured that though the Catholics and Anglicans attend church for reverent worship of God and members of the Reformed tradition gather to be instructed from the Word of God, the Brethren assemble to see one another. It is recognized that such is an oversimplification of each of the traditions. The Brethren have indeed been concerned to carry out the Pauline injunction to gather for corporate acts of worship and correct biblical interpretations. It has been felt, however, that often a special sacramental quality is present in face-to-face relationships. Because of this warm informality and the "low church" nature of some of the Sunday services, the impression has often been given that the Church of the Brethren is not very liturgical. A closer examination will reveal a rich worship tradition with a unifying dynamic in the midst of a variety of forms.

Ordinances

The Brethren spoke of ordinances instead of sacraments in referring to their many covenantal acts. This may have resulted from their desire to follow the New Testament, which does not use words such as *sacraments* or *means of grace* but which does refer to acts instituted by Christ and commended by the apostles. In their desire to obey the commandments of their Lord and to follow the patterns of the New

Testament church, they understood ordinances to be acts of obedience. Worship practices inside or outside of the church building have known special status if they are in some way related to a New Testament reference.

Although not always successfully, Brethren have attempted to avoid a slavish legalism. Alexander Mack, Sr., the leader of the early community, taught that "eternal life is not promised because of baptism, but only through faith in Christ." Nevertheless, a believer will want to do what Jesus wants us to do, which includes his command to be baptized.[1] A 19th century writer, in speaking of the biblical admonition to greet one another with the holy kiss, maintained that the kiss of formality could never be a fulfillment by itself of the apostle's injunction. "There must be something connected with it more than form to make it holy."[2] Nevertheless, sterile formality and legalism have sometimes plagued the body. At times, the teaching has been explicit that commands should be obeyed simply because they are in the New Testament. At other times, the message has implied special rewards for faithfulness.

The Brethren have not been legalistic in holding to an exact number of ordinances or normative criteria about what constitutes a sacrament. They have been Protestant in emphasizing baptism and the love feast (which includes the eucharist) more than other rites. But they have shared with Roman Catholics the inclusion of other practices. These have included feetwashing, the agape meal, anointing, laying on of hands, the holy kiss, covered and uncovered heads, nonswearing, and nonlitigation. The importance of the marriage ceremony has accompanied their traditional beliefs in the sacredness of family life and fidelity in marriage.

Because of the desire to avoid legalism, the decreasing emphasis on some of the above practices, and a growing kinship with other Christians, some contemporary Brethren have appropriated the word *sacrament* for baptism and the communion service. Many still refer to these acts as *ordinances*, while other search for a more appropriate designation. As Brethren very in their terms, so they differ in their theology of these practices. Almost all would deny any inherent sacramental value to elements such as water and bread. Many would be Zwinglian in feeling that the elements are signs pointing to religious truths. Some would follow Paul Tillich in viewing these acts as powerful symbols that not only point beyond themselves but participate in the reality to which they point. Others would stress the real presence of Christ in his body, the people, rather than in the elements themselves. The variety of interpretations is somewhat typical of Brethren, who participate in corporate acts of the tradition without emphasizing dogmatic formulations.

In general the word *sacramental* fits the Brethren only if applied to the total life of the people. It is a wonderful mystery how Christ can be present in this human community. Although the love feast constitutes the essence of worship for many Brethren, Christ's presence is not regarded as qualitatively different in this great worship experience than in other places and occasions. In fact, it is in discerning his presence in this special occasion of communion with God and one another through Christ that believers can be confident of Christ's presence in other times and places where two, three or more are gathered in his name. For this reason it is not appropriate to place the Brethren within the sacramental tradition as defined by most Christians.

Baptism

As with the Anabaptists of the 16th century Radical Reformation, baptism constituted a powerful symbol for the early Brethren. Unlike the Anabaptists, however, these Brethren practiced an immersionist mode of baptism. The typical Brethren practice still includes the following acts: The believer assumes a kneeling position in a body of water in the presence of the church community. Following a public confession of faith and the promise to be faithful to Jesus, his teachings and the church, the applicant for baptism is dipped three times, in the name of the Father, the Son, and the Holy Spirit. Then the hands of the minister are laid on the head and a prayer is offered, requesting the forgiveness of sins and the presence of the Holy Spirit.

Early Brethren literature contains more references to baptism than is true today. A caricature of Brethren preaching in the 19th century claimed that whatever the text, the exhorter eventually came to baptism. On the American frontier, many schoolhouse debates between Brethren elders and advocates of other traditions focused on this practice. Brethren apologists vigorously defended believers' baptism against the pedobaptists. They quoted the church fathers and Luther in support of immersion instead of the sprinkling and pouring used by other denominations. Many arguments were marshalled to buttress the three-fold forward action against Baptist groups who dipped backward one time. These debates over specifics often buried the deeper meanings and purposes of baptism.

More basic than the form was the underlying theology. Baptism was a powerful symbol of the relationship of the believer to the church and society. To baptize or to be baptized was originally an act of civil disobedience, a stance which espoused voluntaryism, religious freedom and separation of church and state. Brethren were Anabaptist in their repudiation of the complete union of church and state that required everyone in a geographical area to be members of the official state church. In this they affirmed a higher allegiance to the Lordship of Christ than to any earthly agents. Alexander Mack, Jr., wrote that Baptist-minded people do not baptize their children because "they firmly believe that the covenant of God under the economy of the New Testament demands only voluntary lovers of God and of His truth."[3]

Because of this belief, Brethren have often been accused of works-righteousness, that is, believing that the work of baptism saves them. Their emphasis on the commitment and response of the individual has seemed to subvert the prior and more important emphasis on God's grace. The Brethren, however, have consistently opposed any idea of baptismal regeneration. How they answered the above concerns may be discerned through a remark of Alexander Mack, Sr., about infant baptism: "Therefore, if a child dies without water baptism, that will not be disadvantageous for it. . . . The children are in a state of grace because of the merit of Jesus Christ, and they will be saved out of grace."[4]

Brethren families have presented their babies to the Lord in the presence of the community to point to the priority of God's grace and its coming through the church. In recent years, church parents are increasingly being chosen to stand with the families to represent this loving concern. In other ways there have been attempts to allow the love of the community to encompass their children through nurture, worship and fellowship. But the act of baptism itself and the biblical metaphors of new birth, of dying and rising, are seen to point to the joining of God's grace with the faith response of the individual believer.

The voluntary response of the believer not only denotes freedom from political and ecclesiastical domination but also points to a vital relationship with the church. Before baptismal acts Brethren have often read and interpreted sections from the 18th chapter of Matthew that contain the method of settling differences and teaching about forgiving one another. Following the action of baptizing, there occurs a Brethren "confirmation," the laying on of hands with prayers. This action embodies the intimate connection between baptism and membership in the community of faith.

In this it is possible to discern a difference between the Brethren and representatives of revivalistic Pietism in colonial America. The latter regarded the most powerful working of the Holy Spirit to be in the conversion experience that preceded and led to baptism. But the predecessors of the contemporary Church of the Brethren followed the story of the 8th chapter of Acts and Paul's own conversion experience, in which the laying on of hands came after baptism and the vision of Christ on the Damascus road. Without denying the working of the Spirit prior to baptism, they felt that there was a special manifestation of the Spirit in relation to the faith community. For the church is not simply a voluntary association of converted Christians; it is an agent of God's saving work. The laying on of hands points to the coming of God's grace through the lives of other people, the church.

Currently, there is a growing recovery of the emphasis of the early church and the early Brethren on baptism as ordination for the "royal" or general priesthood. The model is the baptism of Jesus, which coincided with the beginning of his public ministry and his identification with sinners. Alexander Mack, Jr., in his *Apologia* faults an opponent ("the churchman") for pretending the baptism of Jesus and that of his disciples are not the same, namely an ordination to public ministry. "Just as the Chief High Priest pledged himself . . . through his baptism to make the entire rebelling creation subject to Him, so all of His followers with their baptism have pledged themselves . . . to assist Him in this important task. That is why Peter calls them a royal priesthood" (1 Peter 2:9).[5] In Mack's view, baptism is not viewed primarily as a rite saving one for heaven (though that is a precious promise). Rather in baptism believers are saved from self-centeredness to be persons for others. In baptism we join others in the church to begin our public ministry.

In light of these convictions, there is less emphasis today on the form of baptism, though it is rarely changed in actual practice. Brethren receive persons from other communions on the basis of their previous baptisms and confessions of faith. Some feel that most basic differences on baptism have disappeared, as the Brethren dedication of infants corresponds essentially with infant baptism, and Brethren baptism functionally resembles confirmation in other traditions. Others criticize what they regard as movement toward infant baptism in progressively lowering the usual age of baptism from late adolescence to 12 years of age, or, in some cases, to an even lower age. It is claimed that this violates the principle of voluntaryism because it urges baptism at a time when it is easier to gain acceptance. Some would like to return to the earlier practice of believers' baptism, corresponding in most cases to late adolescence or the time of accepting basic responsibilities of marriage, parenting, and vocation.

Current practice ordinarily involves church membership classes preceding baptism. However, there are emerging at Annual Conferences and in some other circles proposals for some kind of rite that could recognize the near-universal desire of adolescents to join the adult world. Such a rite might initiate participation in the love feast and require a promise to begin a period of study. Baptism would come at the time of accepting greater responsibilities. It would become a rite of ordination for ministry. In Christian history, renewal has often been marked by the revival of the practice of the priesthood of all believers.

The Love Feast

The love feast, historically, has been the high point of Brethren worship. With the shortening of the love feast service and its decline in importance, Brethren may be a people in search of a liturgy.

In preparation for the love feast of past times, deacons conducted the annual church visit to each home of the congregation asking whether the members were still in the faith, still in peace with the church, and still willing to labor with the Brethren for an increase of faithfulness. Opportunity was given for the family to bring any matter to the attention of the church which they thought might serve its welfare and ministry. If the members were in sufficient harmony, the date for the love feast was announced. Large crowds, including Brethren from neighboring and distant congregations and often many visitors, gathered for the hospitality of free food and lodging offered by the host congregation. Preaching on Saturday prepared for the three-to-five hour love feast beginning Saturday evening. The weekend concluded with a worship service on Sunday morning, followed by dinner for all.

The love feast weekend provided opportunities for a youth gathering, a great social occasion for all of the Brethren, a frequent attraction for the activities of rowdy young men who disrupted the meetings, and for witness by the community to children, visitors, and hecklers. Martin G. Brumbaugh, Brethren historian and governor of Pennsylvania in the first part of the 20th century, described in his own way the first love feast at Germantown:

> It is evening now. The old-time tallow-dips are lighted. They gather around a long table, a hymn is sung, and in the silent evening hour, with no witness but God, and curious children, these people begin the observation of the ordinances in God's house on Christmas evening, 1723. The sisters on one side, the brethren on the other, arise and wash one another's feet. Then they eat the Lord's Supper, pass the kiss of charity with the right hand of fellowship, partake of the holy communion, sing a hymn, and go out.[6]

In the 20th century the weekend love feast has been replaced by shorter meetings, often on World Communion Sunday and Maundy Thursday of Holy Week. In addition to two feasts, many congregations have additional communion services, similar to those of other Protestants, partaking just of the bread and the cup during a Sunday morning church service. The annual deacon's visit has been replaced by a brief self-examination service preceding the love feast.

The love feast is an attempt to dramatize the central events of the Upper Room. It is based on a literalistic piecing together of the biblical narratives concerning the Last Supper. It has been said that on the American frontier where neighbors and strangers came to observe, the Brethren provided the community passion play for the pioneer community.

The first part of the service is based on the 13th chapter of John. Jesus washed the feet of his disciples and commanded his disciples to do the same. The second part comes from the primitive practice of an agape meal, a common supper around the tables. The men usually gather around one group of tables, the women around the others. In some instances it is now arranged so that families can sit together, in which case the feetwashing service usually takes place in adjoining rooms. It is in the same table setting that the Brethren share the third part of the love feast in continuity with much of Christendom, that is the breaking and eating of the bread and the drinking of the cup.

Throughout the love feast, hymns are sung, prayers are offered, silence is observed, scriptural passages are read and interpreted, and confessions and exhortations are offered by the minister and various members of the community. The Lord's Supper usually refers just to the meal. Holy communion and eucharist are common designations for the service of the bread and cup.

The general structure of the three-part service has known basic continuity but variations concerning the specifics have been legion. Alexander Mack, Jr., recounted how the Brethren originally practiced feetwashing following the meal and communion, then following the meal, and then changed to wash feet first when instructed by a brother who knew Greek.[7] For several decades the Brethren living in the Eastern part of the United States differed from the "Far Western Brethren" in that the former practiced the "double mode" of feetwashing (one washed and another dried the feet of several), while the latter adopted the "single mode," (the present practice in which each participant washes and dries the feet of the next one, and in turn receives the service from another). Generally, it has been the practice to greet one another with a "holy kiss" following the washing of feet. Historically, the passing of the kiss of peace in a complete circle occurred between the meal and the communion. This observance, known as binding the community, has disappeared for the most part except among the Old German Baptist Brethren.

The agricultural style brought a change from biblical mutton to the common beef of the American farm as the main substance of the meal. Today, the menus vary widely from congregation to congregation. The temperance movement in America brought a change from biblical wine to the use of grape juice, and medical hygiene was used as the rationale for the substitution of individual communion cups for the common cup or glass which was passed from one person to another. Occasional experiments have included the shining of shoes instead of the washing of feet or the clearing away of the dishes as an alternative symbol of service. Instead of traditional unleavened bread and grape juice, a few congregations have attempted to appropriate whatever may have been used for the fellowship meal such as tea, milk, coffee, rolls, or crackers. Though there are frequent attempts at novel experimentation and a widespread freedom to attempt the new, most love feasts still incorporate the washing of feet, a common meal, and specially-baked unleavened bread and grape juice.

Theologically speaking, the Brethren have in the love feast the visible manifestation of their fundamental emphasis, the inseparable relationship of the two great commandments—a loving response to God's love and our love for one another, which belong together. This Johannine emphasis has been basic: "If we love one another, God abides in us . . ." (1 John 4:12). The feetwashing rite and meal point to the love for the sister and brother, the neighbor and the world. The eucharist symbolizes the believers' relationship to Christ and the signifance of his death for them and the world. But this neat distinction is difficult to maintain, for all three parts manifest the reality of the presence of God in the midst of his body. In the love feast the people celebrate, witness to, and participate in the fellowship and mission of the body of Christ.

The reading of the 13th chapter of John introduces the feetwashing service; it has often been referred to as the symbol of servanthood. In addition, the Johannine reference to washing as cleansing has become a part of the basic meaning for some Brethren. As baptism refers to justification and regeneration, the washing of feet becomes a continuation of the cleansing without which believers, like Peter, would have no part of Jesus. A new forgiveness, a new purification or a new sanctification is always needed. Moreover, each one should be open to be served as well as to serve in order to combat the sin of self-sufficiency, pride and the striving for power. For this reason each person should have his or her feet washed. Each also needs to wash another's feet, for this act participates in the egalitarianism of the body of Christ as well as the call to adopt the servant role in relation to the world.

Thought of as worship, the washing of the feet of another may sometimes seem crude, awkward, and lacking in aesthetic finesse. Yet the washing of feet may lead to acts, for example the changing of bedpans, feeding the hungry, clothing the naked, or binding raw wounds, that have the same characteristics. Some Brethren have been embarrassed to participate in such a service in our contemporary culture; others feel that the attitude and manner of the participants often lead to pride rather than humility. For most Brethren, however, the rite of feetwashing remains an integral, meaningful part of the total love feast.

The Lord's Supper has reminded Brethren of the last meal Jesus shared with his disciples. They think of the instructions on observing it that were given by Paul (1 Cor. 11: 20–21). However, the meal represents more than a legalistic attempt to duplicate literally the biblical accounts. This becomes clear in a statement by Alexander Mack, Jr.: "For Christ did not say that one should recognize His disciples by the feetwashing or the breaking of bread, but He said that by this shall every man know that you are my disciples, that you have love for one another."[8] For this reason the meal has often been referred to as the symbol of community. The meal represents more than a mere togetherness; it is togetherness as a divine gift and an eschatological expectation. Some Brethren homilies have pointed to the meal as a sign of the messianic banquet. By grace the community is granted a foretaste of the bond of peace which God wants for all peoples.

In the breaking of bread and the drinking of the cup, Brethren share the practices and theology of other Christians. They remember and participate in the death, redemption, and resurrected body of Jesus. The breaking of bread expresses brokenness in the midst of a community which is open to healing love. The true mission of the church lies in its identification with the body and blood of Christ given for the world. Brethren have not believed in the transubstantiation of the elements nor in the complete absence of the real presence of their Lord. Rather, they articulate the mystery that in the breaking of bread is sensed the real bodily presence of their Lord in the lives of the people.

Other Ordinances

There are other practices which have been derived from New Testament admonitions. A literalistic following of some of these has prompted some to see in the Brethren a New Testament Phariseeism, the making of a new law out of the commandments and practices of the early church. But a deeper examination may reveal symbolic meanings comparable to the significance of liturgical colors, orders of worship and special customs in other traditions. If religion is life, acts of worship will be found in ethical contexts. Many 20th century Brethren feel that some of these practices should be regarded as *adiaphora*, acts which have no special merit or demerit. Yet, others would regard them more highly because of their symbolic and pedagogical value and biblical rootage. There is often a lack of extensive preaching and teaching supporting these practices. Many youth and members only learn about them within their families or in the context of life experiences.

The anointing service finds its basis in James 5:14–16. In following the text about calling the elders of the church, initiative, for the most part, comes from the person who is ill or hurting in other ways. The condition usually involves more than a minor illness, although the person need not be critically ill. Sometimes anointing is requested before surgery. It is increasingly called for in times of emotional or relational alienation. Traditionally, two elders administered the anointing; today the patient often receives a pastor and a deacon or another member. The service is conducted simply in a home or hospital, often in the presence of a few intimates or members of the family.

Typically, the passage from James is read; an opportunity is given for confession of sins and of faith; a brief hymn, prayer, or scriptural passage may precede or follow; then, with oil on the fingertips, the pastor anoints the person on the forehead three times—for the forgiveness of sins, for the strengthening of faith, and for the restoration of health to body and mind. Then, both ministers lay hands on the head of the anointed and offer prayer. Usually brief parting words of love and encouragement conclude the service.

For the most part Brethren have desired to avoid making faith a work that insures physical health or as a manipulative act to use God for their purposes. On the other hand, Brethren have not held rigidly to naturalistic philosophy that rejects possibilities of the miraculous working of God. Their prayers have tended to be in the name and spirit of One who prayed: "Nevertheless, not as I will, but as thou wilt" (Matt.26:39). Customarily, healings are not highly publicized. Brethren have perhaps followed too literally the command of Jesus to "tell no one" (Luke 5:14); so much so, many observe, that often the members and the larger community are not informed of the nature and availability of the anointing service.

Reference has been made to laying on of hands as a part of services of baptism and anointing. This rite has also been used in the service of special ordination for the preaching or pastoral ministry beyond the temporary licensing period. Further, it has been appropriated for special acts for commissioning of missionary, service and pastoral ministries at closing convocations of Annual Conferences. In recent years there have been a plurality of practices in the use of the laying on of hands in relationship to special gifts and tasks in the life of the church and the world. Following the clues of the Book of Acts, the rite has symbolized the enabling power of the Holy Spirit to be present with the one commissioned for ministry. For Brethren this power is related to the love, choice, and support of the community. For many decades it was not considered in good taste to desire to become a set-apart minister. Brethren believed that the Holy Spirit worked more effectively through the call of the body. In recent decades, however, the call of the individual and the choice of the congregation have both been regarded as valid contexts for the working of the Spirit.

Because of the many biblical references to the posture of kneeling in prayer, Brethren often assumed this position, more so in earlier times than in recent decades. They also sought to follow the special instructions of Paul (1 Cor. 11: 3-15) that in prophesying or praying, women should have their heads covered and men should appear with uncovered heads. In some parts of the church, one will still find uniformity in that all or many of the women of a particular congregation wear for worship the traditional small white lace caps or veils. In other places there will be only a few thus attired and in many congregations the practice is extinct. At present, there seems to be a great latitude of freedom and respect for the feelings and practices of others. In some congregations prayer veils appear in greater numbers during the observation of the love feast. In the Pennsylvania German country, which includes Mennonite, Amish, and other plain people, one may still find the prayer veil and other plain clothes worn for all activities during the week.

The observance of covered and uncovered heads has not only represented an attempt to take seriously the instructions of Paul, it has also symbolized reverence for God and life. In referring to teachings about this practice, two quite opposite strands have been cited. One taught that the covering symbolized submission in order to point to proper Christian vocational roles for women. The other strand emphasized the covering as a symbol of woman's authority to speak and participate equally in the life of the community of faith.

To a great extent, the special religious garb, which characterized members during the late 18th, the 19th, and early 20th centuries, is disappearing. Successive Annual Conferences see fewer bearded, tieless Brethren with their broadbrimmed hats and straight-cut coats and plainly dressed sisters in black bonnets, sober-colored dresses, and black stockings. Actually such dress remains for some a living symbol which not only points to but participates in Brethren convictions about nonconformity, simplicity of life, and the priesthood of all believers.

The origin of the costume is uncertain. Some have speculated that it was borrowed from the early Friends in order to identify with them in their struggle to remain nonviolent while exercising authority over the commonwealth of Pennsylvania. Today, the Brethren dress as other people. In a society of prevailing materialism and dominant militarism, however, increasing numbers know a nostalgic hunger for contemporary symbols of nonconformity and witness to the Way of peace.

As with other New Testament instructions, the Brethren took seriously the five references in the epistles to greet each other with a holy kiss. The exchange of a kiss accompanied by a warm handshake— intimate nature of the denominational family. In the 19th century it was taught that the kiss is a confirmation of baptism, feetwashing, and ordination. A person who had just been baptized or ordained was greeted with kiss and handclasp by the members of the church. The following explanation was given in the *Monthly Gospel Visitor* in 1852: "We meet in baptism our brother for the first time upon the heavenly road, as a member of the body of Christ; . . . in feetwashing we show by the kiss, that love prompts us to perform this lowly service; . . . in establishing a deacon, a teacher, etc., we salute a brother for the first time in that capacity, and show our willingness, in laying on him a burden, also to help him [in] bearing it."[9] To a great degree the kiss has been replaced by a friendly handclasp as the customary form of greeting but the practice of exchanging the kiss survives as a part of the feetwashing service. The warm greetings by members to new members and ministers often remains as a legacy to the spirit of the practice.

From the Sermon on the Mount (Matt.5–7) and the letter of James (5:12) the Brethren appropriated the prohibition regarding the swearing of oaths. Not only was profanity forbidden, but other civil oaths were not allowed. When called to a court of justice, Brethren historically have shared the mood of Quakers and Anabaptists who have regarded it foolish to swear on the Book that commands one not to swear. For this reason civil law often recognizes those who affirm or promise to tell the truth instead of swearing an oath in signing legal documents and appearing in courts. Again, more than literalistic adherence to the letter has been involved. More basic has been the pedagogical and symbolic value of pointing to a style of basic integrity, a higher allegiance than civil authority, and to the refusal to compartmentalize the sacred from the secular.

The strictures against oaths led naturally to a prejudice against secret oath-bound societies. Though Christians are to be in mission to all, it was emphasized that they were not to be "unequally yoked together with unbelievers" (2 Cor. 6:14). Christians are to be completely open; they are to hide nothing; they are not to acquire allegiances that would interfere with their being completely honest with brothers and sisters in Christ. Of all of the reasons proposed against the oath-bound societies, probably the most basic was the reluctance to relinquish a style of community life that was primary in terms of allegiance. Because the church was regarded as an exemplary community to point to God's intention for all of humanity, Brethren were cautious in allowing basic loyalties to lodges. The Brethren may have been too fearful of the fruit of such divided loyalties. Today, belonging to oath-bound societies is no longer a test of membership, although the Annual Conference has encouraged maintaining the traditional doctrine concerning oath-bound societies.

The church regarded the methodology in Matthew 18:15–22 as the way to settle disputes. One should first confront the brother, then others, and if necessary the entire church. In this context the Brethren stressed the principle of nonlitigation spelled out by Paul (1Cor. 6: 1–7). A Christian is not to go to law against her sister. She may go to court when called to be a witness. She may even appear to defend the rights of others. But she is not to take to civil authorities what should be settled in the life of the faith community. Insofar as possible a Christian should attempt to live at peace with all people. Here is a small incarnation of the role of the suffering servant. The chief posture in life is not that of defending one's own rights and interests, but one of service.

Gathering for Worship

Although the early Brethren emphasized the necessity of prayer and instruction in the home, they did not intend to neglect their regular assembling for corporate worship. They were not as strict in their observance of the Sabbath (Lord's Day) as their Puritan neighbors but habits of faithfulness emerged in setting aside special times for church meetings and fellowship. In the colonial period and into the 19th century, members rotated from house to house to hold worship in many parts of the church community. Some members built their farm houses with hinged walls, which could be raised in order to accommodate the gathering of the members for worship. Larger gatherings such as love feasts and annual business meetings often needed to be held in barns.

The first church building was erected by the parent congregation in Germantown in 1770. In other areas the first buildings were called *love-feast houses* with fireplaces and the beginnings of church kitchens in one end for the purpose of preparing the agape meal. They had upper lofts designed for sleeping guests, with a wall dividing the women's quarters from those of men. Some have speculated that early Brethren architecture, which needed to be designed for cooking, might have been a contributing factor to the unique American phenomenon of the centrality of the kitchen and fellowship dinners in the life of Protestants.

The stark simplicity of the architecture and the designation of *meetinghouse* for the building reflect the egalitarian church-view of the Brethren as well as their disaffection from the more institutional and formalized modes of worship of the mainline churches. The meetinghouse always had two front doors, one for the women and another for men. The uncomfortable benches were frequently made with a dual-purpose back that could be lifted to serve as a tabletop during love feasts. The walls were barren except for hooks on which rows of broad-brimmed black hats or black bonnets were placed at the time of meeting. Frequently a wood stove occupied the center of the room. There was no pulpit, no lectern, and no altar. Instead a long table was placed along the broad side of the room around which sat the elders and ministers who were in charge of the meetings.

On the American frontier the Brethren borrowed schoolhouses for the purpose of engaging in public debaters on doctrinal questions, conducting singing schools, and holding preaching missions. As they settled in communities, however, their meetinghouses evolved into church buildings, which in architecture began to resemble those of their Protestant neighbors. With the advent of the salaried pastor in the 20th century, the central pulpit on a raised chancel replaced the long table. Increasingly the open chancel has become more common with a pulpit on one side, a lectern on the other, and often a table in the center. this is sometimes called an altar, sometimes a communion table, and sometimes a worship center. The introduction of Sunday schools in the last part of the 19th century led to the provision for classroom space for Christian education and often a fellowship hall for special assemblies and dinners. In the post-World War II period, many Brethren communities erected beautiful edifices, churchlike in appearance, and reverent in mood. The chief characteristic of contemporary Brethren architecture is variety in style and in size of buildings. Many small plain meeting places remain to provide a sense of continuity with the past. A continuity in atmosphere is also in evidence in the many large church kitchens, fellowship halls, and large foyers, which provide visiting places for familial faith communities.

The early order of worship gave an appearance of spontaneity as the elders would exhort one another to "be free, Brethren." But often planning took place through a prior huddle of ministers or through preparation of exhortations on the part of the participants. Often a text emerged as a theme on which several ministers spoke, referring to the remarks made by a previous brother. A Baptist historian, Morgan Edwards, gave this description of the Brethren in 1770, containing some hints as to their manner of worship:

> Their church government and discipline are the same with those of the English Baptists; except that every brother is allowed to stand up in the congregation to speak in a way of exhortation and expounding; and when by these means they find a man eminent for *knowledge* and *aptness* to teach, they choose him to be a minister, and ordain him with imposition of hands, attended with fasting and prayer and giving the right hand of fellowship. They also have *deacons*; and ancient widows for *deaconesses*; and *exhorters*; who are licenced to use their gifts statedly. They pay not their ministers unless it be in a way of presents, though they admit their right to pay; neither do the ministers assert the right, esteeming it *more blessed to give than to receive.* Their acquaintance with the Bible is admirable. In a word, they are meek and pious Christians; and have justly acquired the character of the *Harmless Tunkers.*[10]

Worship in the 19th century probably became more ordered and controlled by the ministers than might be indicated in the above passage. In 1887 Henry B. Brumbaugh compiled *The Brethren's Church Manual Containing the Declaration of Faith, Rules of Order, How to Conduct Religious Meetings, etc.*[11] The last such manual, *Book of Worship: Church of the Brethren* (1964) focuses more on worship helps and less on doctrinal statements.[12] Today, one finds a wide appropriation of resources from other traditions and a freedom to use books of prayers and liturgical manuals from many sources.

The most consistent characteristic of Brethren worship today is its growing variety. It is true that some congregations may be enslaved by the necessity of maintaining the typical Protestant style of worship of several decades ago. Others may be faddish in their compulsion to experiment with the new. For the most part, however, there is growing freedom to appropriate from others and experiment with new forms. In some congregations there has been a movement to more formal worship with congregational participation and classical choral music. At the same time in many places there has been a movement toward greater spontaneity and informality as evidenced in the popularity of the time of "sharing of joys and concerns".

Some observers in colonial America regarded the Brethren to be among the more zealous and spirited of the sectarian groups. Since the Brethren were peaceful and orderly in daily life, such references no doubt referred to their singing. They shared the Pietist legacy of devotion, edifying writings, and the composition of new hymns. The Solingen Brethren composed hymns while in prison. In the preface to the first Brethren hymnal, *Geistreiches Gesang-Buch* (1720), is found this statement of purpose: "[T]hese hymns will be able to serve to the awakening and joy of their hearts to look even more steadfastly to Jesus.[13] Brethren in America published a relatively large number of hymnals; the first in English was *The Christian's Duty* (1791). This points to the adjustment made by the Brethren from the German to the English in the course of the 19th century.

Brethren originally sang *a cappella*; organs and pianos did not come into church buildings until the early decades of the 20th century. The large selection of hymns and worship resources in the present *Brethren Hymnal* (1951) indicates the ecumenical nature of contemporary Brethren worship; it contains social gospel hymns, classical Protestant chorales, revivalistic gospel songs, and new selections from Brethren authors and composers.

The poetry and hymns written by Brethren contain many references to Jesus. Phrases such as "looking to Jesus," "lover of Jesus," and "Jesus' beauty" may signify a Jesus mysticism. The most common christological title used by Alexander Mack, Sr., was "Lord Jesus." Such a devotion does not imply a repudiation of belief in the divinity of Christ. It does point to a strong emphasis on his lordship. In one way or another the Brethren have often identified with the *imitatio Christo* motif of Christian piety. Such identification with the mind and spirit of the Jesus of the Gospels may be one of the basic deductions which can be made about Brethren beliefs from early documents of devotional and worship literature.

It has been noted that the Brethren are not united by common creedal affirmations, book of prayer or liturgy. They have possessed a common tradition of rites and ordinances, ethnic bonds, and an Annual Meeting for fellowship, inspiration, and business. their communal feeling and style have been basic to their theological and worship gatherings. but basic to the tradition has been a spirit of openness to changing forms and practices and to new light, as to the consensus of the community develops in relation to the Word. In the midst of the resultant plurality of practices and beliefs, one finds both the tensions and unity of the denomination.

Notes

1. Alexander Mack, Sr., "Basic Questions," in Donald F. Durnbaugh, ed. *European Origins of the Brethren* (Elgin, IL: 1958), 331–332.
2. *The Monthly Gospel Visitor*, 2 (October, 1852): 103.
3. Alexander Mack, Jr., "Apologia," in Donald F. Durnbaugh, ed., *The Brethren in Colonial American* (Elgin, IL: 1967), 483.
4. Durnbaugh, *European Origins* (1958), 352.
5. Durnbaugh, *Colonial America* (1967), 510.
6. Martin G. Brumbaugh, *A History of the German Baptist Brethren* (Elgin, IL: 1899), 156.
7. Durnbaugh, *Brethren in Colonial America* (1967), 467.
8. Durnbaugh, *Brethren in Colonial America* (1967), 467.
9. *Monthly Gospel Visitor*, 2 (October, 1852): 104.
10. Durnbaugh, *Brethren in Colonial America* (1967), 175.
11. (Huntingdon, PA, and Mt. Morris, IL:, 1887).
12. (Elgin, IL: 1964).
13. (Berleburg: 1720); Durnbaugh, *European Origins* (1958), 407.

5

Polity

S. Loren Bowman

Church polity is not a consuming issue in Brethren circles. In fact, there appears to be a low level of interest in the governing system that gives order to the corporate life of the denomination.[1] It is difficult to discern the reasons for this situation. Do Brethren consider administration and legislative structures as tangential to the church's mission? Are the responsibilities of operating the church's institutions less worthy than other ministry functions? Do members lack information about the polity of the church? Or do they feel polity is some hidden ministry?

Perhaps the issue goes deeper. The apparent lack of interest may be related to certain elements in the Brethren view of the church. While the gradual developments of many generations added some of the accouterments of a denomination, there are vital residues from this history that speak of the church as a movement, a sect, a family, a faith community. There are familiar Brethren refrains in the air reflecting subterranean feelings that point toward the open, personal, and intimate character of faith: "the church is the body of Christ"; "the exercise of freedom of conscience, with no force in matters of religion"; "in the presence of Christ, it is expected that new light will break forth from the Word"; "the New Testament is the only rule in matters of faith and practice"; "there shall be no creed"; "members shall be priests to each other, within the context of the priesthood of all believers."

These underlying assumptions give support to the concept of the church as a dynamic, open movement, composed of a group of believers with an intimate relationship with Christ and with each other. Personal guidance flows from these relationships as members to Christ and engage in prayerful study of the Scriptures. The primacy of such relationships tends to rank organizational structures as a peripheral concern. So, it is difficult for some Brethren to get excited about the way the church orders its corporate life.

During the present century, however, the personal nature of faith has been modified by an understanding that the church, as well as individual Christians, should be doing "the work of Christ" in the world. The glory of the inner life of faith should not be hoarded but is to be translated into acts of mercy and reconciliation among one's neighbors. Over several decades, "the call of Christ to go" generated a high level of enthusiasm among Brethren for overseas missions, for service to neighbors near and far, for acts of mercy, for reconciliation and peacemaking. In order to implement these commitments around the world, the church was required to create organizations, secure staff personnel, and to raise funds. These developments, coupled with the need to maintain order within the church, led to the gradual evolvement of a comprehensive, functional plan of church government.

Even so, polity has not moved to the top of the list of discussion topics among the Brethren. The need for structures, for leaders, and for programs seems to be taken for granted. But such manifestations of the church's mission are viewed by many as less spiritual than internal items of faith. This makes church structure a secondary concern. Actually, the instruments that make the ministries available to the recipients become basic to the church's mission. This means that church structures need to receive the thoughtful appreciation of the members— viewing them as significant contributors in fulfilling the church's mission.

Polity Defined

In ecclesiastical language, *polity denotes the form of government a church employs to order its corporate life*. Technically, polity describes the plan of operation of the group and names the agencies and persons that are authorized to administer, evaluate, and revise this governing process. In other words, polity describes the way the church operates, how it describes what it wishes to be, what it wishes to do, who participates in making these decisions, who is authorized to act in its name, and where authority is lodged. Strictly speaking, then, *polity* refers to the form of government the church chooses, while *policy* denotes the adopted principles of operation for its institutions.

Common Polity Types

The modern Christian church is a worldwide institution and speaks glowingly of its universal character. Actually, the church presents many faces to the modern world. Its scope includes the Roman Catholic, Coptic, Eastern and Roman Orthodox traditions, along with hundreds of Protestant bodies, and a host of independent groups. All claim, however, to be rooted in Christ and to belong to one body (Rom. 12:4–8; 1 Cor. 12:12–13, 20; Eph. 4:4–7).[2]

This professed oneness is not readily accepted as a reality by those outside the church. The multiplicity of voices, institutional structures, and styles of operation that characterize the modern church tend to give a hollow sound to its claim to be one body. In the 20th century, a number of ecumenical expressions have attempted to point to the essential unity of the church. The World Council of Churches, with 310 member denominations from more than 100 nations, is the most comprehensive of such organizations. However, the separate identity of each member is maintained, and, as yet, all have not joined in communion at the Lord's Table. Nationally, there are efforts in America, and elsewhere, to express common allegiance to Christ through national, regional, and area councils or conferences of churches.

In spite of the large number of denominations and the broad diversity of beliefs and practices, there are only a few basic forms of church government in operation within the Christian community. There are four types identified historically: monarchial, episcopal, presbyterial, and congregational polities. Currently, the monarchial form is not considered operative, at least, not as it functioned in the pre-Reformation and immediate post-Reformation eras when the autocratic ruler of a particular area dictated the religion to be followed by all the people. This leaves three basic forms of church government in the churches today, although variations cloud the theoretical purity of the models.

Episcopal Government

The episcopal form of government places authority for the life of the church in the hands of the clergy and rests this claim upon the concept of the apostolic succession of the bishops. But there are variations regarding the nature and significance of the unbroken line of clerics. The Roman Catholic tradition, with a pope whose office is traced to the Apostle Peter and who has ultimate authority for the life of the church, represents the purest form of the episcopal type of government.

Other familiar denominations within the episcopal tradition include the Anglican (Episcopal), Lutheran, and Methodist bodies. The authority of the bishops is tempered in each of these cases, with other members of the clergy and lay persons participating in the governance of their respective churches. Further, the Methodists give no significance to the concept of apostolic succession—they claim simply that it is the most efficient form of church government.

Presbyterial Government

Presbyterians, as members of the Reformed Church family, provide the illustration of a middle-of-the-road type of church government. It draws its basic idea from the organization of the Jewish synagogues of New Testament times and puts the primary responsibility of government in a board of elders. This was the early church pattern of the New Testament, the Presbyterians say, with routine services handled by deacons, and the ruling powers handled by the elders (Acts 11:30, 14:23, 15:22, 20:17; Titus 1:5-7; Philem. 1:1). As the early Christian community developed, *bishops, elders,* and *overseers* became interchangeable terms.

In current Presbyterian practice, *Presbytery* denotes a legislative, executive, and judicial court system that is presided over by an annually elected moderator. The ministers and elders of the congregations of a specified area constitutes *presbytery* and assume responsibility for the life of the congregations through quarterly meetings. Its functions include administrative, legislative, and judicial responsibilities. In denominational perspective, the presbytery fits into an interlocking governing system of Consistory (congregation), Presbytery (congregations of a prescribed area), Synod (a cluster of presbyteries), and General Assembly (the denomination). The General Assembly, the final voice of authority, is made up of equal number of ministers and elders chosen and commissioned by the presbyteries.

Congregational Government

Theoretically, congregational polity is the least systematized of the three familiar forms of church government and is open to numerous local expressions. Simply stated, in this form each local congregation functions as an independent unit and is free to order its life in keeping with the wishes of its members. The principle of democracy is assumed, with all members being eligible to share in the decision-making process of the congregation. Baptist churches are good illustration of this type of government.

Two assumptions of the Believers' Church support this approach to church government: the head of the church is Jesus Christ—no earthly bishop can be tolerated; the believers themselves are priests unto God, who need no intermediary. Moreover, they are priests to each other and are capable of full responsibility for the life of the congregation. At times, this autonomy has resulted in anarchy or oligarchy, but congregational polity has continued as a vigorous form of church government since the days of the Reformation.

In most denominations that follow congregational polity today, responsibility for true welfare of the congregations is shared by specified structures and officers, as directed by the members in their business meetings. Although the ultimate authority rests with the full membership of the congregation, the established administrative and program agencies exert a major influence upon the decision-making of the congregation.

There is little evidence to indicate that any of these three forms of church government are found in pure form in the mainline churches. There have been borrowings across the lines, and the populist movement has brought an increasing role to the lay members of the churches. To govern, in most instances, means to share in an extensive, consultative network, even if one is a bishop!

Brethren Government—A Blended Version

When asked, a number of Brethren say that the church is among the denominations that practice congregational polity. They assume the congregation is free to order its internal affairs and to determine the nature of its witness. When asked, a number of other Christians feel that Brethren polity is a modified form of presbyterianism. They sense the connectedness of the congregation, district, and denomination as resembling the interlocking units in the presbyterial form of government.

Actually, Brethren polity is a particular blend of congregational autonomy and representative, denominational authority. Limitations apply in both directions: the congregation is granted authority to order its internal life by the actions of its members; the denomination is granted authority to act representatively upon matters that affect the total church. An interlocking of congregation, district, and denomination (the Annual Conference), with approved responsibilities specified for each, provides for a two-way flow of information and action. Although less specific and authoritative than the system of Presbyterian Graded

Courts, the Brethren blend does involve the participation of representative members (delegates) in all deliberations at district and denominational levels. This movement from local to district, to denomination, and from denomination, to district and/or congregation is abetted, and sometimes modified, by the active participation of denominationally authorized boards and agencies. The process is rather complicated at times: it is an ongoing process; it is dynamic, not fixed; it is open to evaluation and revision at any time on the initiative of any of the basic participants.

But it was not always so among the Brethren. A number of polity approaches were tried. Initially, the founding Brethren espoused government by consensus. For local groups, this merged into the more formal decisions of a council meeting, with a majority vote required, if consensus could not be reached. As Brethren spread across the wilderness of the New World, governing responsibilities were shared by the congregations and the emerging Yearly (Big) Meeting. Rather rapidly, the Yearly Meeting assumed the decisive role in determining the nature and shape of the new church. For decades the Yearly Meeting, dominated by elders, functioned as a centralized authority, leaving only the more routine aspects of congregational life for local action. Gradually, as general boards were created near the end of the 19th century, and education became popular, the authority of Yearly Meeting was distributed to new agencies and participation in decision-making was broadened. These developments evolved into the present two-way flow of action from congregation to district, to Annual Conference, and back again. It is an interlocking governing system involving the congregation, the districts, and the Annual Conference, with specified responsibilities for each. In the emerging plan of government, there were variations of practice and outcome. Theoretical purity of congregational polity was seldom a reality.

With this abbreviated examination of what church polity is, and summary of the Brethren experience in church government given, it will be helpful to describe more fully how the Brethren arrived at their current practice. It involves many steps—some sharp turns, some surprises, some failures. An overview of developments, with a functional description of present practice, will give greater reality to the corporate life of the church.

Early Beginnings

The eight founders at Schwarzenau were interested in getting away from authority rather than establishing a new form of church government. They were familiar with the abuses of the Roman Church that spawned the Protestant Reformation, and they were disgusted with the arbitrary exercise of power in the state churches of their day. As a group determined to recapture the essence of the New Testament church, Bible study constituted one of the major activities of this group of searchers for a different expression of the Christian faith. Among other things, the group became convinced that the Christian experience called for

—an intimate, direct, personal faith relationship to Jesus Christ, based upon free adult choice;

—individual Christians to serve as priests, one to the other, based upon the "priesthood of all believers;"

—each to respect the freedom of conscience of another, with no coercion in matters of faith;

—a readiness to accept new insight under the guidance of the Holy Spirit as one searched the Scriptures;

—the practice of the New Testament ordinances as observed by the early church;

—an honest effort to live out the teachings of Jesus in all human relationships;

—and an open sharing of the believers in a caring, non-discriminating community.

There assumptions were not expressed in these terms; this list may also suggest a more definitive statement than existed in the early Schwarzenau community. It does seem clear, however, that the first Brethren were determined to create a faith community that approximated, as nearly as possible, the New Testament church. For them, the Christian faith represented a journey with Christ, an open sharing/searching with each other, and a witness to the world of what it means to live by the demands of love and peace. The church was viewed as a movement, as a spiritual family, and could not be portrayed faithfully as an ecclesiastical or hierarchial institution.

In the light of such a general perspective, it was natural for that original group to govern its life by decisions based upon consensus. Since members had little concern for structure, and shared a distaste for ecclesiastical considerations, their goal seemed to be to talk, to pray, and to search—repeating the process as many times as necessary—until they arrived at a common mind. This formula applied to biblical insights as well as to operational procedures. It was congregational polity in its simplest and purest terms.

As members were added to the Schwarzenau group, and as new groups were formed in other communities, the consensus approach was severely tested. Apparently, the decisions continued to be made largely in the respective groups, but it became evident rather early that Alexander Mack, Sr., exercised a strong leadership role in the early congregations. Persecution, coupled with the appeal of freedom in Penn's Woods, brought Brethren efforts to a close in Europe before any formal plan of church government emerged.

The move to Germantown involved different groups arriving at different times, with little evidence of definite plans for transplanting a church in a new country. For the first few years in the New Land, the Brethren were occupied with the tasks of settling in and there are no records of planned activities. There were associations with other German immigrants of the area as Brethren pondered their course. Soon they began to gather at Germantown and a congregation took shape. An elder was chosen and council meetings developed in connection with the yearly love feast. Again, with only one congregation, it was easy to operate by congregational polity.

As families moved into the surrounding rural areas, it became customary in those early years in America for church members to return for the yearly council and love feast at Germantown. The decisions that emerged from these deliberations provided the limited guidelines for the developing church. Gradually, church members in larger numbers moved into the Western wilderness and new congregations were created. For a while, Germantown was a primary center of guidance but outlying congregations soon began to hold their own council meetings, with the assistance of adjoining elders. It was commonplace for elders to visit among the congregations to share the news and to help resolve local problems. Polity remained primarily congregational, with the elders assuming a position of primary influence in the life of the emerging church.

The next major step in church government came with the expansion of the Germantown council concept into a Yearly Meeting for all the Brethren. (The stimulus of synods called by the Moravians in 1742 is usually given credit for this change.) During the experimental years, this "Big Council" alternated between open discussion of the total body and decision making by a committee of elders, which was appointed by the elders in attendance from the various congregations. It was clear, however, that the actions of the Yearly Meeting applied to all the congregations and represented the voice of the church. A new element was introduced in Brethren polity: a denominational body assumed responsibility for the general character of the church. This divided the authority and restricted congregations to decisions related to their internal life. By direct initiative, albeit by action of persons from the congregations, the Yearly Meeting dealt with all items affecting the Brethren in the areas of polity, doctrine, and discipline. Church government now had two focal points: the local council meetings for the ordering of its local affairs; the denominational Yearly Meeting for ordering the life of the church as a whole. If a question arose regarding responsibility for a particular area or issue, the Yearly Meeting provided the answer. It was a significant, but logical, step from the "study group" in Schwarzenau and the initial "community meetings" at Germantown.

Yearly Meeting Takes Center Stage

As the church moved across the American wilderness, the position of the elders and the power of the Yearly Meeting increased steadily throughout the church. In the congregations, the presiding elder, assisted by the elders' body, governed with a strong hand. Yet, the members elected the ministers, and participated in making the decisions about the operations of the congregations. In this respect, congregational polity was operative, but the elders' body functioned as policy shapers and primary administrators.

Gradually, the Yearly Meeting—through the Standing Committee (a denominational elders' body, as it were)—expanded and consolidated its control of the church. During much of the 19th century the decisions of the Yearly Meeting (later called Annual Meeting) were considered binding upon all members. For a period of time, committees of elders were sent to congregations to interpret the actions and to discipline leaders or congregations that failed to conform to the decisions. It was clear the Annual Meeting was the voice of authority among the Brethren. And that voice touched a wide variety of topics: from proper dress to baptism, from taking an oath to taking out insurance, from the proper mode of feetwashing to membership in secret societies, from receiving interest on loans to misrepresenting a sale item, from the treatment of a divorced member to the bearing of false witness against a neighbor.

This detailed, comprehensive control by the Annual Meeting was achieved by a representative form of government. Delegates were sent from the congregations on a specified ratio basis to act upon the items before the meeting. In a strict, technical sense the congregations representatively expressed the will of the church. From this perspective, it could be claimed that congregational polity reached beyond the decisions regarding local services and operations. This was evidenced as congregations brought issues to the Annual Meeting. Nevertheless, when local delegates came together from across the denomination, and cooperation with the Standing Committee (which sorted out the business items and proposed answers), it was a very different situation than in a local council meeting.

Representation at Annual Meeting was expanded slightly with the emergence of districts in 1856. Initially, however, this development had no real impact upon the governing system. Clusters of congregations were permitted to meet in annual gatherings to share experiences and to discuss problems of their particular area. Any issue bearing upon the life of the denomination had to be presented to the Annual Meeting. In fact, the districts were not allowed to keep minutes of their proceedings during the early years of their existence. Only the items for the Annual Meeting could be recorded—an illustration of the extent of the control of the Annual Meeting over the life of the church. The role of the districts expanded slowly, and elders from the districts were named to serve on the Standing Committee of Annual Meeting. Although there was little transfer of authority to the districts, the church had arrived at an interlocking structure of congregation, district, and annual conference, with prescribed areas of responsibility for each.[3]

Appearance of Boards

As the Brethren neared the end of the 19th century, a new perspective began to take shape regarding the role of the church in the world. The vigorous publishing efforts within the church, the wide involvement of key members in expanding higher education programs, and the exciting drama of moving from Pennsylvania to California challenged the parochial views of an earlier era. In the larger Christian community, the rapid growth of foreign missions and the rise of a dynamic Sunday school movement increased Brethren awareness of other churches and created a desire to share in a Christian witness to the world. The combined effect of these forces resulted in a keener awareness of a world community and a desire to see the denomination participate in "the evangelization of the world in this generation."

The first concrete expression of the need for plans that would make possible Brethren participation in mission beyond their borders appeared in 1880 with the creation of a Foreign and Domestic Missionary Board, forerunner of the General Mission Board. Other primary interests were soon able to secure boards to further their concerns: a General Educational Board, a General Sunday School Board, and a Publishing House followed in rapid succession. These general boards did not change the structure of the governing system, as they functioned as administrative or program agencies of the Annual Conference (as the Annual Meeting was now called). Governing power was still concentrated in the elders of the church, as all board and committee members had to be ordained elders at that time.

Dynamics of the business sessions of Annual Conference did undergo change as general boards made regular reports and raised concerns for Conference consideration. Discussion of timely issues in church periodicals, and the contacts of staff members of the general boards with local members tended to broaden the perimeter of Conference discussions. As a result, the kinds of issues and the outcomes of the deliberations underwent significant change, even though the emerging boards were not technically a part of the governing structures. The shift was from personal behavior—moral and church order issues—to organizational issues for the denomination and to social issues in the society. Boards were influential in this shift, even though without an assigned legislative role.

In the closing years of the 19th century and the opening years of the 20th century, the General Mission Board was the dominant body. Other boards secured their funds from that board and cleared their major programs through it. This included the publishing efforts and the Sunday school curriculum materials. Eventually, this control came under question and there was slow evolution in the direction of cooperation. Joint staff efforts were followed by the creation in 1928 of the Council of Boards, resulting in some increased degree of independence for the individual boards that had been under the General Mission Board. Pressures from within the Council of Boards, and from the general constituency, continued for greater coordination of the denominational ministries.

In 1946 the Annual Conference approved a recommendation of the Commission of Fifteen that called for the consolidation of the general boards into a single board to be known as the General Brotherhood Board. It was a comprehensive assignment:

> The General Brotherhood Board as a whole will consider the total brotherhood program, evaluate all phases of the program, and determine the general policies and budget needs in each area of its work. It will corre-

late and unify the work of all commissions, and assign to the commissions the responsibility for the detailed planning of the general program in their particular areas of service.[4]

In order to facilitate its work, the General Brotherhood Board was to provide for the varied ministries through five program commissions. These were: Foreign Missions, Christian Education, Ministry and Home Missions, Brethren Service, and Finance. Brethren Publishing House operations were assigned to the Finance Commission. The Board moved promptly to consolidate program and staff operations. It then moved gradually to a prominent position of influence in shaping the life and the mission of the denomination.

In 1947 the Annual Conference, upon recommendation of the Commission of the Fifteen, adopted a revised organizational structure for the entire denomination.[5] The centerpiece was the extension of the one-board concept to the districts and the congregations. Although options were offered at the congregational level, the preference was obviously for a *one-board structure*, with commissions throughout the church. The plan spelled out the detailed structures and responsibilities for the congregation, the district, the General Brotherhood Board, and the Annual Conference.

In 1968 the General Brotherhood Board was further consolidated by reducing the five commissions to three, namely: World Ministries, Parish Ministries, and General Services, with the three commission executives also named as Associate General Secretaries, working under a General Secretary. The name was shortened to the Church of the Brethren General Board. Although the board structure is not a governing entity from a policy viewpoint, the Board (and its staff) has exerted a tremendous influence upon all phases of the life of the church over the past four decades. During these years a number of polity changes occurred. Boards of Administration at district and local levels replaced the elders' body, District Boards were assigned primary responsibility for recruiting, ordaining, and disciplining ordained ministers: appointments to committees and church offices were opened to lay persons.

Actually, the basic structures of shared responsibilities between congregations, district, and denomination was not changed drastically. The role of districts has been upgraded significantly, with special responsibilities in the area of set-apart ministry. The query process has been refined, with criteria for congregations and districts in processing requests to Annual Conference. The 1947 plan added specificity to the responsibilities to be assumed at each point in the relationship. However, the interlocking of congregation, district, and denomination, through Annual Conference-approved responsibilities, leaves the Brethren form of representative government intact. There is congregational polity within certain boundaries in the congregation. There is a kind of presbyterial polity in operation in the shared decision making of the District and Annual Conferences, with the Standing Committee serving as the final court of appeal. In theory, the Annual Conference is the ultimate voice of authority and has power to implement its decisions. In practice, however, today, those decisions invite support on the basis of their merits and are rarely enforced.

Polity in Operation

In operational terms, the success of the Brethren blend of government depends upon the acceptance of specific areas of responsibility by each unit, and a careful observation of the prescribed connectedness between them. Each congregation is a member of a district, and, in turn, each congregation and each district participates in the Annual Conference. This interrelatedness allows information and decision making to flow in either direction: from the local unit to the area unit, to the denominational unit or from the denominational to the district and/or the local group.

In legislative terms, or matters of polity, this means that an individual member or any group of members who can get the support of a congregation may present a proposal, through the district conference, for action by the Annual Conference. The initiating process is known as the *query* approach and has been used as an avenue of effecting numerous changes in the life of the denomination. At the same time the Annual Conference, through Standing Committee, study committees, and authorized boards, may take actions on behalf of the church which are addressed to districts and congregations.

While there have been some minor adjustments in recent years, the basic division of responsibilities, along with the detailed structures of the various denominational units—the description of this system sharing of authority—may be found in the 1947 Annual Conference *Minutes*. A functional picture, without the listing of all the details, may be found in the current issue of the *Church of the Brethren Manual of Organization and Polity*. Here it should suffice to indicate the nature of the responsibility—the areas of respective authority—by giving a few illustrations of the types of action appropriate in each case.

Autonomy for the congregations prevails in such matters as: location, name, and care of buildings (though districts should receive property that ceases to be used for congregational purposes; districts and

General Board consult in founding new congregations). Congregations also decide on: budgets, educational programs, schedules, membership in local ecumenical agencies, election of officers, election of delegates to District and Annual Conferences, employment of staff (with district participation in calling of pastors). The congregation is jointly involved with the district in the licensing and ordaining of members to the set-apart ministry.

The districts have authority for their internal organization; select needed staff, with consultation with the General Board in calling a district executive; plan and implement their own programs; establish budgets; assist congregations in programs of nurture; serve as a connecting link between congregations and denominational agencies; participate, through their executives, in General Board planning and goal setting.

In terms of governance, the district Boards of Administration are charged with the recruiting, licensing, ordaining, classifying, and disciplining of ministers. This is facilitated through the Ministry Commission, with the Board of Administration as the point of first appeal and the Standing Committee of Annual Conference as the point of final appeal. The districts also process queries from the congregations that are addressed to Annual Conference. Their options include: rejection; referral back to the initiating congregation for clarification or restructuring; and passing on to Annual Conference, with or without instruction. Although guidelines for the creation and processing of queries have been issued by the Annual Conference, the criteria for District Conference consideration are seldom followed. More often than not, the districts forward the queries on to Annual Conference in preference to challenging the merits of an item from one of their congregations.

The general denominational agencies are the Annual Conference and the General Board; the former functions as the legislative, policy-making body; the latter serves as an administrative, program-development body. As a creature of the Annual Conference, the General Board is responsible to the Conference for its stewardship. The Board reports annually, seeks counsel from time to time, and maintains a close relationship with the Conference at all times. In theory, the division of responsibilities is explicitly stated:

> Annual Conference: The delegate body assembled in Conference is the ultimate legislative authority of the church of the Brethren. It is composed of the Standing Committee (district delegates) and the local church delegates. It functions primarily as a deliberating legislative assembly, determining the polity and setting forth the primary courses of action and relationships in which the church should be involved.[6]

The General Board shall be the principal administrative body for the total church program. In keeping with general policies determined by the Annual Conference, it shall plan, administer, and evaluate all phases of denominational program and structure, and project its budget needs . . . It shall correlate and unify the work assigned to the Board by the Annual Conference. Each year, the Board shall report to Annual Conference, present such recommendations as seem advisable, and seek guidance and direction on the total church program.[7]

In specific terms, the Annual Conference determines issues of polity, doctrine, and denominational structure. It acts on queries coming from the districts or from Standing Committee, as well as on other problems or requests coming from the General Board and other Conference-related bodies. It elects Annual Conference officers; these consist of a moderator, moderator-elect, and secretary. It also elects members of the General Board, a majority of Bethany Theological Seminary directors, members of the Central Committee (planners of the Annual Conference), and members of the Committee on Interchurch Relations. The Conference confirms appointments to Annual Conference study committees, representatives to ecumenical agencies, and any special committees dictated by Conference actions. The Conference may instruct, revise, or over-rule the General Board; it may approve, revise, or disapprove policy statements brought by the General Board. It may accept, amend, or reject the work of study committees.

While the separation of powers seems clear in theory, the line of demarcation becomes blurred in practice at times. The Annual Conference, on occasion, may assign study tasks to the General Board that border on polity issues. Or, the General Board may wander across the policy line to the polity area. A random sampling of several categories of Church of the Brethren members in connection with another project indicated that both agencies exercise care in acting within their respective areas of responsibility. At least, the limited sample of respondents indicated no awareness of major abuses of power in these basic denominational agencies.

The structure of governance are clear—congregations, districts, and Annual Conference in prescribed relationships—and the process rests upon the easy flow of issues through the system with the nature of the decision designating which unit casts the decisive vote. The connectedness of this plan of government is well established, and decisions may be initiated at any point and flow from local level to denomination or from Annual Conference to district and congregation. A polity issue may be raised by a congregation in a query and be processed through a district to Annual Conference. Likewise, Annual Conference, through Standing Committee or an established agency, may initiate polity changes and report the changes to the district and congregations.

While the General Board is not a part of the basic governing system, it exerts direct and powerful influence upon the polity of the church. This develops naturally out of the Board's extensive involvement in the ongoing life of the church and out of the issues that arise in the Board's administration of the church's worldwide mission. In the interpretation of programs, in staff exchanges with the general church constituency, in its comprehensive reports to Annual Conference, in dialogue with other denominations through ecumenical agencies, and in evaluative and goal-setting sessions of the Board, issues of concern, proposals for revision, or needs for additions to polity may surface and be picked up for action. Although the Board is not a legislative body, it is appropriate that it provide leadership in aiding the denomination to become as effective as possible in its corporate life and witness. It is the responsibility of the Annual Conference to see that polity decisions remain the prerogative of that body.

The obvious difference between current Brethren governance and that of the 19th century lies in the enforcement of Annual Conference decisions. In the former era, the Annual Conference (Yearly Meeting) was in full control of denominational decisions, and systematically enforced these decisions throughout the church—using the ban when necessary to achieve compliance. Today, while full reporting of Annual Conference actions occurs, seldom is a systematic effort made to check on acceptance by congregations or districts. Almost no attempt is made to enforce Conference actions. Informal channels of communication work well, and it becomes relatively easy to discover the lack of adherence to approved policy. However, it is assumed that the merits of the decision and the pressure from those who take Conference actions seriously will bring about majority adherence over a period of time.

From practice, rather than by design, the church has moved toward a flexible view of government. Even though there are structures that could exercise authority in implementing decisions, the stance in recent years anticipates voluntary compliance based upon the rightness of the actions. In fact, few decisions have been enforced by any organizational level in recent years. This suggests that the church continues to feel comfortable with the family spirit as an appropriate approach to its corporate life. Heavy-handed authority runs the risk of endangering the Brethren commitment to freedom of conscience and the priesthood of all believers. From a strict polity perspective, the Brethren practice is vulnerable—open to potential abuses but also open to new insights and improved structures.

Actually, the church rarely gets excited about polity in its more formal dimensions. It does not spend time devising precise definitions of government or in describing the degree of authority entrusted to the different units. Instead, the focus is upon the practical, functional efficiency of the church's organizations and upon the widely participative nature of the decision making process. This opens the door to some confusion and tension, frequently blurring the lines between policy and polity, between policy and administration. At times, this decreases the effectiveness of the church's operations and allows differences to continue without honest confrontation. But this is the way the Brethren now prefer it; this is who the Brethren are. When a system of government is affirmed that balances local autonomy and denominational responsibility, there are numerous procedural details for the community of believers to resolve as it moves forward in mutual respect with a commitment to faithfulness in light of the Brethren understanding of the Gospel. Currently, there is a high level of tolerance for diversity among the Brethren.

Notes

1. Brethren literature on polity includes: Martin G. Brumbaugh, *History of the German Baptist Brethren* (Elgin, IL: 1899), 471–508; I. D. Parker, "Church Polity," in *Two Centuries of the Church of the Brethren,* ed. D. L. Miller (Elgin, IL: 1908), 152–169; Warren F. Groff, "Polity," in *Church of the Brethren: Past and Present,* ed. D. F. Durnbaugh (Elgin, IL: 1971), 67–75; *Church of the Brethren Manual of Organization and Polity* (Elgin, IL: 1979); Robert G. Clouse, "Polity," in *The Brethren Encyclopedia* (1983–1984), 1041–1045, with extensive bibliography. Some historical studies include brief treatment of polity.

2. Basic sources used as background for the description of current forms of church government are: *Encyclopedic Dictionary of Religion* (Washington, DC: 1979); F. L. Cross and E. A. Livingstone, eds., *The Oxford Dictionary of the Christian Church,* 2nd. ed. (London and New York: 1974); *Minutes of the Annual Conferences of the Annual Conference of the Church of the Brethren, 1965–1970* (Elgin, IL: 1970), 316–320, 334–344.

3. This blend represented the middle-of-the-road position following the 1881–83 division into three bodies: the Old German Baptist

Brethren opted for the enforceable rights of the Yearly Meeting; the Brethren Church chose to emphasize congregational authority; the Church of the Brethren held the two in balance/tension.

4. *Minutes of the Annual Conferences of the Church of the Brethren, 1945–1954* (Elgin, IL: 1956), 54. A more definitive statement occurs in the General Brotherhood Board Revision of 1968; see *Minutes* (1970), 340–344, and *Manual* (1979), B: 1–7.

5. See *Minutes* (1956), 52–80, for a full description of church structures and assignments of responsibilities.

6. *Manual* (1979), A: 6.

7. *Manual* (1979), B: 1–2.

6

Education

Allen C. Deeter

Brethren attitudes toward education have varied greatly over the years. At times Brethren have simply taken education for granted. At other times Brethren have gone to the extremes of fearing it, on the one hand, or having an exaggerated faith in its possibilities, on the other. Yet, there has been one constant in the Brethren concern for education from the beginning—the concern that the Brethren receive, whether in schools, home, or church, the education needed to live a rich and productive Christian life. What has changed in 275 years is the Brethren understanding of what kind of education is required to live a full and fruitful life and exactly what that life is.

In their first 150 years of existence, Brethren understood training for a fruitful life to be centered in families living as part of a close-knit Christian community faithful to the New Testament. The early Brethren were literate and their leaders articulate in making their Christian witness. Brethren, however, had to focus most of their energies and resources on survival, originally as refugees, later as immigrants, and at times as a persecuted minority. Brethren saw themselves as primarily responsible to one another, caring for their own needy, and sharing in material and spiritual ways. This was their way of living out the pattern of faith and life seen in the New Testament church. Everyday practical concerns crowded out thoughts of more advanced education.

Still, in this close community the study of the New and Old Testaments, as well as of early church history, was a genuine interest. To be able to read, to form questions, to find answers in the Bible were all-important. Living the Christian life depended upon understanding what that life was, especially if it differed from the life of their neighbors.

The importance of basic educational skills was taken for granted, and some, at least, among the Brethren attended, taught in, and actively supported schools, first in Germantown and then on the frontier. But most Brethren, even the most able writers and speakers among them, had little formal training beyond elementary schooling; often they were educated at home and largely self-taught through much reading. Being prepared to witness to the faith that was in them (1 Pet. 3:15) was demanded of the early Brethren. Confrontations with the authorities in the state churches in Europe and with their neighbors in the New World motivated literary productivity, as well as diligent searching of their Bibles. Most of the writings of the Brethren until the 1850s set forth and defended what they felt God required of them as a community of believers based on the New Testament.

Thus, the early Brethren concern for education was determined in part by their own needs but also by their relationships with the society around them. These are the keys to interpreting the Brethren involvement in formal schooling. The story of the Brethren and their educational concerns can be divided into four eras. These eras are marked by shifts in the focus of their attention between internal and external problems and by varying degrees of participation in the wider society and its formal educational endeavors.

Four Eras of Brethren Education

The first era, from their founding in 1708 to the imposition of the loyalty oath in 1778 during the Revolutionary War, was a period of limited acceptance by Brethren of education and participation in society. Brethren were for a time alienated from the larger society and became refugees. This was in Europe when rulers, at the prompting of the established churches, persecuted and, in several cases, imprisoned them. From 1743 in America, many took advantage of the new law which enabled "foreign Protestants" to be naturalized and, at the urging of Christopher Sauer, Sr., began to vote. They felt at home among the Quakers and German immigrants.

But then again, when the Brethren refused to take the loyalty oath to the Revolutionary Congress in 1778 and refused to serve in the military, there came confiscation of their property and renewed alienation. Many Brethren fled to the frontiers, leaving the areas where their refusal to participate in the Revolution would be a cause for further persecution. Some of the more established Brethren, such as Alexander Mack, Jr., Christopher Sauer II, and Martin Urner, Sr., who had been most active in supporting education, suffered persecution. Sauer II, particularly, had been influential among the whole German community as the leading publisher; he had supported the Germantown Academy financially and served as chairman of its board of trustees. Despite persecution and migration to the frontiers, Brethren did not completely reject schools and growing participation in the wider culture through the use of the English language, although German was still spoken by the majority of the Brethren well into the 19th century. Many Brethren were bilingual.

During the second period from 1778 to 1851, most Brethren settled in areas where education was not well established. Until the Revolutionary War scattered them, many Brethren had lived in and around Philadelphia, with the most influential Brethren deeply involved in the economic and religious life of the colonies, especially of the large German-speaking minority.

Thereafter, most Brethren were dispersed into rural, frontier areas largely cutoff from the new nations's developing culture and intellectual life. Some Brethren were alienated by language and more by memories of persecution for not supporting the Revolutionary War. Nonetheless, Brethren sent their children to whatever schools existed where they settled. Often these were limited in subject matter to reading, writing, and arithmetic, and limited in time to the few winter months when the children's labor was not needed on the farms. Often, they received Bible study and moral training along with the "three r's." Whereas many Brethren earlier had been businessmen, artisans, and craftsmen (such as weavers, printers, tanners, and woodworkers), the majority now became pioneers, clearing and farming land never before under cultivation and building homes and barns for themselves and their neighbors in relatively isolated areas.

Frontier religious life tended to be looked upon skeptically by the Brethren because of its focus on the emotions and dependence on periodic revival meetings in the absence of resident ministers. Brethren found suspect evangelistic meetings that called for conversions and baptisms on the basis of threats and emotional appeals to consider one's eternal well-being. Brethren sought sober, thoroughly-informed adult decisions for participation in a community and a way of life not based primarily on hope of heaven or fear of damnation. Until the mid-19th century Brethren cautioned against and tended to avoid these emotion-charged revival meetings.[1] Yet, Brethren gradually joined in this form of encouraging Christian commitments. In many ways, Brethren on the frontier were like their neighbors. As there were few churches, the Brethren pattern of holding their meetings for prayer and study in homes was not unusual. It was not unusual either that Brethren worship centered more in singing and group study, along with non-professional preaching from the New Testament, rather than in traditional services led by ministers who earned their living as full-time pastors and evangelists. The Methodist class meetings and services of other frontier groups were similar in their lack of dependence on traditional worship in church buildings.

Similarly, much of the basic education for those on the frontier came in the homes, not in the schools. So it was with Brethren education. Gradually many Brethren became more suspicious of formal schooling, specially of high school and college education, which were seen as incompatible with Christian simplicity. In 1831, 1852, and 1857 queries to the Yearly Meeting concerning Brethren attending higher schools were answered with the word that Brethren disapproved. However, "common" or elementary school attendance was taken for granted as these opportunities became available, despite the fact that this schooling was available only in English. The schools undermined one bulwark of Brethren separateness, the use of the German language in their homes and congregational affairs, but few seemed to notice.

The third period of about 75 years followed the founding of the *Gospel Visitor* in 1851. This period encompassed the Brethren shift to a much fuller participation in the general cultural and religious life of the times, symbolized and furthered by the predominant use of English. Gradually, the Brethren began cooperating with other religious groups, sometimes debating with them and at other times sharing in preaching missions. One example was the often-cited encounter of Elder George Wolfe II with a Baptist minister named Jones, whose handshake at the end of joint debate ca. 1817 was later memorialized on a county seal in Illinois. In a religiously competitive environment Brethren won many to their ways of thinking and believing. The last half of the 19th century was a period of rapid growth for the Brethren, because of natural increase through large families and "marriage evangelism," and because many came in as neighbors and friends impressed by Brethren lifestyle, integrity, and evangelism. Estimates indicate that the Brethren grew from a membership of about 10,000 in 1850 to over 75,000 by 1900.[2]

From the mid-19th century until today, the sense among the Brethren of their own uniqueness has diminished. The earlier Brethren saw themselves as set apart both religiously and culturally. Their distinctiveness became less clear as the vast majority of Brethren accepted the English language and began attended the more widely-available private and public schools. Brethren also gradually lost their uniqueness as they increasingly adopted the religious strategies and causes common among their neighbors. Brethren joined those around them when they took up the temperance movement, Sunday schools, "protracted" (revival) meetings, and eventually a college-educated, salaried ministry. They also copied other religious groups in sponsoring schools and colleges. Their similarities to their neighbors were fast becoming more notable than their differences. That pleased the progressive element among them and worried many others.

The *Gospel Visitor* and a half-dozen other periodicals begun over the 35 years following 1851 provided a church-wide medium of communication at a time when much greater numbers of Brethren were moving with the frontiers to the West. Brethren scattered widely as transportation greatly improved with the coming of the railways. Letter-writing and articles in these new church periodicals served to knit the Brethren together as they discussed issues with the fellowship. This was a period of expanding horizons for the whole society as well as for the Brethren. The elementary school was replacing the home as the primary place for basic learning. Some Brethren began to attend higher schools. In the end additional schooling and new publications contributed not only to harmony but also to disharmony among the Brethren.

During the first half of the 19th century, Brethren had rather carefully defined their life in terms of simplicity in dress and household furnishings, and in responsibilities of mutual economic aid and admonition. These and other Christian obligations, such as renunciation of slavery, nonparticipation in war, and nonlitigation, seem to have been settled relatively easily by clear biblical guidance, ratified by agreement of the church in decisions of Annual Meeting. On the other hand, it was long and fiercely debated whether Brethren should attend schools of higher learning, participate in revival meetings with other Christians, take out insurance policies, take advantage of land settlement schemes, hire salaried pastors, and possess organs in their churches and homes. These questions were settled, not by queries to Annual Meeting, but individuals and congregations going their own ways, gradually accepting these general societal practices, and by division of the Brethren into three separate bodies. Debates over the issues of accommodation to American culture were church-wide as well as local. However, individual Brethren and local congregations increasingly relied on their own judgments, not those of elders' bodies or the total church in Annual Meeting. Certain congregations, such as the original urban church in Philadelphia, periodically were investigated by district elders and admonished for breaking with traditional patterns.[3]

This turbulent second half of the 19th century was the period when Brethren began founding schools and colleges, a further source of tension among Brethren. Most of the local public schools were limited to the first eight grades. High schools, or academies as they were often called, and colleges were largely private and often sponsored by denominations or founded by religious leaders. Brethren joining in this process caused widespread conflict within the fraternity; much of the debate within the pages of the *Gospel Visitor*, other periodicals, and at Annual Meeting concerned the issue whether Brethren should sponsor higher schools. Some Brethren had come to feel that preserving the Brethren way of life demanded isolation from higher education and the more sophisticated culture it represented. Brethren wore strict garb and beards and kept their homes and farms relatively plain or unostentatious to symbolize their separation from the world and its values. Participation in higher education, in the eyes of many, was unnecessary and dangerous and a denial of Brethren simplicity.

Education was a central issue in the three-way schism (1881–83) between those who eventually pulled away as the strict "Old Orders" (Old German Baptist Brethren), the "Progressives" (Brethren Church), and the "Conservatives" (later Church of the Brethren) who formed the majority of the 19th century Brethren. Participation in such innovations as Sunday schools, colleges, and musical training was widely debated. Most of the "Conservatives," even while seeking to maintain an unique Brethren identity, gradually were absorbed into the mainstream life and values of the late 19th and 20th century America.

The final period, which roughly corresponds to the time since World War I, is one of increasing recognition that this acculturation has in fact happened. Education in the Church of the Brethren, as well as the general congregational and individual life, has gone through a process of adaptation to the new Brethren status as a small denomination with special concerns for service, peace, and world ministry. Brethren are no longer marked by their earlier, isolated sectarian character. Most of the people who have come into the Brethren fold in the late 19th and 20th centuries have had neither German or sectarian roots. Recently, Brethren have struggled to know how to relate to their heritage of isolation and sectarianism. While a few Brethren have romanticized their past, most have willingly let it disappear. Educationally, this has meant that gradually the Brethren schools have been transformed from carefully protected environments for the children of Brethren families, fearful of the temptations and allurements of the wider culture, to institutions that are fully a part of the wider culture.

Thus, for the past 50 years or so, most congregations within the Church of the Brethren, along with their educational institutions, have been hardly distinguishable from those of other American Protestants. They fit along a range from relatively conservative to liberal in their beliefs and approaches. So, too, most individual Brethren do not stand apart from their neighbors. A few Brethren have retained the distinctive 19th century garb and a minority of Brethren, in obedience to church teachings, have refused to participate in war. Yet, especially since World War II, Brethren have not been much concerned about uniquely Brethren beliefs and practices. The central concern of the original Brethren—to form a disciplined community of Christians responsible to each other in living out New Testament teachings—has been largely forgotten. Instead, family and individual fulfillment of the American dream of success and prosperity, while maintaining a Christian stewardship of God's gifts, has become a top priority.

Education and Accommodation

Floyd E. Mallott, longtime church historian at Bethany Seminary, saw education as playing a major role in this Brethren absorption into the American mainstream. He detected a pattern of unfaithfulness to New Testament teachings, as the Church of the Brethren became organizationally complex and oriented toward modern management practices. Members became diverse in their theologies, sophisticated in their lifestyles, and tolerant of divorce and remarriage, even among ministers. Vernard Eller made similar charges, although he has focused more on theological than on sociological or historical changes in what he sees as the loss of New Testament norms of behavior and belief.[4]

While most Brethren may not lament, as did Mallott, the transformation of the Brethren from a small, exclusive sect into a modern denomination, there is much to argue for his thesis that education was a key determinant in Brethren societal accommodation. Formal education has been a powerful impetus to change for the Brethren, as they have rejoined the societal mainstream, just as it has been for other ethnic and religious minorities. The onset of universal free public education was not resisted by Brethren, as it was by the Amish, who saw it as threatening their way of life. Schools replaced the home not only in teaching basic skills but to some extent in inculcating morals and loyalties. Brethren joined the American mainstream, became patriotic citizens, and shared in the generalized piety of American "civil religion" in part because of their participation in public schools. Soon many

Brethren were going beyond the schools to the colleges to prepare themselves to be teachers, ministers, doctors, lawyers, scientists, and business people. Whether secular or church-related colleges were attended, the effect has been to diversify, secularize, and transform Brethren into 20th century Americans who share most of the value patterns of their neighbors.

Against those who see the Brethren as unfaithful, it can be pointed out that accommodations to the wider culture in the last half of the 19th and in the 20th century were not entirely new or without historical precedents. As noted, Brethren left the mainstream of early 18th century European society because of persecution. The original Brethren valued the literacy that enabled them to study the sources of their faith. From the beginning Brethren leaders defended their beliefs in tracts and public debate, as well as in written confessions of faith when imprisoned and under examination by religious and civil authorities, often appealing to common elements of Christian tradition. After the Brethren came to the New World they had nearly 60 years of limited participation in the society of colonial America, attending and supporting schools. Individual Brethren published a wide range of materials secular and religious, not only for their own use but for the whole German population of the colonies.

With the renewal of persecution resulting from the Brethren refusal to participate in the Revolutionary War, Brethren withdrew more completely from the mainstream of society and focused their energies on differentiating themselves from other German and English settlers. Their adoption of "plain dress" and many external marks of plain living was as much identification with the Mennonites and other "New Testament Christians" as it was rejection of the culture around them. Brethren, Moravians, and Mennonites had differences among themselves but, nevertheless, often settled in the same areas, intermarried, and aided one another in material and spiritual ways. In their relations with other churches, Brethren evidenced competition and suspicion but also cooperation. Brethren did not end up in spiritually isolated communities such as the Ephrata Cloister or the Amana colonies in Iowa.

Even the adoption of English as the language of the Brethren indicates that they did not totally reject the wider culture of the 18th and 19th century America. The Amish, for example, still maintain the German language as a mark of their distance from the "English." If the Brethren had wished to shut themselves off completely from their neighbors, there would have been much less intermarriage, less growth by conversions, and fewer debates and joint evangelistic meetings with their Christian neighbors. Brethren were acquainted with religious groups who did close themselves off from the outside world but they did not choose that path. Instead, Brethren slowly but steadily tore down the barriers themselves and the society around them. The Civil War, and to a lesser extent, the First and Second World Wars provided jolts and doubts as to how fully they could accommodate themselves to the American mainstream, but few Brethren looked back regretfully. Education and accommodation have long since won the day. Through it all education was a major factor in Brethren involvement within the wider society.

Institutional Development

It will prove helpful to examine various aspects of the educational activity of the several Brethren groups and specifically of the Church of the Brethren. The first refers to the increasing participation of Brethren in schools, colleges, and organized educational programs both public and private from the 1850s onward. The second discusses the group of formal educational ventures owned, supported, and sponsored by the Brethren. The third involves programs of the church not aimed at formal educational attainments but were ministries of the church— publications, service, missions—having significant educational impact on participants, the church at large and those served. These three elements were operative at the same time and can, therefore, not be discussed without reference to each other.

Brethren were concerned to found their own schools and colleges, in part, because of the experience of young members who went off to schools sponsored by other churches and did not return to the Brethren fold. Many Brethren reacted negatively to this first era of beginning Brethren attendance at higher schools. Annual Meeting advised against permitting Brethren youth to attend such schools. Others argued that the tide of interest in advanced schooling could not be turned back and, therefore Brethren should operate their own schools. These schools could teach Brethren about New Testament understandings of life along with the academic disciplines. While many Brethren pondered and debated, other Brethren went ahead, secured the education necessary to lead and to teach, and persuaded others to join them in founding Brethren schools. Brethren publications carried the debate and information about the new educational ventures, and in several cases delivered steady editorial propaganda supporting their legitimacy.

Between 1852 and 1923 some 39 schools and colleges were founded by Brethren. Seven of these have survived and matured into accredited institutions of higher education, and one (Bethany) became the graduate theological seminary of the Church of the Brethren. One of the seven, Ashland College in Ohio, went in 1882 with the "Progressives" or the Brethren Church; it also developed an accredited theological seminary. (A schism in the late 1930s within the Brethren Church resulted in the Grace Schools at Winona Lake, a liberal arts college and large theological school.) While all of these institutions were founded by Brethren primarily for Brethren, from the beginning they welcomed non-Brethren; now each of the seven colleges serves a much wider, predominantly non-Brethren constituency. Non-Brethren students and faculty were always essential to their success. Most of these schools at first met the local need for secondary as well as college-level work in an era before most rural communities had public or parochial high schools. As public high schools became available near the surviving Brethren institutions with such academies, and as accrediting agencies increasingly discouraged their perpetuation, the secondary levels were phased out.

Clearly, a relatively small denomination such as the Church of the Brethren could not adequately support the large number of schools that sprang up in the second half of the 19th century, or even the smaller number that survived until 1908 (when Brethren celebrated 200 years of existence). The Annual Meeting of 1908 signaled the end of the debate over whether Brethren were to be involved in higher education. In the bicentennial volume of speeches and statistics heralding Brethren advances, the schools were used as prime evidence for the optimistic assessment of developments within the mission, and foreign missions.[5] Each of these had strong aspects of educational concern. As the conservative opposition to these developments was overcome, these new projects and the schools themselves began to compete with each other for Brethren resources and support.

In the first decades of Brethren higher education, from 1852 to the 1890s, failures were attributed largely to opposition or lack of interest among Brethren and to unforeseen circumstances such as the Civil War, recessions, deaths of their founders, and the like. But it soon became evident that the Brethren were simply over-extended as they sought to support and strengthen more than a dozen schools and colleges in the first decade of the 20th century. After experimenting with various forms of supervision of the colleges, the Annual Meeting transformed their "official visitors" into the General Education Board, which in 1923 hired John S. Noffsinger as its first full-time secretary.

Noffsinger prepared a study comparing the Brethren with 14 other Protestant denominations active in sponsoring higher education. He discovered that the Brethren were next to last in number of members per school and in the value of the schools' physical facilities but first in the percentage of their own membership enrolled in their schools. He concluded from this that the Brethren had too many schools for their needs, and the ones they had were too poorly-supported financially to succeed in competition with their better-equipped competitors with large church constituencies. Noffsinger also made a thorough study of each college in relation to both Brethren and non-Brethren populations in its area, its finances, and competing schools, He proposed a sweeping reorganization which would have consolidated Brethren higher education: the four colleges considered at that time to be the strongest—Bridgewater (Virginia), Juniata (Pennsylvania), Manchester (Indiana), and McPherson (Kansas)—should become the four-year "standard" liberal arts colleges. The other schools and colleges would be reduced to two-year colleges (with associated academies), affiliated with the four-year colleges and serving as feeders for them. Thus, Daleville, which was already functioning in this way, and Blue Ridge were to feed Bridgewater and serve the South. Elizabethtown was to feed Juniata, serving the East. Mount Morris was to serve as a junior college feeding Manchester and McPherson in the Midwest. In the West, La Verne was to provide an academy and two years of college work for those who would proceed to McPherson.[6]

There was logic in these proposals, for, in fact, Daleville, Blue Ridge, and Mount Morris were soon forced to close or to combine with other Brethren colleges. However, the devotion and pride of the students, leaders, and constituencies of the six colleges that survived would not permit them to accept the proposal. Annual Conference did not act on the recommendations.

The colleges then turned increasingly to recruitment of non-Brethren students. The percentage of Brethren students—over 66% in 1920—fell to slightly above 40% in the 1930s. Except for the years of World War II, when all colleges were down in total numbers so that percentages mean little, Brethren colleges continued until about 1960 to have about 40% of their student body members of the Church of the Brethren. From 1960 to 1985 the Brethren colleges composite full-time student numbers have grown from about 4,000 to 7,145, plus almost 3,700 part-time students. Approximately 8% (576) of present full-time students are members of the Church of the Brethren.[7] This percentage may be somewhat misleading, as an unknown number of students of the Brethren colleges have Brethren roots or relatives but because of population mobility and the ease of changing church affiliation are currently members of other denominations. Nonetheless, in order to survive as financially viable, accredited colleges, the Brethren-related schools have increasingly served a much broader constituency and served it well.

Continuity and Change

Brethren schools that have survived to the present have grown into strong, respected institutions of higher learning. Just as the Brethren have become adjusted to, and largely assimilated within the larger American culture, so too these colleges have adapted to the general expectations of what church-related liberal arts colleges should be. This process has involved major transformation but also continuity of purpose.

The early Brethren schools and colleges were concerned, as are the Brethren-related colleges today, for solid academic programs. There has continued to be a strong emphasis on a high quality of teaching by instructors who are concerned for a well-rounded education for their students. The physical, intellectual, and spiritual growth of the co-educational student body is noted as a goal in nearly all institutional statements of purpose and was so from the beginning. A healthy, useful Christian life was to be modeled, taught, and lived by the community of teachers and students. Rules for campus life have been formulated and reformulated to attempt to create a climate for learning, personal growth, and maturation. But even more than rules, personal influence, precept, and inspiration have been consciously utilized to challenge and call forth the best in students.

Again, as with the changes in the Church of the Brethren generally, it is important to note how the changing understandings of the good and productive life have altered the way Brethren-related colleges structured their programs and campus life. Whereas a restrictive attitude toward leisure activities reigned in the first half-century of Brethren educational institutions, freer environment in the church and society and perhaps also smaller proportions of Brethren faculty and students since the 1930s have resulted in major changes on the campuses. Smoking, drinking, social dancing, card-playing and even intercollegiate sports were ruled out in the earlier days. They were considered time-wasting preoccupations and bad habits at best or positively sinful by many in the church and college.

Amusing and endearing stories of college life have been passed on by alumni about how they sought to outwit the presidents and deans, who often made regular rounds in the dormitories to check on student adherence to the letter and spirit of the rules. "Rook" and other card games were quickly converted into Bible studies by having a large Bible to put on top of the cards when the familiar footsteps of the "prexy" or dean were heard in the halls. The monotony of dining-hall meals is no new complaint. On occasion, illicit food was dangled out of dormitory windows when someone came, only to have the string break or come loose, with local cats and dogs then enjoying the feast. For the most part these "games" seem to have been mischievous, lighthearted fun, and the penalties when students were caught to have been meted out with sympathy and lack of severity.

Extra-curricular activities included debating societies, campus papers and literary magazines, mission and evangelism teams, religious deputation groups to nearby churches, and Sunday school instruction for unchurched children. Students often helped raise money to keep the schools and colleges open in hard times, just as students today help in fund raising by telephoning alumni. Tuition was sometimes paid in foodstuffs for the college kitchen or in materials for a construction project under way. To support their studies students helped to clean, build, and repair college buildings and sometimes worked on farms that had been donated to the institutions. In the early days most students came from farms or small towns; they found the combination of hard work and study at college quite normal after years of juggling school attendance and lessons around chores. In some cases they were able to attend college only sporadically during spring and fall, when the family farm required their labor. During the periods when the institutional struggle to survive and grow involved great effort and self-sacrifice from everyone connected with them, the colleges provided a remarkable sense of unity and significance beyond merely personal goals and accomplishments. They were indeed "schools of Christian living."

In later and less strenuous times, their small size as well as the genuine interest of faculty, students, and administrations in each other and in academic and personal growth have often given a special ethos or sense of close community and common striving, which has made their alumni grateful and proud. Today, although large numbers of Brethren college students continue the tradition of work on or near campus and during the summers, fewer numbers are from farms and small towns where family livelihood depends on their contribution. The student bodies of the Brethren-related colleges today are predominantly non-Brethren, non-rural, and much more cosmopolitan in their pre-college experiences and life style than the students of 50 years ago.

In contrast to earlier generations, before arriving at college most students today have been exposed to alcohol, tobacco, or other drugs while in public schools. A vast majority of them do not have family backgrounds of total abstinence, frugality, and simple dress, nor do they come from common ethnic origins. A large number own cars and have stereo systems, television sets, and small refrigerators in their dormitory rooms. Many go home on most weekends. Films on campus, dances, intercollegiate and intramural athletics, a host of clubs and student activities, including political and social activism, take up much student time and attention.

Most students (and their parents) expect attendance at college to enable them to secure better-paying and more challenging jobs than they could get without it. While a large number see the possibility of service to society as an exciting possibility at the end of their college careers, many others have no such interests. Whereas some students organize campus fasts to raise money for food for starving people around the world and for dozens of other causes, and while class assignments include service projects such as direct medical aid to suffering people in Latin America or other needy settings, many students show no interest in such action.

Religious activities on campuses of Brethren-related colleges involve a minority of students; most of these programs are ecumenical rather than denominational. Many students are active in local congregations or attend church at home regularly. Chapel attendance has become voluntary and convocation programs are conceived as part of the general cultural and intellectual life of the campuses. There is little or no official effort to inculcate Brethren beliefs, although these are certainly discussed and promoted by some students and faculty. The percentage of Brethren students on these campuses varies from 5% to 30%. The number of Brethren faculty members has decreased significantly, although in 1985 22% of full-time and part-time faculty and administration are Brethren; academic qualifications have clearly taken precedence in employment over religious interests and affiliations.[8]

Still, a significant Brethren presence and imprint is clear on each campus. College administrations and some faculty have sought to perpetuate Brethren values. Cases in point are the peace studies institutes on several Brethren campuses. One, the Peace Studies Institute founded by Gladdys E. Muir at Manchester College in 1948, has been recognized as the first such program offering a college major in American higher education. By 1981 more than 1,000 students had taken its courses and some peace studies graduates had found work in social service agencies in the USA and abroad. Juniata College developed a program in Peace and Conflict Studies in 1974 with a grant from Elizabeth E. Baker and John C. Baker.

Yet, these values are not identical with traditional 19th and early 20th century Brethrenism; rather they tend to represent a set of concerns generated by modern Brethren and non-Brethren faculty and youth engaged in the major issues of today's world and in the subjects they are studying. Brethren campuses are alive with religious, political, and intellectual diversity. Thus the greatest transformation in the Brethren colleges (and seminary) is in the continuing growth of diversity, openness to the outside world, and engagement in the same national and international issues and causes about which educated people are concerned everywhere.

Brethren Colleges Abroad (BCA), a cooperative overseas study program founded in 1962, has demonstrated the world awareness of the six colleges related to the Church of the Brethren. As it has grown from the first group of 16 students and one faculty couple to nearly 200 students and 8 faculty couples per year from America and Europe currently exchanging and working under BCA auspices, both educational opportunities and Brethren concerns for world understanding have been furthered. Exchange relationships have been developed with universities and colleges in: Marburg, Germany; Strasbourg, France; Barcelona, Spain; Cheltenham, England; and most recently, Dalian, China. Over 2,000 students have each spent a semester or year fully integrated into an overseas educational institution, for study in a wide range of academic disciplines. BCA has not only emphasized study of the language and culture of the host country but also work in the major fields of the participants, the majority of whom are not majoring in foreign languages. Most overseas study programs are primarily language and cultural study, or else are made up almost entirely of courses taught only to the visiting students. To be able to study chemistry, political science, sociology, or psychology in an overseas university in the same classes with students of the host country enriches the students' educational goals and provides language and cultural experience as well.

Students from more than 120 colleges and universities have taken advantage of the respected BCA program, but most students have come from the six BCA colleges (and four cooperating Mennonite colleges). Similarly, the six colleges have been imaginative in developing interterm and summer study travel courses. Students and faculty members visit other parts of the United States, Third World countries, or European nations. There they can see at first hand the problems, economic conditions, historical monuments, and cultural treasures under study. In the same way, internships and independent research have been made available to give "hands-on" opportunities for learning.

Colleges related to the Church of the Brethren have reached out to serve a much wider community, as off-campus centers and short-term courses have brought education to thousands who would not otherwise have been touched by a Brethren institution. This has included, in the case of the University of La Verne, classes on military bases in the USA and overseas, as well as cooperative centers such as that at Harrisburg, Pennsylvania, where Elizabethtown College has provided faculty and administrative staff. Faculty members from all of the colleges have offered special courses and programs in congregations, camps and public schools. Over the past 50 years thousands of teachers and church leaders have benefited from on-campus and off-campus programs arranged by the six colleges. They have served the church and their communities in many different ways, in addition to providing high-quality education to their own student bodies.

Moreover, alumni of the Brethren-related colleges numbering in the tens of thousands, have contributed to the well-being of their communities in all walks of life. Unusually large numbers of their graduates have gone into the professions and service vocations. These colleges have established outstanding reputations for the number and quality of their students going on to graduate schools and particularly for the large percentage of their graduates earning research doctorates. Motivation for service and a concern for the whole life of the student continue to be stressed. Closeness between faculty members, students, and administrators has created lifelong bonds. Not just intellectual growth or vocational preparation but also moral, spiritual, and physical health and development continued to be emphasized. It is not surprising that among the alumni of the six colleges there have been Nobel Prize winners, governors, and other leaders.

Bethany and an Educated Ministry

During the last half of the 19th century it was feared that academic study of the Bible would result in a professionalized ministry. The Brethren had always called pastors from their midst to the "free ministry." These unpaid ministers served with their older colleagues as apprentice pastors while their skills in preaching and serving the needs of the congregations were developed. There were usually two to four ministers per congregation under the leadership of a presiding elder, either from that congregation or another nearby. After some years of ministry the most trusted among the younger ministers were advanced to the degree of elder. The elders then had special responsibilities, increasingly in the area (district) and at the Annual Meeting in preparing business items for discussion land decision by the whole conference.

Ministerial responsibilities were widely shared, as free ministers earned their living by farming or some other secular occupation.

Brethren expected their free ministers to be self-educated, to know their Bibles, and, because they were not formally educated beyond their brothers and sisters, not to preach the Word "too high." The pastor's flock would thus be able to reach the level of their spiritual food, helping to maintain essential equality and unity of the congregations. So long as a "common school" or limited elementary education was all that was available to most Brethren, and even later, so long as many were resistant to any further schooling as endangering the simplicity and faithfulness of Brethren, this system seemed to meet their needs.

Increasingly, however, in the second half of the 19th century after the founding of Brethren periodicals and "higher schools," Brethren were receiving further education. Brethren began to become teachers and get advanced training. Moreover, in the city congregations, such as Philadelphia, and among the ministers and elders who were founding the schools, Brethren ministers were receiving various kinds of support for essentially pastoral functions. While some Brethren spoke out against an educated, professionalized ministry, others were ministering on a full-time or part-time basis along with teaching and administering the new schools. The new Brethren schools required chapel attendance and Bible study outside of regular classes led by their Brethren minister/teachers. The schools were seeking to build character and to make the church's New Testament rule of faith and practice meaningful in these young lives.

For a time the founders of the new Brethren schools and colleges carefully avoided the academic study of the Bible and religion. There was much resistance to the possible development of educational standards for the ministry. Nonetheless, the "Progressives" were concerned to have salaried pastors, Sunday schools, colleges, and "protracted" (revival) meetings. These educational issues were prominent among the debates which led to the three-way schism of 1881–1883. Ironically, within 30 years all of the specific desires of the Progressives had been accepted within the much larger body of "Conservative" Brethren. The separation of the three groups had allowed the issues to recede from prominence and their substance to be settled by the course of events.

E. S. Young, along with other Brethren who attended universities and theological seminaries, brought Bible study into the church colleges. Young became president of Manchester College in 1895 and proceeded to build a Bible school building to go along with the existing college buildings purchased from the previous operators of the college.

In the period 1890–1920, Brethren-related schools and colleges developed Bible departments, which trained lay people and ministers alike, at the same time that degrees were earned in commercial subjects, teaching, the sciences, and the like. The emergence among Brethren of the home and foreign mission movements, salaried pastors and Sunday schools coincided with the growth and acceptance of the Brethren colleges and of higher education in general.

From its founding in 1905, Bethany Bible School in Chicago, Illinois, increasingly met the growing interest among Brethren for specific training for professionalized ministries at home and abroad. For some years, Bethany's college-level training school, as well as its graduate-level seminary program, competed with the Bible departments of the colleges, and particularly after 1918, with the School of Theology at Juniata College. Between 1899 and 1921, four Brethren colleges awarded 24 Bachelor of Sacred Theology degrees. Finally, after debate, Bethany was adopted in 1925 by Annual Meeting as the sole theological school of the denomination. This settled the lingering issue of theological education and focused at Bethany the work of preparing professional church workers.

Juniata College graciously phased out its School of Theology, ending the competition with Bethany in the professional training of ministers.[9] Gradually, under pressure from its accrediting body, Bethany reduced the extent of its college-level work and closed the training school in 1962, to concentrate on graduate theological education. Today Bethany Theological Seminary is noted for its innovative curriculum, the scholarly productivity and service to the church of its faculty, and its cooperative ecumenical stance in relation to the seminaries and denominations of Chicago. Like the Brethren-related colleges, Bethany serves students from many denominational backgrounds; still its faculty and student bodies are predominantly members of the Church of the Brethren.

World Awareness Through Missions and Service

In the last decades of the 19th century Brethren became increasingly aware of the world around them. The activities that furthered this world awareness served to educate the Brethren and helped transform them into the modern denomination they are today. As far back as the 1850s, there has been queries to the Annual Meetings and letters to the *Gospel Visitor* raising the cry for more systematic efforts to carry out the Great Commission. Brethren had from the beginning actively shared their faith with their neighbors and sought to increase their numbers by conversion. It must also be remembered that the Brethren arrived in America and then moved westward in the midst of spiritual stirrings and the fervent evangelism of frontier communities touched by the repeated waves of revivalism.

Thus, the Brethren calls in the 19th century for home missions, and later for foreign missions, were new forms of a continuing concern. Yet, the effect from the 1850s on was increasingly to bring the Brethren into the mainstream of American religious life. Mission concerns sometimes led to competition in local communities but increasingly led to cooperation with other Christians, particularly overseas. The need for training for missions added support for Brethren participation in education, thus helping to overcome Brethren isolation. But more importantly, interest in missions opened vast new worlds to the Brethren, who had finally emerged from the period when nearly all their energies were absorbed by the requirements of setting and resettling, and developing productive farms and businesses. Home missions were mainly to the cities, where the Brethren were now beginning to live in larger numbers. The many unchurched families encountered in the cities of many Brethren in their rural communities.

Brethren horizons were expanded as they were increasingly caught up in the American ethos. National expansionism, faith in education, technological and social progress, democratic participation in the development of their communities, and desire for personal success—all in varying degrees captured Brethren imagination.

Simply entering fully into American life, with increasing numbers of respected Brethren in public life and the professions, educated the entire membership. Carrying out special mission and service projects, such as aid to the Armenians persecuted in Turkey or material aid and resettlement, and establishing missions in Europe, Africa, India, and China, brought a vision of interaction with the whole world as their Christian responsibility. The outpouring of help victims of war in Spain, and after World War II, elsewhere in Europe, put thousands of Brethren into direct contact with other peoples, other cultures, and other ways of understanding the world. A worldmindedness emerged among Brethren, which led to their pioneering in the creation of service programs. These programs later came also to be supported by other Christian denominations and became ecumenical efforts. Among these programs pioneered by Brethren were the Heifer Project, International Christian Youth Exchange for high school students, the material aid and refugee processing center at New Windsor, Maryland, and the Christian Rural Overseas Program (CROP).

As hundreds of younger and older Brethren served as shipboard and airfreight "cowboys," as volunteer service workers, as short-term and long-term missionaries, as teachers and development workers overseas, the Brethren were transformed. Outpourings of Christian love in the form of gifts of food, animals clothing, as well as time and energies over a number of years, gave the Brethren a new sense of their own identity. No longer an isolated, small, sectarian group, the Brethren proudly stood among the leaders of Christendom in their concern to reconcile and serve God's human family. Brethren leaders served high offices in the National and World Council of Churches, and were called upon to advise presidents in establishing the Peace Corps and educational exchange.

As Brethren stand poised on the threshold of the 21st century, the Church of the Brethren has more educated members and stronger, better-equipped educational institutions than ever before. Moreover, more Brethren are writing and publishing, both through the Brethren Press and other publishing houses, than ever before. An excellent denominational magazine, *Messenger* and a fine journal, *Brethren Life and Thought*, inform and stimulate discussion of issues. There is good reason to believe that education will serve well in the years ahead as it has in the past as the Brethren continue to be transformed and to be creative in service in mission enterprises "for the glory of God and their neighbor's good."

Notes

1. Roger E. Sappington, *The Brethren in the New Nation* (Elgin, IL: 1976), 245–246; cf. *Minutes of the Annual Meetings of the Church of the Brethren* (Elgin, IL: 1909), 75 (1842: Art. 2) and 174 (1858: Art. 31).

2. Donald F. Durnbaugh, ed., *The Church of the Brethren: Past and Present* (Elgin, IL: 1976), 55. 145 (a study prepared for the Conference on High Education and the Church of the Brethren, Richmond, IN, June 24–27, 1976).

3. Roland L. Howe, *The History of the Church (Dunker) . . . The First Church of the Brethren of Philadelphia, Pa., 1813#1943* (Philadelphia, PA: 1943), 475–491.

4. Floyd E. Mallott, *Studies in Brethren History* (Elgin, IL: 1954), passim; Vernard M. Eller, *Towering Babble* (Elgin, IL: 1981), passim.

5. D. L. Miller, ed., *Two Centuries of the Church of the Brethren)* (Elgin, IL: 1908).

6. Lehman, *Beyond Anything Foreseen* (1976), 67–70; J. S. Noffsinger, *A Program for Higher Education in the Church of the Brethren* (New York: 1925).
7. *Church of the Brethren Yearbook: Directory 1985, Statistics 1984* (Elgin, IL: 1985), 311.
8. *Yearbook* (1985), 311.
9. Lehman, *Beyond Anything Foreseen* (1976), 50–54, 64–66.

7

Social Outreach

David B. Eller

"Above all, preserve love, for then we will preserve light."[1] These words from the pen of Alexander Mack, Jr., express an ethic of love and service which has characterized the Brethren since the first baptisms in 1708. Throughout their history this love ethic has manifested itself in various ways, but a central theme has remained constant. Brethren have believed that devotion and love for Christ may be best expressed in loving service.

This chapter surveys two key aspects of this love and service ministry. The first is Brethren response to war, militarism, and the search for alternatives to participation in military forces. The second section discusses other avenues of social witness, such as attempts to alleviate human suffering and care for orphans and widows. There has been considerable overlap of these two concerns.

Nonresistance and Conscientious Objection

Traditionally, Brethren have based their opposition to war on the teachings of Jesus in the Sermon on the Mount (Matt. 5–7) and other New Testament passages. War and military service were understood to be completely contrary to the example of Jesus Christ and of the early Christian church. This biblical pacifism and loving opposition to militarism was historically called "nonresistance." The term was coined from Jesus' instruction to "resist not one who is evil" and to "turn the other cheek." It meant that the believer willingly chose to suffer wrong and personal injury rather than to retaliate with violence.

Unquestionably, the first Brethren arrived at this understanding not only from biblical study and the example of the early Christians but also from the heroic witness of the 16th century Anabaptist reformers and their descendants, the Mennonites, with whom they shared many beliefs. Significant, too, was the historical context in which the Brethren were rooted. Memory was still vivid of the horrible Thirty Years' War (1618–1648) that had devasted much of Germany. The harsh occupation of the Rhine Valley by French troops during the War of the Spanish Succession in the 1680s did not end until the Treaty of Ryswick (1697). The effects of war were everywhere. Given their Anabaptist leanings, it was hardly surprising that the Brethren, as well as other Pietist reform groups, called for a biblically-based peace ethic.

Unfortunately, other than a few references to the example of Anabaptist nonresistance in the writing of Alexander Mack, Sr., there is little that documents the peace position of the Brethren in Europe. A story preserved by the 19th century antiquarian and book collector Abraham H. Cassel, however, provides a clue to their attitude toward military conscription. According to this tradition, Johannes Naas, a powerful preacher, was a tall and powerfully built man. Because of his stature, Naas came to the attention of recruiting officers for the personal guard of a Prussian ruler. He refused conscription. Naas was subsequently arrested and tortured but still did not consent to join the guard. Eventually, he was brought before the ruler where the preacher explained that he had already enlisted in the service of Jesus Christ and could not forsake him. Impressed with this witness, the ruler released him and rewarded him with a gold coin.[2]

In the New World the Brethren, along with the Society of Friends (Quakers) and Mennonites, constituted an important peace church element in William Penn's "holy experiment" of Pennsylvania. For the first time these and other groups enjoyed religious freedom and were free to spread their views and to prosper without state interference. Neither were they faced with the prospect of military harassment for their refusal to bear arms. Continued unrest in the English colonies, however, caused the Quakers to lose control of the Pennsylvania legislature during the French and Indian War (1754–1763). At the same time the peace principles of these churches was severely tested, especially in frontier areas. A small settlement of Brethren in Morrisons Cove, Pennsylvania, was destroyed by Indians in 1762 (a second attack occurred in this area in 1777).

Revolutionary War

During the Revolutionary War period (1775–1783), numerous Brethren experienced hardship and persecution as a result of their nonresistant beliefs. There was no national conscription by the Continental Congress and most of the colonies where Brethren lived did not require military service of religious objectors. Still, the Brethren faced various types of local militia enrollments and intense public pressure to support the Revolution. Peace groups suffered mob violence in Lancaster County, Pennsylvania, and in Frederick County, Maryland.

Annual Meeting decisions from this period make clear that Brethren could not join the army or hire substitutes. Throughout the war most members acted consistently in refusing to bear arms but less so when it came to paying for the war effort through fines, special taxes, and providing substitutes. Some Brethren refused to make such payments. In other cases local congregations were called on to provide financial assistance.

Equally serious was the issue of taking an oath of allegiance ("attest") to the new revolutionary state governments. Because Brethren were conservative in their views of civil government and because they had affirmed loyalty to the British crown when they arrived as immigrants, most were reluctant to counter the admonition of Paul (Rom. 13:1) to be "subject to governing authorities." It is often overlooked that the American Revolution had many of the characteristics of a civil war, with brother fighting brother. These circumstances made it difficult for the Loyalist-minded Brethren to remain neutral.

The first recorded Annual Meeting decision called upon members who had taken attests to renounce them publicly and to ask their local congregations for forgiveness. It was the refusal of Christopher Sauer, Jr., to take the oath that led to the confiscation of his personal property and destruction of his famous printing press. Sauer, who was one of the most wealthy and influential men in colonial Pennsylvania before the Revolution, was arrested, harshly treated, and publicly humiliated. Other Brethren in Pennsylvania and elsewhere were arrested or levied with heavy fines. Clearly, the issues presented to the church in the Revolutionary era shaped Brethren attitudes toward the state and military service throughout most of the 19th century.

The Brethren response to the war for independence also took a positive turn with numerous expressions of charity. A classic statement to the Pennsylvania Assembly, issued jointly in 1775 with the Mennonites, articulated the theme of service. It acknowledged the advice of the Assembly that "they ought to be helpful to those who are in Need and distressed Circumstances towards all men of what Station they may be," for it was their "Principle to feed the Hungry and give the Thirsty Drink." Maintaining that they had dedicated themselves "to serve all Men in every Thing that can be helpful to the Preservation of Men's lives," they asserted they found "no Freedom in giving, or doing, or assisting in anything by which Men's lives are destroyed or hurt."[3]

Civil War

American wars before 1861 touched relatively few Brethren, other than the impact that these conflicts had upon the nation's economy, particularly on agriculture. Many states mandated participation in militia drills, but such laws were seldom strictly enforced, and commutation fines or substitutes were generally allowed. The United States maintained a small army and navy during this period without conscription. Consequently the War of 1812 and the brief Mexican War (1846) were fought primarily with volunteer military forces. In frontier Illinois it is believed that Elder George Wolfe II obtained exemption for Brethren during the Black Hawk War in 1831.

By contrast, the Civil War (1861–1865) deeply touched the church. While clearly still a closed sectarian group, many Brethren were comfortable enough with the wider social order about them to openly support the Union side. The church had also long opposed slavery; members who continued to own slaves were disciplined. Brethren who resided in the Confederacy sought to remain neutral; but as the war dragged on, and Southern resources dwindled, this became increasingly difficult, if not impossible. Without doubt, Brethren in the South, especially those who resided in the strategically important Shenandoah Valley of Virginia, suffered personal injuries and losses to a greater extent than Brethren who resided in the Northern states.

The Union passed its first conscription law in 1863, but states such as Ohio and Indiana had earlier enacted draft legislation. Generally, Brethren and other religious objectors were able to obtain exemption by paying fees and, later, by hiring substitutes. When conscripted, peace church members were often allowed to serve in hospital units or were assigned to other noncombatant duties. Annual Meeting minutes opposed conscription and directed local congregations to help pay for exemption fees according to need.

In the Confederacy exemption from military duty was more difficult to obtain. A Virginia conscription law passed in 1862 reluctantly provided for religious objectors and required both a $500 fee and a property tax. When the Confederate government passed a similar act shortly thereafter, some Brethren were forced to pay for exemption again. In both the North and the South there was confusion about the status of young men from Brethren homes who were opposed to military service but who had not yet joined the church. These young men frequently ended up in the army.

These and other unfavorable circumstances led to two organized attempts in 1862 by Mennonites and Brethren from the Shenandoah Valley to cross illegally into Northern territory. Both groups were captured, arrested, and placed in prisons in Harrisonburg and Richmond. Although the men were released shortly thereafter, they and other nonresistant people were viewed with increased suspicion by their secessionist neighbors.

Many Protestant denominations had split in earlier decades along North/South lines over the slavery issue. The Brethren remained unified during the war, a fact symbolized by the selection of Elder John Kline, a Virginian, as moderator of Annual Meetings from 1861 to 1864. He managed to obtain safe passage through the lines to meetings held in Northern states, but communication was cut off with most Brethren in the South. Sadly, both Kline and John P. Bowman of Tennessee were martyred in 1864 by Confederate sympathizers. Following the war many congregations in the North sent love offerings to assist in the rebuilding of destroyed homes and farms.

Although the church remained one body and expected conformity from its members, the decades which followed brought increasing tensions. Between 1865 and 1915 the church expanded rapidly, both in members and geographic location. Accommodation to the mainstream culture quickened. Progressively minded Brethren undertook new ventures in higher education, home and foreign missions, and publishing, although the price of these changes was two painful divisions—the Old German Baptist Brethren and the Brethren Church.

World War I

During this period of transition much of the membership also underwent a fundamental change in their attitudes toward the secular world, and with it participation in civic affairs, including military service. The peace witness of the church was assumed and personally affirmed at baptism, but otherwise nonresistance and peace issues were seldom discussed. Prior to World War I (1914–1918) there had been little in the way of peace education materials available to local congregational leaders. The Spanish American War (1898) had been but a brief episode in American imperialism, fought with volunteer troops, and it had little impact on the church. Although a Peace Committee was appointed by the Annual Conference in 1911 with ambitious goals, it received little funding. Consequently, when in 1917 draft legislation was passed that provided only noncombatant military assignments for conscientious objectors, church leaders were largely unprepared.

At the same time, however, Brethren were becoming more politically aware. The earlier Grange and Populist movements caught the attention of some Brethren but it was support for the temperance crusade that brought many Brethren into polling booths, and with it a rethinking of the meaning of Christian citizenship. The older Anabaptist position was of "honoring the emperor [the state]" and paying lawful taxes but not seeking to influence or change government policies; this view was weakened considerably. When the United States entered the war against Germany in 1917, some Brethren bought Liberty [War] Bonds and exhibited a patriotic spirit. No doubt some were thankful that only a few years earlier the name of the church had been changed from German Baptist Brethren to Church of the Brethren.

The result of these changes was that during World War I, for the first time, most members of draft age accepted some form of noncombatant military duty in the engineering, quartermaster, or medical corps; a small percentage of Brethren entered the regular service. A significant number, however, felt that any form of military service was wrong. They refused to put on the uniform or drill. In various camps this minority was cruelly harassed by officers and others who wanted them to become regular combatants. A few of these objectors were placed in military prisons, most notably at Fort Leavenworth, Kansas, for their refusal to cooperate. One member of the Old German Baptist Brethren, Maurice Hess, was placed in solitary confinement.

The counsel of local church leadership to this situation was mixed. Some urged acceptance of noncombatant duties, even though it meant becoming part of the military service. Others advised strict noncomformity, discouraging the wearing of uniforms and drilling. Such confusion led to the calling of a special conference, with delegates from all the districts and many local churches, at Goshen, Indiana, in January, 1918. Through a specially appointed Central Service Committee, the conference sent a resolution to the government detailing the historic opposition of the Brethren to military service. More importantly, the assembly issued a statement to be used by members when drafted. It counseled that "we cannot conscientiously engage in any activity or perform any function contributing to the destruction of human life." With respect to the key questions of wearing a uniform and participation in drills, the document urged the Brethren "not to enlist in any service which would, in any way, compromise our time-honored position in relation to war; also that they refrain from wearing the military uniform." Finally, the resolution concluded that "the tenets of the church forbid military drilling, or learning the art . . . of war."[4]

The Goshen Conference resolution was distributed among the congregations and taken to young men in the camps. Eventually it came to the attention of military officials in Washington, D.C. In July, J. M. Henry, a member of the Central Service Committee, was called to the War Department and informed that the officers of the Goshen conference faced charges of sedition unless the "Goshen Statement" was immediately withdrawn. Reluctantly and prayerfully, the members of the Central Service Committee agreed to recall the resolution and to discontinue its use. From the perspective of the committee, this action saved the church from "impending tragedy." It also left the church without any clear policy regarding military service—other than tradition—for the duration of the war. Young men who continued to be drafted were left for themselves to decide which type of service, if any, to accept.

This largely negative experience of dealing with military and governmental officials gave some new dedication to the peace work of church in the 1920s and 1930s. These years were also marked by the influence of the Social Gospel movement and increasing ecumenical commitment on the part of church leaders. A new, ethically-based and activist vision of peacemaking, which was more politically sensitive, captured the hearts of many. For numerous Brethren, religious or ethical pacifism replaced the older view of biblical nonresistance.

The activist careers of M. R. Zigler, Dan West, and Kermit Eby illustrate the changed attitude of Brethren leadership. These three leaders and others urged the church to turn to the world in loving service. Sunday school classes, peace caravans, summer camps, and work camps became vehicles through which this new optimism was expressed. A new and more vocal understanding of peace witness stimulated Annual Conference to proclaim in 1935 that "all war is sin" and reassert its conviction that the church could not accept any form of military participation. "[I]t is wrong for Christians to support or engage in it; war is incompatible with the spirit, example and teachings of Jesus."[5]

World War II

As war clouds gathered across Europe in the 1930s, members of the "Historic Peace Churches" began to explore ways in which they could work together. An important meeting of Brethren, Mennonites, and Friends held in 1935 in Newton, Kansas, discussed common beliefs and appointed a Continuation Committee to plan united action in event of war. There was a shared determination not to repeat the situation of World War I in which large numbers of religious objectors found themselves in the military. These discussions resulted in delegations that visited high-level government and military officials in 1937 and 1940. As a result of these lobbying efforts, the Selective Training and Service Act of 1940 provided that conscientious objectors (COs) were to be assigned nonmilitary service, specifically "work of national importance under civilian direction."[6] At the same time the peace churches created the National Service Board for Religious Objectors (NSBRO, later called the National Interreligious Service Board for Conscientious Objectors) to work with Selective Service officials. The United States entered World War II during the following year, the last major power to do so.

The alternative service program, Civilian Public Service (CPS), was officially established in February, 1941, by presidential executive order. With NSBRO serving as a liaison to the government, Brethren, Mennonites, and Quakers administered CPS base camps where the draftees worked at government approved jobs, primarily in forest and soil conservation. Other units, detached from the camps, were later created in public health projects, mental health facilities, and dairy farming. One of the best known projects was an experiment in starvation conducted at the University of Minnesota.

Church leaders cooperated closely with government officials in the CPS program, which operated from 1941 to 1947. This arrangement seemed to work well, although some of the projects may have been of questionable "national importance." The irony, however, is that only a small minority of Brethren men of draft age, perhaps 10% of all those eligible, opted for any type of alternative service. Most entered service when drafted and served in combatant roles. Unquestionably, there were many volunteers for the regular armed forces. Although the church officially opposed war, most Brethren were by now comfortably part of the world they had sought so long to avoid.

Many argued that the conditions leading to World War II were unique. Democratic citizenship required military service. Most denominations that had earlier opposed US entry into the war changed positions after the attack on Pearl Harbor. The popular pacifist movement of the 1920s and 1930s dissolved. Here was clearly a just war, fought to check the evil expansion of the Axis powers. While the war was not promoted frantically at home—as had been the case in World War I—stopping Hitler, Mussolini, and Tojo was seen as necessary for living in a peaceful world.

Recent Wars

Allied victory in 1945 set the world stage for the decades of "super-power" confrontation and "limited wars" that followed. The United States and the Union of Soviet Socialist Republics have been important antagonists in the Korean War (1951–1953), the Vietnamese War (1948–1975), continued conflict between Israel and her Arab neighbors (1948ff.), and various wars of "national liberation" in the 1970s and 1980s. Brethren response to conflicts in which the United States used conscripted troops (Korea, Vietnam) and Brethren attitudes toward the US role in other international conflicts have been mixed. Generally, denominational leaders have been critical of American military policy. Since the late 1940s much effort has gone into political witness against peacetime conscription and into efforts to provide alternative service for draftees. Beginning in 1951 alternative service projects for COs, normally of two-year duration, were greatly expanded. The church was also allowed to create and administer its own alternative service programs. Much of this was done through Brethren Volunteer Service (BVS), created by the Annual Conference in 1948. BVS challenged the youth of the denomination to give a year of humanitarian service without financial compensation.

During the turbulent late 1960s the horrors of the tragedy in Vietnam led a few young people and others to ask if the church had become too comfortable in a militarized society and if its national staff should cooperate with Selective Service. An informal network of peace activists known as the Brethren Action Movement challenged both the government through noncooperation and denominational officials with appeals to sanction civil disobedience. Some even held that religious pacifism should be a test of church membership.

A particularly tense moment occurred during the Annual Conference of 1970 when one young man publicly burned his draft card. That same conference significantly revised an earlier position paper on war. The resulting document, "A Statement of the Church of the Brethren on War," remains the official position of the denomination. It reaffirms the historic witness of the Brethren against war and militarism, yet at the same time holds "in respect" those members who in good conscience disagree. For draft-age youth the church "commends" either civilian alternative service or noncooperation with the Selective Service system, and pledges support for both. Further, members are urged to avoid work in defense industries and to oppose taxes for war purposes.[7]

During the war in Southeast Asia, many young Brethren men continued to do alternative service through BVS or a similar agency, perhaps 35 to 40% of those drafted. One Brethren noncooperator, Bob Gross of Northern Indiana, served a federal prison term. After the war the conscription issue for many youth shifted to that of Selective Service registration for a possible future draft (1980). A Brethren college student, Enten Eller, refused to register and, after a highly publicized trial in 1982, was the first young American to be convicted for nonregistration.

In the late 1970s and 1980s, in the midst of the most deadly buildup of armaments the world has seen, there is new evidence that many Brethren are seriously examining the peace heritage of the church. In a now thoroughly pluralistic denomination, this examination has taken quite different directions. For some it has meant emphasizing a more traditional Anabaptist theology, including nonresistance and the "suffering way of the cross." Others have linked peace with justice issues and identify strongly with movements around the world against military, economic, and political oppression. New ecumenical peace efforts with Mennonites, Quakers, and other peace groups, such as the New Call to Peacemaking, have provided both a sense of renewed discipleship and an urgency about the nuclear arms race. Peace networks such as the Brethren Peace Fellowship (1967ff.), On Earth Peace Assembly (1974 ff.), and denominational programs keep issues—including the arms race and disarmament, war taxes, nuclear free zones, resumption of conscription, opportunities for East-West dialogue and understanding, and other peace-related concerns—before the Church of the Brethren.

Service Activities

Another dimension to Church of the Brethren social outreach has been its service activities. Although Brethren have consistently sought to avoid war, they have also looked for ways to give humanitarian aid when possible. Much of this effort might be termed "mutual aid" and was first directed to members of the fellowship. Biblical passages such as "If one member suffers, all suffer together" (1 Cor. 12:26) and "Bear one another's burdens" (Gal. 6:2) have been taken to mean that the welfare of each member is the burden of the whole church. These concerns fit squarely with the Anabaptist vision of the church as a community of God's people *(Gemeinschaft)* and the Pietist emphasis upon living a life of charity. At Schwarzenau those who became Brethren may have experimented with common ownership of property, a "community of goods" (Acts 2:44–45, 4:32). Such economic systems were practiced by certain monastic orders, the Hutterian Brethren, some Radical Pietist groups, and the Ephrata community.

In the New World congregations were expected to look after the physical as well as spiritual needs of their members. By the 1770s the office of deacon/deaconess had been established; part of its duties included care ("oversight") of the poor. The Germantown congregation kept a "poor box" into which members made donations for those in need. After the turn of the century, mutual aid frequently took the form of barn raising, financial support, and performing farm chores for others during times of family crisis. On several occasions during the 19th century, organized collections of funds by individuals and congregations were made for distribution to needy Brethren. Following the Civil War financial aid was sent Southern congregations for use in rebuilding damaged or destroyed houses and farmbuildings. Two droughts and grasshopper plagues affecting Brethren in Missouri and Kansas (1895–1860), 1874–1875), also brought a generous response.

Because it was the duty of the church to care for its members, Annual Conference was slow to sanction the use of insurance, especially life insurance. Eventually, however, attitudes shifted and several members were instrumental in organizing commercial insurance companies. The Mutual Aid Association of the Church of the Brethren (1885ff.) with offices in Abilene, Kansas, insures real and personal property on a mutual aid basis. More recently, various Brethren-related credit unions have been formed to offer a range of financial services.

Orphans and Aged

Another aspect of the love and service ethic was the care given orphans and the aged. Many in the church have considered it their duty to provide homes for destitute children. Customarily, orphans from Brethren families were placed in homes where they might continue to be raised in the Brethren faith. In the early 20th century Frank Fisher and others promoted "child rescue work" to reach out beyond the Brethren and the idea received popular support. Orphanages had earlier been established on the mission fields, both in India and China. In the 1910s and 1920s several districts began to sponsor homes for children, sometimes combined with homes for the aged. This effort was to provide social services but was also for the purpose of evangelization. These institutions typically were small, underfunded, and provided only temporary shelter. Placing children with suitable Christian families remained a high priority. As the state and federal governments established public welfare programs in the 1940s and 1950s, these homes no longer met higher licensing standards and the need itself diminished. Denominational attention shifted to comprehensive programs of Christian education, which included camping.

Aging Brethren typically lived with their children, until shifts in lifestyle in the mid-20th century brought a surge of interest in retirement homes for "senior citizens." Traditionally, poor and aged Brethren were to be cared for by local congregations if the immediate family was unable to do so, rather than allowing them to be placed in the county "poorhouses." Beginning in 1883, districts began to sponsor "old folks" homes. Residents of these early homes were usually those who had nowhere else to turn or retired church leaders with limited financial resources.

Following World War II several new retirement homes were built, many offering full nursing services. In 1985 there were 27 such homes related to the Church of the Brethren in operation, with approximately 6,000 residents. Because most of these homes secured major funding beyond the church, particularly from government agencies, residence has been open without regard to church affiliation.

Social Welfare

The social welfare ministries of the Brethren have not only been directed toward members. Indeed, Brethren may best be known by others for their relief and service activities that have spanned the globe, although this story has never been completed documented. The biblical foundation for this ministry was the teaching of Jesus: ". . . for I was hungry and you gave me food, I was thirsty and you gave me drink . . . As you did it to the least of these . . . you did it unto me" (Matt. 25:34–40). For many Brethren in the 20th century, "service"—symbolized by the washing of feet during the love feast—became the most important priority of the denomination.

An important principle was that aid has been given to those suffering because of war and natural disasters, without regard to race, political ideology, or religious affiliation. It has also included giving aid to the enemy. A story from the colonial era of America illustrates this point. George Miller was the first minister of the Big Swatara congregation in Pennsylvania. When a neighbor stole Miller's ox and was apprehended, the preacher is said to have walked 20 miles to the jail at Lancaster; he carried a bed in cold weather to make sure that the thief would be warm.[8] A more recent example is the financial contribution made by Brethren during the Vietnamese War to North Vietnam for rebuilding bombed-out hospitals and for medical supplies. In both the Revolutionary War and the Civil War, Brethren homes and meeting-houses were used as temporary hospitals by armies on both sides of the conflict.

An illustration of Brethren concern for social welfare is attention given to American Blacks in the late 19th and early 20th centuries. Given the prevailing pattern of racism and the Brethren expectations of nonconformity, it was very difficult for blacks to fit into white congregations. A few black congregations were started in Southern Ohio and mission projects were initiated in Arkansas and Colorado. Unfortunately, all of these were relatively short-lived. Attempts to begin church work in the Deep South, where there were no Brethren, also failed. Later, in the 1960s, BVS began several projects working with black youth in urban areas; those in Baltimore and Washington, D.C., were the most successful. A few black congregations with community outreach programs have since developed from older churches in racially-changing neighborhoods. Brethren were also active in civil rights efforts, particularly in Selma, Alabama.

Work with Hispanics also dates from the early decades of the 20th century. A long-term project was started at Falfurrias, Texas, in 1918 when John Stump provided funds to establish a farm and trade school for Mexicans. The school closed in 1925 but, after World War II, BVS took over the operation of the farm. In 1942 Brethren CPS men began working at Castaner, Puerto Rico. A hospital, school, and community improvement projects were soon in operation.

Relief Activities

Brethren began to respond to international relief opportunities in an organized way in 1917 when the Annual Conference authorized taking up collections for famine relief in Armenia; the generosity of the church was unprecedented. In 1921 about $267,000 had been raised, much of it through the efforts of J. E. Miller. Although the aid went to Christians who had been systematically persecuted by the Turks, for the first time a relief program was supported by Brethren for people they did not know.

There was little followup on this effort during the "return to normalcy" decade of the 1920s. In the crisis years of the 1930s, however, new opportunities for service developed. One of the most significant was sending a small group of relief workers to Spain during the Spanish Civil War (1937–1938) under the sponsorship of the American Friends Service Committee (AFSC). The volunteer staff (which included Mennonites) was able to give assistance on both sides of the conflict. Several tons of material aid and approximately $20,000 had been collected by mid-1939. The experience of one relief worker, Dan West, laid the foundation for the Heifer Project, a program of sending overseas heifers (and later other livestock) for distribution to those in need. Shortly after the end of World War II, the Heifer Project sent thousands of animals to the war-torn countries of Europe, Africa, and Asia.

Brethren Service

Perhaps the most important result of Brethren work in Spain was the establishment in 1939 of the Brethren Service Committee (BSC, later Brethren Service Commission) to coordinate relief efforts. As reorganized by the Annual Conference in 1941, the BSC initially worked with the other peace churches and government officials in operating CPS camps during and after World War II. Much of the early vision and administration of the committee was provided by M. R. Zigler and W. Harold Row, both of whom served as BSC executive secretaries. Zigler was called in 1948 to oversee Brethren Service work in Europe and to represent the Church of the Brethren in the newly organized World Council of Churches. An office in Geneva, Switzerland, has continued to this day to be the center for directing Brethren projects in Europe and the Near East.

During World War II, the Brethren Service Committee established hostels in several urban areas in the USA to assist in the resettlement of Japanese-Americans. This was in response to the forced evacuation of Japanese from the west coast. Ralph and Mary Blocher Smeltzer organized this effort, which resettled in the Chicago area alone more than 1,000 persons in 1943–1944.

Between 1945 and 1947 the emphasis of Brethren Service shifted from Civilian Public Service to providing relief and rehabilitation projects in Europe and around the world. A full listing of these projects to the late 1950s is not possible in a few paragraphs. By any standards, however, Brethren Service accomplishments have been impressive. Relief work started in Europe through the International YMCA, with volunteers working in prisoner-of-war camps in several countries. This was followed by teams of "sea-going cowboys," who tended relief shipments of livestock on trans-Atlantic voyages.

In Europe, BSC initiated substantial programs in France, the Netherlands, Germany, Austria, Poland, Greece, and Italy. Brethren were among the first to work with the Council for Relief Agencies Licensed to Operate in Germany (CRALOG) in 1946. Programs for aid distribution were centered in Kassel in central Germany. In Bremen, Brethren Service staff members worked with the Evangelical Church on successful projects to retrain handicapped war victims. One long-lasting program was a student exchange project, initiated in 1949. Selected refugee youth of high-school age were sent to the USA for one year. The US government provided ocean-transportation, BSC provided the administration, and Brethren families in the United States provided the homes. The student exchange project was so successful, it became a permanent ecumenical agency, International Christian Youth Exchange.

In Austria, BSC work centered on material aid, health care, agricultural assistance, and the resettlement of *Volksdeutsche* refugees. These ethnic Germans had lived in Eastern Europe but were forced to leave their homes after the war. Several million fled to the West but, as former enemies, were refused government aid. In Poland, BSC programs were terminated by the Communist government in 1949, although fruitful agricultural exchanges were allowed to resume in 1957 as cold war tensions eased.

Greece was the scene of an innovative BSC project devoted to improving the agricultural economy of a desperately poor area near the Albanian border. Organized in 1951 on an ecumenical basis with endorsement by the Greek Orthodox Church, this Interchurch Service to Greek villages was centered in the northwest Epirus province. It succeeded in returning large areas of land to cultivation, introduced what is now a flourishing poultry industry, and trained villagers in improved agricultural and home economics practices.

Elsewhere, one of the most unusual of early BSC projects was undertaken in 1946–1947 in cooperation with the United States Relief and Rehabilitation Administration (UNRRA) and the Nationalist Chinese government. The "tractor units" involved sending 50 volunteers to China as mechanics, drivers, and agricultural advisors in order to teach the Chinese to use US-built tractors provided by UNRRA. Hundreds of Chinese were trained and several thousand acres placed under cultivation by these units.

Volunteers for a variety of Brethren Service assignments, both men and women, were recruited by BSC. Training (until 1968) took place at New Windsor, Maryland, on a former college campus which the Commission had purchased in 1944. The Brethren Service Center quickly became a processing and distribution center for clothing, food, medical supplies, and other material aid. The New Windsor facility has also developed into an ecumenical service center, with offices for Church World Service (an agency of the National Council of Churches), Lutheran World Relief, Sales Exchange for Refugee Rehabilitation

(SERRV), Brethren Disaster Network (1973ff.), Christian Rural Overseas Program (CROP), and other aid groups as well. Both CROP (1947ff.) and SERRV (1949ff.) began as Brethren initiatives, with considerable Brethren Service investment, both in personnel and funding.

In 1969 the work of the Brethren Service Commission was merged with the World Ministries Commission (WMC) of the denomination's newly organized General Board. As Europe recovered from the war, the scope of Brethren Service activity has been reduced, although Brethren continue to respond to the needs of suffering people around the world. A strong BVS program continues; thousands of dollars are channeled each year to ecumenical relief and rehabilitation agencies, particularly to Church World Service. Mission staff workers responsible to WMC also carry on assignments, formerly a part of BSC. In the 1970s and 1980s emphasis has been placed on economic development programs, hunger relief, and peace and justice advocacy.

Clearly, the Brethren continue to be a people with a strong social outreach. The witness of the church to peace concerns and her ministries to give a "cup of cold water" in the name of Jesus Christ have made a significant impact not only on other Christians but also on the global community. The sacrifice of the church to these ends has been far beyond what might be expected of a small denomination with a sectarian heritage.

Notes

1. "Letter on Feetwashing," *The Brethren in Colonial America*, ed. Donald F. Durnbaugh (Elgin, IL: 1967), 468.
2. *Brethren Family Almanac*, (1874), 24.
3. "A Short and Sincere Declaration, 7 November, 1775," in Durnbaugh, *Colonial America*, (1967), 364.
4. *Minutes of the Special General Conference, January 9, 1918* (1918), in the Brethren Historical Library and Archives, Elgin, IL.
5. *Minutes of the Annual Conferences of the Church of the Brethren, 1923-1944* (1945), 110-111.
6. Rufus D. Bowman, *The Church of the Brethren and War, 1708-1941* (1944), 292.
7. Revised from a "Statement on Position and Practices of the Church of the Brethren in Relation to War" (1948); revised (1957, 1958). The 1970 statement is taken from *Minutes of the Annual Conferences of the Church of the Brethren, 1970-1974* (1975), 63-67; it also was issued separately by Brethren Press (1970).
8. J. E. Miller, *Stories from Brethren Life* (1942), 36-37.

8

Mission

B. Merle Crouse
Karen Spohr Carter

The Brethren are a people with a sense of mission. Even though they have used the Great Commission text (Matt. 28:19–20) more for justifying the practice of trine immersion baptism than for sending God's people into the world, its constant missionary imperative has always been heeded to some extent. Brethren have a rich history of missionary endeavor. Their participation in the world missionary movement has been serious. The Church of the Brethren sees mission as an essential element of the faith and as a consistent theme in its life. Members hold living as disciples of Christ to be essential; it is emphasized in the Brethren interpretation of the gospel.

Brethren have felt called to places of mission both near and far. Although there has been considerable diversity regarding the mission of the church, there has also been considerable unanimity that it has to with Jesus Christ, people, the church, love, servanthood, peace, community, and doing the will of God. The ebb and flow of history through the years have given varying emphases to the Brethren missionary intention.

Missionary Attitude and Activities of the Early Brethren in Europe (1708–1723)

The early Brethren in Europe were recognized for their zealous missionary spirit and activity. They were both respected for their sincerity and denounced for their persistent and bothersome inroads among the established churches. They were convinced that God had ordained them to take their message to the world. Alexander Mack, Jr., in his preface to the first American edition (1774) of his father's writings, reflected the urgent call to witness and growth that the first Brethren felt on the occasion of their foundational baptism: "Thus all eight were baptized in an early morning hour. After they had all emerged from the water, and had dressed themselves again, they were all immediately clothed inwardly with great joyfulness. This significant word was then impressed on them through grace: 'Be fruitful and multiply.' "[1]

The first eight Brethren at Schwarzenau had been members of the Reformed and Lutheran state churches before their baptism in the river Eder. All of them had taken spiritual pilgrimages away from the churches and had met in the Radical Pietist circle of Schwarzenau. Their new baptism now disassociated them from the Pietists and set them apart in a sectarian movement of their own. Their reasons for forming a new church reveal their missionary intention and the source of their zeal. They believed that true Christianity had been lost with the spiritual decline evident in the established churches. They sought to restore the faithfulness of the primitive church by uniting likeminded, awakened Christians in a new body, free of traditional creeds and rites but commited to New Testament teachings and practices—as they understood them after much searching and study together.

The letter of Alexander Mack, Sr., in 1711 to Charles August, count of Marienborn, contained a clear statement of his missionary message:

> Now I will freely and publicly confess that my crime is that Jesus Christ, the King of kings and Lord of lords, desires that we do what we are doing—that the sinner shall repent and believe in the Lord Jesus and should be baptized in water upon his confession of faith. He should then seek to carry out everything Jesus has commanded and publicly bequeathed in His Testament. If we are doing wrong herein, against the revealed word of the Holy Scriptures, be it in teaching, way of life, or conduct, we would gladly receive instruction. If, however, no one can prove this on the basis of the Holy Scriptures, and yet persecutes us despite this, we would gladly suffer and bear it for the sake of the teachings of Jesus Christ.[2]

Before the baptism at Schwarzenau in 1708 that gave birth to the Brethren, Alexander Mack, Sr., had been an associate of the Radical Pietist leader, Ernst Christoph Hochmann von Hochenau. For a time Hochmann preached earnest missionary sermons to the Jews, exhorting them to seek conversion to Christ in view of His imminent return.

Mack often accompanied Hochmann on missionary journeys in Germany, during which they preached for Christ-centered faith among their countrymen of the established churches.

Later, Mack led the Brethren missionary efforts. Members went out to teach, evangelize, and baptize converts. Their mission was the Christian world of their time. They won adherents from the Reformed, Lutherans, Separatists, and Mennonites. Their appeal to each group was different though their intention was the same: to be instrumental in bringing about a faithful and obedient New Testament church. The message to the Reformed and Lutherans was new life in Christ for a spiritually barren church. The Separatists had found new wine but provided no wineskin in which to hold it. To them the appeal was for an outward church in agreement with the inward spiritual church of which they were already a part. The Brethren essentially agreed with the Mennonites in everything but their form of baptism; Brethren insisted that pouring was not a biblical form. Some Mennonites were rebaptized in the Brethren mode of trine immersion, having been convinced by biblical argument.

Brethren missionary success drew opposition from the established churches, from the Radical Pietists, and from civil authorities, who were not eager to have the delicate religious situation disturbed. That which for Brethren was authentic and necessary missionary work for true conversion to Christ, was understood as offensive proselytism by the groups which lost members because of it.

Brethren grew in numbers in Europe. The Schwarzenau group, under the care of Alexander Mack, Sr., became a well-organized, active congregation that sent out preachers into the Rhine Valley and as far as Switzerland. Scattered converts were baptized in the Palatinate and in the Marienborn area, as well as in Wittgenstein. Most of the Marienborn congregation eventually moved to Krefeld. The Krefeld Brethren baptized a group of six men from Solingen whose story of steadfastness and faith as prisoners in Düsseldorf and Jülich illustrates the zeal of the early Brethren spirit.

Mounting suppression and economic need led to emigration of the Brethren from Germany, beginning in 1719. The Schwarzenau congregation moved in 1720 to Surhuisterveen in West Friesland, where they received Dutch converts from the Collegiant Society. Estimates of the European membership of the Brethren range from the 255 names compiled by Martin G. Brumbaugh to the figure of 1,000 cited by a later leader. The latter estimate is certainly an exaggeration, while Brumbaugh's list was hardly complete. The total population of baptized Brethren in Europe may have included about 300 persons.[3]

Missionary Efforts and Expansion of the Colonial Brethren (1723-1778)

It took time for the Brethren in colonial America to regain the missionary momentum once theirs in Europe. The first group of immigrants from Krefeld, with Peter Becker as leader, arrived in Philadelphia in 1719 and scattered from nearby Germantown into the surrounding region in search of land and work. Some bitter misunderstandings of the church in Krefeld certainly made for cautiousness and loss of motivation for a time among these former members. Their new homeland was strange and they had to learn how to live in the world of colonial Pennsylvania. After four years in the colonies, Brethren reorganized themselves on Christmas Day, 1723, baptized six new members, and held a love feast.

These Germantown Brethren, reorganized and with renewed unity, began to seek out the scattered Brethren in the hinterland and to witness to others of the German-speaking communities with renewed joy and fervor. They were caught up in an awakening that brought rapid growth to the group and moved the spirits of their neighbors over a broad region. In October, 1723, the entire male membership set out from Germantown on a missionary tour to strengthen members of the Brethren diaspora and to preach for the awakening of others. Their journey took them as far as the Conestoga territory in present-day Lancaster County. They organized a second congregation at Coventry and a third at Conestoga, baptizing new members at both places.

The ordinances of baptism and the love feast and their meaning for Brethren were the key to their missionary message and method. Baptism meant that an old life of compromise with the world was now buried forever. It represented cleansing and commitment to a holy life of obedience as called for by Jesus in the Sermon on the Mount. The baptismal rite itself was a first step of obedience. Baptism was an ordinance authorized and performed by the church, that is, by the community of believers and not by sacerdotal clergy. Candidates were approved by the church and the service of baptism was a highly significant and joyful worship service of the whole congregation. It was the outer symbol of an inner reality for the believer. Baptism cut the converts off from many former relationships and made them part of a new family, with Christ as Lord and the other baptized members as brothers and sisters. Baptism meant a leaving of one world and the joining of another.

The love feast was the celebration of the principal elements of the believer's new world. Feetwashing was both a symbol and an experience of service and humility, a renewal of the church's readiness to love one another and to obey Christ. The common supper affirmed the fraternal bonds of the Brethren. The receiving of the broken bread and the wine renewed their baptismal vows, binding the believers to their Lord. Brethren evangelism was related very directly to these rites. The organization of the new congregations were sealed with the love feast celebration.

Colonial congregations met in the homes of members, often on a rotating basis. Many Brethren homes and barns were built with church meetings in mind. The White Oak congregation held its first love feast in 1736 and met in the homes of its members until 1859. Church meetings in the homes encouraged a warm social dimension within the fellowship. The first simple meetinghouse was built in 1770 by the Germantown congregation.

The expansion of the Brethren from Germantown through the colonies to the West and South was dependent upon two patterns of missionary work. The "home community missionary" method was responsible for the rapid growth of the Brethren in the colonial period. This involved evangelism by members and leaders of the congregation within their immediate communities and surrounding neighborhoods. When distant members could form a group of eight or more baptized members and when leadership could be provided, a new congregation was formed. Like the growth and division of cells in living tissue, the home community missionary method was effective in forming new congregations and inspiring them to be fruitful and multiply.

The Conestoga congregation illustrates the effectiveness of this method. The congregation was organized in 1724, then divided in 1732 when Conrad Beissel and his followers left (later to form the Ephrata Community). By 1908, after repeated growth, weakening by emigration, and separation into daughter churches, there were within its original boundaries 20 congregations with a total membership of nearly 5,000. Eventually Conestoga became the parent church of all the congregations in Lancaster, Dauphin, Lebanon, Berks and Schuylkill counties.[4]

The "emigration or colonization" method was used with the movement of the congregations within Germany and continued in West Friesland and later in the American colonies. The westward expansion of the church was largely dependent upon this pattern. Extension of the colonial church into Maryland and farther south was by emigration of Brethren families from established congregations to new territories. In 1770 Morgan Edwards, the Baptist historian, reported statistics for the colonial Brethren. According to his research there were 5 congregations in Maryland with 452 members, 1 congregation in Virginia with 36 members, 3 congregations in North Carolina with 100 members, and 3 congregations in South Carolina with about 100 members. Two of the last named were English-speaking and one had a black member. Edwards counted in all 1,505 adult members of the Brethren in 28 congregations from New Jersey to South Carolina, which number, he estimated, should be multiplied by five to include adherents.[5] More migration into Virginia took place in 1775.

Expansion of the Brethren in Home Mission and Church Extension (1778–1918)

The Revolutionary War hurried the exodus of the Brethren from Pennsylvania to settlement on new frontier land. In an analysis made in 1932 by Frederick D. Dove of the reasons for Brethren migration, along with several economic factors he found that "missionary zeal led Brethren to plant their religion and culture in new territories."[6] The result of this migration was rapid church development in other territories. The Brethren from Eastern Pennsylvania moved into Middle and Western Pennsylvania and down through Maryland and Virginia to North Carolina. They also moved westward into Tennessee and to the Ohio and Mississippi valleys. In spite of war and Indian disturbances, membership doubled by 1825. Ohio and Indiana became strongholds of the Brethren. By 1820 there were 4 congregations in Indiana; by 1866 there were 55 congregations in the state, divided into 3 districts.[7]

In 1882 total membership had increased to about 60,000 and had followed the frontier development to the west coast. The first members to late in the Far West arrived in Oregon in 1850 from Indiana. Brethren colonization had thus reached its farthest extension on the American continent by mid-century, but migration continued to Kansas, North Dakota, Canada, California, and other states.

Congregations were established through the promotion of land sales, sponsored in some cases by Brethren and in other cases by agents of the railroads and real estate interests, who took note of the Brethren and Mennonite patterns of colonization. The Brethren congregations in North Dakota, Idaho, and Washington owe their existence in large measure to enterprising land promoters of the Great Northern Railroad, the Oregon Short Line, and the Northern Pacific Railway. The Canadian Pacific Railroad was responsible for Brethren settlement in Western Canada.

The missionary movement of the Brethren by land purchase and colonization was over by 1918. In later years a few Brethren moved to

Florida and organized rural churches. One small colony existed in Cuba for several years but eventually moved back to the mainland. Brethren expansion in Europe had been determined to a large extent by the level of tolerance of civil government. In the United States up to World War I, it was determined by the availability of fertile land.

During the first half of the 19th century, the Brethren tended to close themselves off from others. Their German language and culture were threatened by the English language and the developing American culture. Fraternal relations with other churches were disapproved. Education was thought a door to vanity and worldliness. The group-consciousness that held the Brethren together was still undergirded by sincere Bible study but tended toward a restricted, sectarian unity rather than one which helped persons discover spiritual truths. The tenor of Annual Meeting minutes suggest defensiveness and self-conscious protectionism. Yet, the church grew.

By 1850 the Brethren had begun to change. There came both interest and agitation for higher education, publishing enterprises, and organized mission work. The life and work of Elder John Kline of Virginia was an example. Kline was a farmer and self-taught physician. He traveled and corresponded with church and political leaders in his opposition to slavery and in his concern to save the unity of the nation and of the denomination during the Civil War crisis. He was a zealous missionary who preached and developed new churches, traveling thousands of miles on horseback. He urged the Brethren to a renewed missionary consciousness, proposing the sending of two men to the Oregon territory to raise up congregations among the scattered Brethren settlers.

John Kline was one of the mid-19th century leaders with a lofty vision for the church. In his time Brethren began to promote higher education and the *Gospel Visitor* was first published. John S. Flory described the first stirrings of foreign mission interest among Brethren: "In 1852 a query from Virginia asked the Annual Conference to consider a plan for foreign mission work. Brother Kline heartily endorsed and urged the matter. While the Conference took no action, a committee was later appointed, of which he was a member, to consider the matter and bring a report to the Conference. He was heartily interested in preaching the Gospel of Christ to the whole world."[8]

The Yearly Meeting of 1853 recommended that any members wishing to move westward should locate where they were most needed by the church. In 1860 the conference appointed James Quinter and Daniel P. Sayler as secretary and treasurer of a board set up to seek personnel for strengthening the members in Oregon and California. In 1870 two ministers from Indiana, Jacob Miller and Daniel Sturgis, were appointed for the work in the West and were provided expense monies for the mission. Appeals for mission workers for the states of Maine, Alabama, and Tennessee came to the church in 1872 and 1875. In 1885, city work was begun in Chicago. Foreign work was established in Denmark in 1876. Mission activities began to be coordinated with the appointment of a mission board in 1880. Brethren missions had entered a new era in which the church's energies were directed to new fields both at home and in other lands.

Recent Mission Work Among the Brethren Bodies (1918–1985)

Those Brethren bodies which resulted from the schism of the 1880s and later have developed their own missionary stances. The Old German Baptist Brethren hold that the Great Commission was fulfilled when the gospel was preached to all nations in the apostolic period. Therefore no specific mission programs have been organized but some congregations have been planted by migration. The Dunkard Brethren formed some congregations in the 1920s and 1930s and sponsored work with the Navajo people since 1955.[9]

The Brethren Church entered home mission activity during the reorganization period following 1883, when evangelists organized dozens of Progressive Brethren congregations. City missions were initiated across the country; over half of new congregations in the Brethren Church between 1905 and 1920 were urban congregations. Initial ventures stressed evangelism and many were of the rescue mission type. In the 1939 division which resulted in the formation of the Grace Brethren, both home and foreign mission agencies went to the Grace Brethren. Since that time Grace Brethren mission strategy has included work with Hispanics, Jewish evangelism, and a mission to the Navajo people. Both groups currently emphasize church growth, with the Grace Brethren focusing their work in church extension toward the suburbs.

Church of the Brethren home mission or church extension efforts from the 19th century to the present have been carried on primarily through district initiatives. This is in contrast to the early practice of founding new congregations through the extensions of individual congregations. During the 1950s a denominational strategy for church extension emphasized "community churches" in new subdivisions on the outer edge of metropolitan areas. A church extension statement, adopted by the Annual Conference in 1958, pledged the Brethren to cooperate on a comity basis with other denominations. Comity involved ecumenical agreements on the locating of new congregations. In order to welcome persons from other church backgrounds, new Brethren churches were encouraged to receive them by transfer of membership letter without requiring re-baptism. Bread and cup communions were offered during Sunday morning worship services and denominational differences were not emphasized.

During the 1960s and early 1970s church extension activity was minimal in the Church of the Brethren. Then a new church movement began in the mid-1970s with projects in Florida, Ohio, and Pennsylvania. After 10 years, nearly all districts were sponsoring new churches in a cooperative pattern with the General Board. Denominational direction is now given by the New Church Development Coordinating Committee, made up of local, district, and General Board leaders. Emphasis is given to growing "Sun Belt" neighborhoods. Some districts are assisting as sponsors in partnership outside their territories, such as Southern Pennsylvania in Vermont and Shenandoah in Puerto Rico. The Brethren Revival Fellowship is the primary sponsor establishing new congregations in Maine, in cooperation with the Atlantic Northeast District and the Parish Ministries Commission.

Church extension in the 1980s takes a variety of forms: the community-type congregation, similar to those started in the 1950s; alternative churches with certain emphases and worship patterns determined by their sponsors or leaders; ethnic peoples' churches serving homogeneous non-English language groups; house churches, sometimes affiliated with another denomination; and new congregations rising out of the heritage of former congregations, such as Germantown, Pennsylvania. A number of congregations, already formed, are coming into the Church of the Brethren from other backgrounds, bringing their own leadership and self-support patterns. At the end of 1985, the new church movement includes a black congregation, Cambodian Khmers, Filipinos, Haitians, Koreans, Mexicans, and Puerto Ricans. There is a growing need for translation at denominational gatherings and publication of materials in languages other than English.

By 1882 the membership of the Church of the Brethren was nearly 60,000. By 1916 the membership had doubled. Thirty years later it reached 182,000, and by 1963 it had attained a high point of nearly 203,000 members in the United States and Canada. Since that year there has been a sharp decline in membership, down to about 161,000 by the end of 1984. Membership in other Brethren bodies in 1980 was: Brethren Church, over 15,000; Dunkard Brethren, over 1,000; Fellowship of Grace Brethren Churches, nearly 42,000; Old German Baptist Brethren, over 5,000.[10]

Some observers see the period of decline of membership in the Church of the Brethren at an end. Perhaps the vitality of the new church movement is indicative of a general awakening among the Brethren, a rediscovery of faith and hope to be offered to the world with such confidence of God's leading that a natural byproduct will be growth for the church.

Mission Outside the United States and Canada

The Brethren are a people with a sense of mission. This was true for home mission from the early beginnings of the church. The first stirrings of interest in mission outside of North America were noticeable in the Annual Meetings around the middle of the 19th century. For the next 25 years the church tried to decide whether foreign mission was within God's purpose for the Brethren. This section intends to give an overview of Brethren foreign mission history and to show the major trends in mission philosophy.

Mission in Scandinavia

For approximately 150 years following the reorganization of the church on North American soil, mission efforts were directed at the establishment of new congregations across the continent. The sending in 1876 of Christian Hope as a missionary to Denmark, his native country, marked the beginning of foreign mission history for the Brethren. Hope was a recent convert to the Brethren, having been dissatisfied with the Baptists in this country and with the Lutheran Church in Denmark before that. He reported enthusiastically to his home community about the church he had found in America. This led to a request by Danish Christians for a Brethren minister who would speak their language. The Northern Illinois district chose Hope as the minister. Thus the first foreign mission project was initiated and supervised by a district, while being recommended through the Annual Meeting to the financial support and sympathy of the church at large. The response of the denomination was inadequate and the mission was seriously hampered through lack of funds.[11]

Christian Hope was a tireless missionary, preaching and distributing tracts and meeting people in their homes and workplaces. In 1885 he extended his work to Sweden, where congregations were organized in five different towns. The Brethren mission boards supported the Scandinavian mission until 1947. The 1955 *Yearbook* listed the Brethren members for the last time, recording 15 members for Denmark and 29 for Sweden.

Initially merely supporting the endeavor of one district, the Brethren became more intentional about foreign mission work in 1880 by creating the Foreign and Domestic Mission Board to supervise and facilitate mission. The name changes and realignments of this board are indicative of the church's changing understanding of its mission. In 1884 the board was succeeded by the General Church Erection and Missionary Committee, and in 1894 by the General Missionary and Tract Committee, which combined mission work and literature outreach. After 1908 it was known as the General Mission Board. With the establishment of the Foreign Mission Commission in 1947, home mission and foreign mission were administered separately for the first time. Since the reorganization of the church's administrative structure in 1968, the World Ministries Commission of the General Board, combining the Foreign Mission and Brethren Service commissions, has carried sole responsibility for foreign mission.

Mission in Turkey, Switzerland, and France

The second foreign mission endeavor of the Brethren began in Turkey in 1895, as in Scandinavia, among nominal Christians. The travels of D. L. Miller to Asia Minor, and his enthusiastic reports about the possibility of mission there, led to the appointment of Gaston J. Fercken. An orphanage had been opened at Izmir (Smyrna) and two congregations established at Izmir and Aidin by 1898. An expatriate missionary presence was maintained until 1899, when charges of mismanagement against Fercken and persecution by the Moslem Turkish government caused the mission board to withdraw Fercken from Asia Minor. After his departure, the mission continued for a few more years under the local leadership of Demetrius Chirighotis. Some contact continued between Chirighotis and the General Mission Board until 1909, but the mission in Turkey was no longer mentioned at the Annual Meeting after 1901.[12]

Fercken was reassigned to Switzerland and France in 1899. By June, 1904, there were 57 members in the two mission points. After 1907, the mission venture declined. Fercken left the Brethren, with whom he no longer agreed in doctrine and practice, and the mission came under the leadership of Adrian Pellett, who proved unworthy of the charge. When Paul Mohler and his wife were assigned to France in 1911, the mission was in such disrepute that in 1912 it was officially closed by the decision of the General Mission Board.[13]

Due to insufficient funding and support from the home base, inadequate leadership, hostile governments, and scandals, all of these early foreign mission attempts among nominal Christians floundered soon after they had been started. The comments of mission scholar Elgin S. Moyer about the Scandinavian mission could be applied to others as well:

> . . . Scandinavia does not challenge the Church of the Brethren with such a need as comes from non-Christian countries. It seems to the Board in America, therefore, unwise to spend much of the church's resources in time and money to do missionary work in a nominally Christian country. These countries have a long Christian history, and have developed their own characteristics and ecclesiastical thinking. For fifty years the Brethren have tried rather unsuccessfully to do mission work among them; to continue the mission with any degree of aggressiveness has seemed to the Board unwise.[14]

After the demise of the European mission the Brethren began to concentrate their efforts on non-Christian fields.

Mission in India

The General Mission Board developed a list of qualifications for missionaries which were published in the *Gospel Messenger* in order to encourage applications from persons interested in a new field, India. Applicants had to be sound in the faith, willing to submit themselves wholly to the control and advice of the Board, and be able and willing to teach and defend the principles of the Gospel and the doctrines and peculiarities of the church, as defined and applied by Annual Meeting. Conversation, lifestyle, and character were to be congruent with these principles, and, for those married, the spouse must have similar qualifications and be willing to be a colaborer in the field.[15]

In 1894, Wilbur B. and Mary Emmert Stover and Bertha Ryan were sent to India. Five years later the mission was firmly established and the First German Baptist Brethren Church of Bulsar was organized. That same year stations were opened at Jalapor and Anklesvar, which combined with Bulsar to form the First District of India.[16] The India mission blossomed into a flourishing enterprise. It is the first example of uninterrupted mission work for the Church of the Brethren until the present.

The mission boundaries were determined in comity agreements with other mission agencies and encompassed over 7,000 square miles along the west coast of India in the Gujarati and Marathi language areas. In addition to planting churches the work included the establishment of orphanages, schools, and hospitals; agricultural development; and vocational training. A large proportion of mission resources were invested in social services. During the bubonic plague and a series of famines between 1896 and 1904 Brethren were engaged in relief efforts. Hundreds of Indians desired to become members of the mission during the famine, but Brethren were reluctant to baptize them while the stress of the famine continued, lest the motive for conversion should be food.[17]

The Rural Service Center in Anklesvar was opened in 1952, through Brethren initiative. It is a cooperative institution supported by other denominations as well to improve living conditions for poverty-stricken people in rural areas of India. Founded by veteran missionary Ira W. Moomaw with the aid of dedicated Indian leaders, it received its first Indian director in the person of Shantilal Bhagat, a third-generation member of the church in India. He was assisted by *gram sevaks* (Gujariti for "village worker"), who were community development workers in training.

After World War II and India's independence in 1947, Indian church leadership developed rapidly and expatriate missionary presence decreased. In 1945, the General Mission Board reported that the Church of the Brethren in India had assumed full responsibility for its own members. This was hailed as the most forward-moving step in the history of Brethren missions. It gave the Indian church the power of decision-making, while calling for wisdom and guidance from the missionaries. However, subsequent Annual Conference minutes show that a certain dependency remained until 1970 when the Brethren in India joined the Church of North India (CNI). This union of six different denominations was the long-expected fruit of four decades of dialogue and patient effort. Brethren pastor Ishwarlal L. Christachari served as the first bishop of the Gujarat diocese. From 1970 to 1984 Brethren expatriate personnel from the United States worked under the direction of the Church of North India.

Mission in Cuba

At the end of the Spanish-American War, Cuba became officially an independent republic, with its first Cuban president four years later. Several Brethren families went to Cuba in an attempt to establish a church there. This appears to have been the initiative of a group of interested persons rather than a denominational effort, as the reports of the General Missionary Committee never mention Cuba. A congregation was established at Omaja in 1907 under the leadership of Landa U. Kreider, George W. Snell, Ira P. Eby, and Grant Mahan. After the organizing leaders had returned to the United States by 1912, the church began to decline rather rapidly for lack of resident pastors; yet it was not until 1937 that the congregation was officially disorganized.[18] The minutes of the 1907 and 1909 Annual Meeting quote letters of greeting received from Brethren in Cuba and replies by the delegates gathered at the Annual Meeting.

Mission in China

The first Church of the Brethren mission opened in China in the church's bicentennial year of 1908, with the arrival of Frank and Anna Newland Crumpacker, Emma Horning, and George and Blanche Cover Hilton. The mission program they initiated had a troubled development. Work was interrupted several times because of evacuation due to Japanese occupation, World War II, and the Communist revolution. The mission was mainly concentrated in the Shansi province of North China. After three decades it encompassed five organized congregations with a total membership of 2,670. There were 3 ordained Chinese pastors and 48 paid evangelists, 29 of whom were women. Medical work reached its height in 1924 with three hospitals and a large number of outpatients.[19]

Another field opened up in South China in 1918, largely as a result of a initiative of Moy Gwong Han, a member of the Brethren Chinese Fellowship in Chicago. The mission was located in On Fun, Kwangtung Province. Within 30 years the church had 340 members scattered over 55 villages, and an elementary school with 270 pupils. The Brethren of the Kwangtung Province joined the Kwangtung Synod of the Church of Christ in China in 1949. At that time, Brethren membership in the North was estimated at around 3,000.

Besides establishing churches, schools, and hospitals, the Brethren were heavily involved in relief work during a plague in 1917 and famines in 1920–1921. During 1921–1922 all Brethren missionaries worked in famine relief, underwritten by the Brethren in the USA with large contributions from the International Red Cross. Following World War II, a total of 2,400 heifers were placed in China through the Heifer Project, International. The Brethren Service Commission, in cooperation with UNRRA and the Chinese government, sent volunteers from the United States to China to reclaim land no longer in production and to train Chinese in the use of farm machinery. The "China Tractor

Units," as the Brethren referred to them, won the respect of both Nationalist and Communist authorities.

Nevertheless, missionaries had to leave China in 1949–1950 as a result of the Communist Revolution, and in September, 1953, all Brethren missionary activity was officially terminated. During the 40 years of its active mission about 100 Brethren missionaries served in China. In the late 1970s some contact with China was reestablished by Brethren. Howard E. Royer reported in 1980:

> Yin Ziehzeng, pastor of Peking's only Protestant church and son of the first Church of the Brethren elder in China, saw the closing of churches under both the Japanese occupation and the Cultural Revolution. During the later period he planted rice and grew fruit. When he reopened the Peking congregation (Rice Market Street) in 1971, at first only foreigners and diplomats came. Now the Chinese come in increasing numbers. Much as he rejoices in global Christian contacts, he is insistent that the future of the Chinese church lies in staunch self-reliance.[20]

Since 1981 the Church of the Brethren in the United States has been participating in a Chinese Agricultural Exchange program similar to the one with Poland, which began in 1947 and has functioned without interruption since 1957. Scientists from Poland and China come to study at American universities, while Brethren volunteers are assigned to the respective countries overseas.

Mission in Nigeria

H. Stover Kulp and A. D. Helser initiated the first church of the Brethren mission station in Garkida, Nigeria, in 1923. To avoid suspicion by British civil administrators, the purpose of going to Nigeria was stated by the Brethren as "moral education for the people." Their real intention, preaching the gospel, might have been considered subversive by the colonial government, who feared that the Christian message might incite the people to rebellion.

Kulp was the first white man to address the Bura people in their own language.[21] By comity agreement, the Church of the Brethren mission eventually came to be responsible for an area located in the Bornu and Adamawa provinces, working with Bura, Margi, Higi, Whona, and Chibuk language groups. Evangelistic outreach, secondary education, teacher training, and medical care were the main emphases of the work in Nigeria. It included hospitals at Lassa and Garkida and a leprosarium at Garkida. Lassa came to international attention when a Brethren nurse, Laura Wine, died of a fever of unknown origin. After several more deaths at the mission station, the virus of Lassa fever and its wild-rat carrier eventually were identified.

Teacher education began at Garkida in 1949 under the leadership of Ivan L. Eikenberry. In 1952 the school was moved and became the Waka Teachers' College. A secondary school was opened in Waka in 1959. Basic education emphasizing agriculture and domestic science was combined with Christian teaching. The Waka schools came under government administration in 1972.[22]

The Theological College of Northern Nigeria was opened in 1959 by member churches of the international Fellowship of the Churches of Christ in Nigeria, of which the Church of the Brethren is a member. Mamadu K. Mshelbila became its first Nigerian vice-principal. Kulp Bible School began in 1960 as a joint venture of the Church of the Brethren in Nigeria and expatriate Church of the Brethren missionaries.[23]

A community health program, Lafiya (a Hausa term for "health and well-being"), first projected in 1971, gained international recognition. Its training of rural health care workers and Under Five Clinics were hailed by the World Health Organization and the World Council of Churches as models for health care in developing nations. A decade later it led to Brethren involvement in the Sudan.

In the 1950s the Brethren Church joined forces with the Church of the Brethren in Nigeria, establishing a mission station east of Lassa with the Higi people. It had earlier sent missionaries to French Equatorial Africa in 1914, to expand on the personal initiative of James Gribble in 1908. Hundreds of congregations were founded there, especially after 1921. Following 1939, after the division within the Brethren Church, mission work in this area was continued under the Fellowship of Grace Brethren Churches. A similar change occurred in Argentina, where missionaries from the Brethren Church had been sent in 1909. In this case, however, the Brethren Church began a new mission in Argentina under the pioneer missionary, C. F. Yoder. In 1985 the Brethren Church had missions in Argentina, Colombia, India, Malaysia, and Mexico; Grace Brethren had missions in Argentina, Brazil, Central African Republic, Chad, England, France, Germany, Japan, Mexico, Phillipines, and Spain.

Church membership in Nigeria, after earlier modest growth, has recently grown rapidly. In 1983 it approached 39,000, with a worship attendance estimated as surpassing 80,000. The Nigerian Brethren actively participated in the fellowship of Churches of Christ in Nigeria but since 1972 the church has been autonomous. Known first as *Lardin Gabas* (Eastern District) of the Church of Christ in the Sudan, it is now called the *Ecclyesiyar 'Yan'uwa a Nigeria* (EYN), a Hausa phrase meaning "Church of the Brethren in Nigeria."[24] (*'Yan'uwa* is a more inclusive term than Brethren, meaning "children of the same mother.") Although the EYN has been officially recognized since 1972 as a sister denomination of the Church of the Brethren in the United States, the process of severing "parental" ties still continues among some of the constituencies of both groups.

Mission in Puerto Rico

During World War II, Brethren conscientious objectors, who were prepared for relief work in China under the Civilian Public Service (CPS) program, were denied permission by the US congress to work in overseas projects. They were reassigned in 1942 to Puerto Rico. David and Janine Blickenstaff organized work in the mountains in cooperation with the local government. Physicians Daryl M. Parker and Carl F. Coffman were among those assigned to Puerto Rico from the original China unit. The result of their efforts was a hospital at Castañer. After that date, the primary emphasis was on medical work. A new hospital was constructed in 1959; it was turned over to a local board of directors in 1976. The CPS and later BSC workers held services in the hospital for themselves and interested Puerto Ricans; this led to the organization of the Castañer Church of the Brethren in 1948. The congregation was recognized in 1959 as part of the Florida and Georgia District (now Florida and Puerto Rico District).

Mission in Ecuador

During World War II, Brethren Service workers began an inner-city youth project in Quito, Ecuador. This brought Latin American to the closer attention of the church and prepared the way for J. Benton and Ruby Frantz Rhoades to be sent as the first Brethren missionaries to Ecuador. They began work in the Calderon Valley north of Quito in 1948 and organized the first congregation there in 1953. The mission in Ecuador included primary and secondary education for children, literacy and vocational training for older youth and adults, medical work, agricultural and community development projects. In 1958 the Brethren Foundation (*Fundaciones Brethren y Unida*) was established to hold the property of the Church of the Brethren mission and provide guidance for the mission program. It was the task of the foundation to direct the educational, medical, and agricultural ministries and to guide the social services related to the Brethren mission.[25]

Six congregations joined in 1964 to become the Evangelical Church of the Brethren (*Iglesia Evangélica de los Hermanos*). A year later it merged with the United Andean Indian Mission to form the United Evangelical Church of Ecuador (*Iglesia Evangélica del Ecuador*) and became self-governing at the same time. The World Ministries Commission continues to be related to this church through the Ecuador Concerns Committee, which coordinates the mission effort of the Church of the Brethren and four other US denominations.[26]

Mission in Indonesia

Mission involvement in Indonesia was approved by the church in 1959, and Joel K. and Phyllis Yount Thompson became the first Brethren missionaries to that country in 1960. In accord with the new mission policy of 1955, the Church of the Brethren did not establish its own mission. Rather, the Brethren were intent on strengthening the existing Indonesian evangelical churches in their efforts, in cooperation with other non-Indonesian churches. Thompson taught at the theological seminary, under the local church synod and the direct supervision of the seminary's head administrator. This approach to mission was new for the Brethren. Colleagues from different faith traditions worked together in the same Christian endeavor, and the Brethren were the "junior partners." Mutuality in mission was a real possibility, yet the church at large was not quite ready for this step. Brethren participation in the Indonesian mission stopped about a decade later.

Mission in the Sudan

The much-lauded Lafiya program of the EYN had been brought to the attention of the Ministry of Health of the Sudan. As a result, Brethren missionary J. Roger Schrock, Lafiya's first administrator, was seconded to the Sudan Council of Churches to launch its primary health care program. It eventually encompassed human health care, livestock vaccination, well-digging, demonstration gardening, and other related projects. From one staff person in 1980, the program evolved into a permanent staff of 26, with a temporary support staff of 30–40 at its height in 1983, when civil war forced the expatriates to leave. The program continued on a low-level maintenance basis because the lack of peace in the region inhibited community development.

A simple sharing of faith eventually led to the construction in 1980 of a first church building in Mayom through the joint efforts of a group of Christians. Additional Brethren workers have been requested by the

Presbyterian Church of the Sudan and are on assignment to assist in leadership development. Because of the continuing war they are working out of Khartoum rather than Mayom.

Recent Mission in Latin America

The Church of the Brethren entered with seriousness and intentionality a new era in its mission history when it adopted in 1978 the *Misión Mutua en las Américas* as a design for mission. Conditions leading the church in that direction will be discussed under "Mission Philosophies."

Misión Mutua en las Américas was a proposal for a radical new mission involvement in Latin America. A pilot project for *Misión Mutua* (mutual mission) was initiated in 1980 with the *Iglesia Christiana Pentecostal de Cuba* (ICP) as a partner. It was hoped that ICP personnel would work in the USA side-by-side and under the auspices of the Church of the Brethren, mainly in the area of evangelism and church extension, while Brethren from the USA would work with their Cuban partners and under their direction in Cuba, particularly in pastoral training. Work camps for young people in both countries were to be a vital part of *Misión Mutua*. The pilot project as such came to a premature end in 1982, primarily because of logistical complications stemming from the political relationships between the two countries. However, some contact was reestablished in 1983 and new projects were under discussion in 1985, possibly in a third country such as Nicaragua.

While mission philosophy and polity has undergone many changes in the preceding decades, the Church of the Brethren continued at the end of 1985 to be actively engaged in mission. There was a total of 62 Brethren on assignment outside of the USA in various forms of pastoral, educational, medical, and social services, for whom the World Ministries Commission carried ongoing responsibility. Of these, 12 were working in Latin America and the Caribbean, 22 in Europe (East and West), 24 in Africa, 3 in the Middle East, and 1 in the Republic of China. Close working relationships continued with sister churches in Ecuador, India, and Nigeria, which received direct program grants totaling $83,500.

Mission Philosophies

Evangelism and service have always gone hand-in-hand for the Church of the Brethren. Missionary endeavor found expression not only in establishing congregations but also in schools, orphanages, hospitals, and village clinics. It has included well-digging projects and agricultural development as well as theological education. Foreign mission, which had begun as an *ad hoc* undertaking of one district, soon became a major denominational emphasis. It enjoyed great popularity among the constituency. The General Mission Board was the most influential and best-financed Brethren agency in the early 20th century. Today, the largest segment of the General Board budget is allocated for the work of the World Ministries Commission.

In the periods following World War I and World War II there was great interest in social projects. The Brethren Service Committee was created in 1939; it administered, among other programs, the Civilian Public Service camps for conscientious objectors during World War II. After the war it expanded its work to include a broad range of programs of relief and rehabilitation reaching around the world. From the outset, Brethren Service was ecumenical in spirit and action-oriented in style. By policy decision, it was not the purpose of Brethren Service to establish new congregations. When the Church of the Brethren underwent a major reorganization in 1968, the Brethren Service Commission was merged with the Foreign Mission Commission to become the World Ministries Commission (WMC) of the General Board.

The year 1955 constitutes a landmark in Brethren mission history when a new foreign mission policy was adopted at the Annual Conference in Grand Rapids, Michigan. It refocused mission from "parenting" churches and institutions to "indigenization," the process of passing the leadership and administration from expatriate personnel into local hands. As important factors affecting missionary work in India, Nigeria, and Ecuador, the report listed nationalism, economic upheaval, racial tension, rising tides of population, growth of materialism, and resurging national religions. The report affirmed that no one nation is superior to another and that any feeling of racial superiority is not in keeping with the spirit and teaching of Jesus Christ. Brethren were called upon not to relax their evangelical efforts but to fit their strategy to the changed world in which they work. The report witnessed to Brethren awareness of and sensitivity to the revolutionary changes that had come about in most parts of the world, specifically in the areas where Brethren were in mission.

Reflecting on this strategy of indigenization, WMC executive Joel K. Thompson wrote in 1973: "It has allowed persons in Ecuador, India, and Nigeria more and more to free themselves from various forms of dependency and allowed them to discover who they are, to decide what they wish to become, and to define their own destiny in and through the Church of Jesus Christ." He described the church as a powerful, living stream adapting itself to the "shape and the features of each local landscape, taking even its coloring from the native soil."[27]

Ten years after the new mission policy was adopted by Annual Conference, Kenneth I. Morse explored the idea of foreign mission in reverse. Perhaps the thought was premature but it certainly was one that merited attention. Brethren, Morse observed, regarded mission as a one-way street, with the Brethren being the givers and others the receivers. Rather, mission should be a two-way street to discover together God's redemptive mission for all persons. Such mission in reverse would not be without cost. Morse warned: "We would have to face up to the actualities of our spiritual poverty . . . [our] sub-Christian way of life that has taken on the color of our national surroundings."[28]

Those were challenging words, and generally for the Brethren of the mid-1960s it was an idea for which the time had not yet come. When Brethren mission was not promoting "Brethrenism," little enthusiasm was generated for such involvements among many of the church members, who wanted to continue to wash the feet of the world with a towel monogrammed "Brethren." With regard to the Indonesian mission, for example, WMC staff members tended to be more apologetic than prophetic, when pressed for explanations by constituents. It is a painstakingly slow process to change long-accustomed patterns of thought. In spite of continuous emphasis on indigenous churches, partnership in mission, and talk of mutual cooperation, the challenge to put these thoughts into practice remained.

In some sense, the Polish agricultural exchange program can be considered as a forerunner of mutuality in mission. However, mutuality in mission, as the concept was developed in the Latin American situation, was more than an exchange. The Lafiya project and the Indonesian projects helped prepare the way. Brethren thought was changing from mission *to* persons to mission *with* them. In 1978 the Annual Conference adopted a new design for mission in Latin America: *Misión Mutua en las Américas*. It was the result of a comprehensive study launched in 1975 to investigate mission possibilities in the Latin American context.

The decades prior to the study were wrenched by convulsive and profound changes on the international scene. Young nations, having thrown off the yoke of colonialism, pleaded to have their nationhood respected. Church "imperialism" and "neo-colonialism" were resented by countries which traditionally had been the recipients of Western mission. Issues of distribution of wealth, of social justice and human rights were brought to public attention as never before. Multinational corporations were accused of exploitation of native resources. The US Central Intelligence Agency engaged in plots to oust democratically-elected governments that were deemed "not in our national interest."[29]

For the poor and the oppressed of the so-called Third World the good news of the kingdom had acquired fresh meaning. Liberation theology began to confront ecclesiastical, political, and societal structures. Formerly cowed peasants, dehumanized masses under the control of powerful exploiters, were aroused from their apathy and, like an awakening giant, began to test their strength. A new wine was foaming and fermenting. Mission was not the only area in which new wineskins were badly needed.

On the international mission scene, the 1973 Bangkok conference of the Commission of World Mission and Evangelism of the World Council of Churches stands out as a watershed. It brought to culmination a movement—the first step of which had been discernible in the first international conference on missions at Edinburg in 1910—a movement from dependence to independence of younger churches, from aggressive missionary presence "overseas" to a call for a moratorium on the sending of Western missionaries. Bangkok, as no other missionary conference before, gave high priority to the issue of social justice. It called for a newly converted church, a church liberated to stand with God on the side of the oppressed and to challenge unjust structures.[30]

In Latin America this call had been heard since the Second Assembly of the Latin American Catholic Bishops Conference (CELAM II) at Medellin (Bogota), Colombia, in 1968. Throughout the assembly the bishops were brought face to face with the social, political, economic, and religious realities of their continent, i.e., with class struggle and the possibility of revolution. Institutional or structural violence, the major form of violence against the marginalized people of Latin America, became a household world. Just before CELAM II, Gustavo Gutiérrez had advanced his "theory of liberation."

While the Catholic Church, beginning with the Second Vatican Council and especially at Medellin, became more open to hear the cries of the people and address the reality of injustice and structural violence, Latin American governments became increasingly more repressive. In 1961, Paraguay was the only country with a military dictatorship. After the assassination in 1973 of Chile's president, Salvador Allende, the only democracies left in South America were Venezuela and Colombia.

Thus, by the mid-1970s the Latin American continent was a seething cauldron ready to boil over. It was into this volatile context that the Church of the Brethren launched its study on new mission possibilities in Latin America. The committee entrusted with this task submitted a report to the General Board which reflected not only its findings but also the insights of several notable Latin American church leaders whom the committee had invited as consultants. After the report had been accepted by Annual Conference in June, 1978, Kenneth E. McDowell, then WMC executive secretary, commented that the Church of the Brethren stood on a threshold regarding its mission philosophy, the threshold of mutual mission.

The 11-page document, especially the section entitled "Background," has been hailed by some as the most radical paper on mission that the Church of the Brethren has ever produced. It dealt with the challenge for mission in the context of North-South economic imbalance and military dictatorships with military training and weapons supplied by the USA, and emphasized the need to recognize the United States as a legitimate mission field. The study was based on the biblical model of wholistic salvation, i.e., personal redemption as well as social justice, care as well as confrontation. The paper became a major impetus for developing a new mission philosophy, incorporating the learnings from the Latin American study and applying them to all Church of the Brethren mission endeavors. The statement on "World Mission Philosophy and Program," accepted by the Annual Conference in 1981, with its emphasis upon ecumenical planning, solidarity with the oppressed, and mutuality in mission, reflected this new thrust.

The Church of the Brethren foreign mission efforts thus have passed from planting congregations (1886–1955), to indigenization (1955–1978), to mutuality in mission (1978–present). To live out the philosophy of mutuality in mission, inside and outside of the United States, is a continuing challenge for the church in the present age.

Notes

[The first half of the chapter, dealing with the expansion of the church in North America, was written by B. Merle Crouse. It is based on his essay in *The Church of the Brethren: Past and Present*, (1971), 110–128; the second half, covering mission outside of North America, was written by Karen Spohr Carter. It draws on her monograph, "The Birth of Misión Mutua en las Américas," MATh thesis, Bethany Theological Seminary (1985).]

1. Donald F. Durnbaugh, ed., *European Origins of the Brethren* (Elgin, IL: 1958), 122.
2. Durnbaugh, *European Origins* (1958), 163.
3. Martin G. Brumbaugh, *A History of the German Baptist Brethren in Europe and America* (Elgin, IL: 1899), 54–70; T. T. Myers, "The Birth of the Schwarzenau Church and Its Activities," in *Two Centuries of the Church of the Brethren*, ed. D. L. Miller, (Elgin, IL: 1908), 39.
4. *Chronicon Ephratense* (1786), quoted in Donald F. Durnbaugh, ed., *The Brethren in Colonial America* (Elgin, IL: 1967), 66.
5. Morgan Edwards, *Materials Toward a History of the American Baptists* (1770), quoted in Durnbaugh, *Colonial America* (1967), 186–191.
6. Frederick D. Dove, *Cultural Changes in the Church of the Brethren* (Elgin, IL: 1932), 58.
7. Otho Winger, *History and Doctrines of the Church of the Brethren* (Elgin, IL: 1919), 77–78.
8. John S. Flory, *Builders of the Church of the Brethren* (Elgin, IL: 1925), 94.
9. S. Wayne Beaver and Dennis D. Martin, "Mission," in *The Brethren Encyclopedia* (1983–1984), 857–863.
10. Floyd E. Mallott, *Studies in Brethren History* (Elgin, IL: 1954), 111; *Church of the Brethren Yearbook* (1947, 1967); "Statistics," in *The Brethren Encyclopedia* (1983–1984), 1465–1478.
11. *Minutes of the Annual Meetings of the Church of the Brethren* (Elgin, IL: 1909), 347, 365; Elgin S. Moyer, *Missions in the Church of the Brethren* (Elgin, IL: 1931), 57.
12. Galen B. Royer, *Thirty-Three Years of Missions in the Church of the Brethren* (Elgin, IL: 1914), 193–200.
13. Moyer, *Missions* (1931), 167–168.
14. Moyer, *Missions* (1931), 158–159.
15. Moyer, *Missions* (1931), 171.
16. Moyer, *Missions* (1931), 174.
17. Glen A. Campbell and Dennis D. Martin, "India," in *The Brethren Encyclopedia* (1983–1984), 649–651; Moyer, *Missions* (1931), 176.
18. Dennis D. Martin, "Cuba," in *The Brethren Encyclopedia* (1983–1984), 355.
19. Wendell P. Flory, "A History of Brethren Involvement in China," *Brethren Life and Thought*, 11 (Autumn, 1966): 35–48.

20. Howard E. Royer, "China 30 Years Later," *Messenger* (February, 1980): 14–19.

21. Mamadu K. Mshelbila, "Church of the Brethren in Nigeria, in *The Brethren Encyclopedia* (1983–1984), 305–308.

22. Ivan L. Eikenberry, "Waka Teachers' Training College and Secondary School," in *The Brethren Encyclopedia* (1983–1984), 1312–1313.

23. Mamadu Mshelbila, "Theological College in Northern Nigeria," in *The Brethren Encyclopedia* (1983–1984), 1256; Philip M. Kulp, "Kulp Bible School," in *The Brethren Encyclopedia* (1983–1984), 709–710.

24. Mshelbila, "Nigeria," in *The Brethren Encyclopedia*, 305–308.

25. Donald F. Durnbaugh, "Brethren Foundation," in *The Brethren Encyclopedia* (1983–1984), 186–187.

26. B. Merle Crouse, "Ecuador," in *The Brethren Encyclopedia* (1983–1984), 422.

27. Joel K. Thompson, "No East, No West," *Messenger* (February, 1973): 28.

28. Kenneth I. Morse, "Christian Mission on a Two-Way Street," *Messenger* (June, 1965): 32.

29. For a comprehensive treatment of US policies in Latin America, see Penny Lernoux, *Cry of the People: United States Involvement in the Rise of Fascism, Torture, and Murder and the Persecution of the Catholic Church* (Garden City, NY: 1980).

30. The complete text of this conference is found in *Bangkok Assembly 1973: Minutes and Reports of the Assembly of the Commission on World Mission and Evangelism of the World Council of Churches, December 31, 1972, and January 9–12, 1973* (New York, London, Geneva: 1973).

31. The full text of the document is part of the World Ministries Commission Agenda, Exhibit B, June, 1978.

9

Women

Pamela Brubaker

Women have been actively involved in the life and work of the Brethren movement since its beginnings. Thus their story is part of each chapter of this book. Yet, their participation in the church has been structured formally by specific policies and informally by custom. In this chapter an account will be given of the church's ordering of the relations of women and men and of the activity of women within the church.

The relationships between men and women in the formative period of the Brethren seem to have been relatively fluid. To a certain extent, Brethren broke with the customary expectations for women in the patriarchal culture of which they were a part. Among the charges brought by critics against the Pietists and Anabaptists in Wittgenstein was permitting both women and men "to teach whatever the Spirit moves them" and discarding "respect of wives for husbands."[1]

There is some evidence that seems to support such charges. All of the first eight Brethren, including three women (Anna Margaretha Mack, Johanna Kipping, and Johanna Nöthiger Boni), are said to have witnessed publicly to their faith. The wife of Jacob Schneider was included in a list of European Brethren as one who served as an elder for seven years after her husband's death. Married, widowed, and single women were involved in every area of Brethren expansion. At least one married woman was baptized against her husband's wishes.

But some of the patriarchal expectations remained. An example was the statement by Alexander Mack, Sr., that married women are to be obedient to their husbands.[2] Yet, his baptism of the woman mentioned above implied that an exception is to be made if the husband's wishes go against the commands of scripture. So even here the system of male dominance was not absolute. Appeals to scripture or the leading of the Spirit were to be considered against the claims of patriarchal subordination.

This apparent openness continued after the emigration of the Brethren to America. Two women were among the first six baptized by Brethren in America in 1723—Catherine Urner and the wife of Henry Landis. At least one of the widows cared for by the Germantown congregation, Sister Margaret Bayer, was elected in 1769 a deaconess by the congregation. Harriet Livermore, a traveling, non-Brethren evangelist, was permitted to preach in some Brethren congregations early in the 19th century. The same was true of Sarah Righter Major, who was even included in a list of elders of the Philadelphia congregation.

Yet, during this same period a more traditional, male-dominant system of relations was being formed among the Brethren. Available evidence does not clearly indicate what the factors were which contributed to this development. One may point to the patriarchal character of post-Revolutionary American culture as influential. But events which took place at the Ephrata Cloister may have also been a significant factor. Although the Ephrata community was not part of the main Brethren movement, its founder, Conrad Beissel, had been baptized by the Brethren and had led one of the colonial congregations before he "gave back" his baptism. Several Brethren and others close to the church left their congregations and families to join the celibate orders of sisters and brothers at the Cloister. After Maria Sauer left her husband and child, Catherine Urner's husband pleaded with his wife not to leave him to join the Ephrata community. Not only was disruption of family life painful, a housewife was also an economic necessity for homesteading.

Sisters in the order at Ephrata were subject to no man, except Beissel, the "superintendent." When many of the householders (a third order of members who lived as families nearby) decided to leave their farms and dedicate themselves to the celibate orders, the women asked for decrees of divorce so that their only loyalty would be to the order. But soon after, for some, concern for their children left alone on the farms led them back into their marriage and households.

The difficulty of transforming relationships between women and men to ones with more equality—when it was customarily and legally expected that women were subjugated in marriage or when sexual relations were seen as less worthy as a Christian lifestyle—is evident in this sketch of life at Ephrata. Those who became Brethren at Schwarzenau had experimented with celibacy for a brief period while Radical Pietists but soon decided that marriage was "ordained and blessed by God."[3] As cited above, within marriage women were to be obedient to their husbands. Thus, such expectations and experiences may have contributed to the continuation of a male-dominant system of relations in family life and its establishment in church life during the 19th century.

The 19th Century

Minutes from the Annual Meetings of the Brethren shed light on the ordering of relationships between men and women within the church. It was this body which set policy for the denomination, although the administration of church discipline was primarily the responsibility of the leaders of each congregation. Women did not have a voice in Annual Meetings during the 19th century, but their voice in congregational councils was indirectly upheld by action of the larger body in 1854.[4]

Annual Meeting affirmed the teachings of the early Brethren on marriage and family life. Marriage was to be between believers and to endure for life. Sexual relations were only permitted within marriage. Couples were expected to live together agreeably. Adultery was generally the only acceptable reason for divorce, although a woman with an abusive husband was permitted, but not encouraged, to seek a divorce. Divorced persons were not permitted to remarry. These principles were tests of fellowship until the 20th century; those who disobeyed them were put into avoidance. Family members were also expected to avoid the disobedient member; if they failed to do so, they were themselves to withdraw from communion.

Brethren did not usually keep diaries but accounts left by others indicate some of the contributions made by women to their families and to the church during the 19th century. The Brethren were part of the westward expansion which was intensified after the Revolutionary War. New congregations were formed when a sufficient number of Brethren settled near each other. Women were involved in setting up households and establishing congregations. The story of Sarah Lint Berkey is representative of these women. She moved from Pennsylvania to Indiana in 1848 with her husband, Elder Jacob Berkey, and their five children. Three more children were born to them there. In 1850 they helped to organize the Rock Run congregation. Sarah Berkey cared for the children and with their help "made the garden, cared for the cows, sheared the sheep, spun the yarn and made the clothes for the entire family." She and the children walked three miles to church for services. After her husband became a well-known elder, she entertained "dozens and even hundreds" of Brethren in their home.[5]

Women in settled areas also contributed to the preservation of home and congregation. One such woman was Barbara Yount, whose story was told by her granddaughter:

> Barbara Yount was born near Broadway, Rockingham Co., Va., June 27, 1807 . . . She was married to Benjamin Yount. To them were born six children, two dying in infancy. She was left a widow before her youngest daughter . . . was born. Thus she was left to struggle alone, with the care of her little children . . . Her home was always open for members of the church. Often at love feast she would entertain as many as forty people. That meant much, for so many rode horseback then, and it took a great deal of feed for the horses, yet she did it willingly, even if she did have to support her family by weaving . . . She died April 8, 1893, aged almost eighty-seven years.[6]

These women, like many others, combined the responsibilities of time-consuming household chores with dedicated efforts to build up congregations. When children came, mothering was added to their responsibilities. Their stamina was remarkable. Rather than becoming preoccupied with the cares of home and family, most found time and energy to devote to both home and congregational life.

Early Women Preachers

Women's activity in sustaining congregational life through their presence, support, and hospitality was appreciated. But those who assumed leadership roles were usually challenged. The first recorded instance of this was a query brought to Annual Meeting in 1834 "concerning a sister's preaching." The Annual Meeting stated its disapproval, adding that "such sister being in danger, not only [of] exposing her own state of grace to temptation, but also causing temptations, discord, and disputes among other members" (Article 13).

The sister in question was Sarah Righter (Major), of the Philadelphia congregation. Sarah Righter had been converted in 1826 under the preaching of Harriet Livermore, at the age of 18. Soon after she experienced a calling to preach; she was hesitant to act on this as she knew of the opposition of Brethren to women preachers. She shared her call with her father, John Righter, when he asked her why she was so melancholy. He was sympathetic and suggested that they confer with Peter Keyser, elder of the Philadelphia congregation. Keyser encouraged Sarah to preach, as did Israel Poulson of the Amwell congregation in New Jersey.

Sarah Righter began in 1828 to preach in these and a few other congregations. Following the 1834 Annual Meeting decision, a committee of elders was sent to counsel with her. They decided not to enforce the Meeting's decision, although they did not give her official permission to preach. A committee member later explained: "I could not give my vote to silence someone who could outpreach me." In the following year Sarah Righter wrote a letter giving the biblical basis for her preaching. In reference to those who cited the Apostle Paul's injunction to women to keep silent in church, she wrote: ". . . I conceive it would be very inconsistent in an apostle, who laid his hands on men and women, and pray'd over them, that they might receive the Holy Ghost, to quench the gift of the Spirit of God because it was given to a woman . . ." So she continued to preach.[7]

In 1842 she married Thomas Major, who had been elected a minister in the Philadelphia congregation during the previous year. They moved to Ohio, where they farmed and raised three children. They also conducted preaching missions in Ohio and Indiana. Thomas Major customarily opened the service and then invited his wife to speak. If the congregation had asked that she not preach, she often led in prayer. A query came to the 1859 Annual Meeting asking if "the gospel permit of female preaching." In answering this time, the conference made a distinction between teaching, ministering, and prophesying (Rom. 12:6-7), deciding that a sister could prophesy but not teach (Article 7).

Sarah Righter Major continued to preach until near her death in 1884, including one sermon during the 1878 Annual Meeting. A few other women also began to preach in the latter half of the 19th century. Mattie Lear began preaching in Illinois in the 1870s and continued until her death in 1903. She filled the pulpit in her home congregation and addressed ministerial and Sunday school meetings. She was also a writer and an educator. Yet, official sanction for preaching by women was not to come until the 20th century.

Women and Communion

The slight openness in the pattern of male dominance in regard to preaching by women was not evident when it came to women's participation in the love feast. The elements of communion were distributed by deacons and ministers under the supervision of a presiding elder. As these offices were not open to women, communion was administered by male leaders. After male members of the congregation received the bread and the cup from the administrator, they distributed the elements among themselves. The sisters, however, were individually given the bread and the cup by the administrators; they did not distribute them among themselves.

This practice was first questioned in a query brought to the Annual Meeting of 1849: "Whether it would be more consistent with the Word, if, at the communion, the administrator would give the bread and cup to the sisters, and they divide it, like the brethren, among themselves, and the administrator to pass along, to keep order?" (Article 35). The meeting decided unanimously to continue as before. This question became an item of debate in the pages of the *Gospel Visitor* soon after it began publication in 1851. Various writers cited scriptural support for both continuation and change of the current practice. One writer claimed that women had broken bread with each other, as the men did, in the early days of the church. Those who supported the sisters having bread broken for them claimed that this was done out of respect for them. Yet, they believed that her place in communion and in relation to men generally was to be subordinate.

A few claimed that this hierarchal view could not be challenged as it was divinely ordained. This view was supported by Annual Meeting when it was asked in 1857 why women did not break bread as men did. The answer read: "Man, being the head of the woman, and it having been the practice of the church, from time immemorial, for the officiating brethren to break the bread to the sisters, we know of no scriptural reason for making a change in our practice" (Article 9). But the question continued to be debated in church publications and later Annual Meetings. Those asking for the privilege of the sisters also breaking bread cited Galatians 3:28 and 1 Corinthians 10:16–17 as the scriptural basis for the change. The practice was to remain unchanged throughout the 19th century.

Change in the Church

In this as in other questions Brethren wanted to be faithful to the commands of Christ as recorded in scripture. At the mid-century point, there were some who thought that the command to spread the gospel required a new witness through church publications, educational institutions, and mission programs. As these endeavors were innovative, others saw them as unscriptural and out of keeping with Brethren practice. These differences, and others such as the role of women in the church, contributed to a three-way schism among the Brethren in 1881–83.

A traditionalist group, which opposed these innovations, withdrew from the main body in 1881 to become the Old German Baptist Brethren. The traditionalists, while believing in spiritual equality in the salvation of women and men, held that scripture intended women to be under the headship of men in church and home life. This has remained their position to the present day. The progressives, who supported the innovators, organized the Brethren Church in 1882–83, after one of their leaders was disfellowshiped by the main body in 1882. They at first supported full participation of women in the church. Laura Grossnickle (Hedrick) was ordained in 1891. The 1892 General Conference of the Brethren Church granted to "the sisters all the privileges which the brethren claim for themselves." This church later, under the influence of fundamentalism, became more conservative in regard to ordaining women. The moderate main body, which in 1908 changed its name from German Baptist Brethren to Church of the Brethren, soon supported endeavors such as missions and educational institutions. They were still undecided about participation of women in the church and continued to discuss this issue.

Voting at Annual Meeting

The question of women voting at Annual Meeting was debated during the period of the schisms. During an 1881 debate on sisters wearing hats, a brother commented: "They are not allowed to vote on any matter, but we, their lords, assume the authority to make rules to bind them, and they dare not open their mouths in helping to decide these rules . . ." The next year Annual Meeting agreed to allow sisters to vote. In response, the moderator informed the delegate body that "it has always been their privilege, but it has lain dormant and they were never called on particularly to carry out their privilege" and instructed the sisters to "be active in expressing your sentiments in rising one way or the other."[8]

In 1883 this change was defined by Standing Committee as referring only to questions decided by a rising vote. Women were to be excluded from matters decided by assent or by vote of the delegate body and the Standing Committee. One brother pointed out that if adopted, these rules would deny any voice at all to women, as none were delegates. The rules *were* adopted and the sisters lost their recently-won franchise. A query came to the 1889 Annual Meeting requesting that sisters be eligible to be elected delegates; it was not approved. Thus, women were denied votes in setting policy for the life and work of the church in which they were so actively involved.

Women continued in their traditional patterns of participation but also joined in new endeavors undertaken by the church. Many articles in the new church periodicals were written by women. In 1876 Wealthy Clark (Burkholder) became the first woman to edit a Brethren publication (*The Young Disciple*). Women were part of the student body and faculty of every educational institution initiated by the Brethren. Women were often the organizers of congregational Sunday school programs; they also taught most of the classes and occasionally served as Sunday school superintendents. Women also helped support and participate in the home and foreign mission programs begun by the church.

Women's Mission Organizations

During the 1885 Annual Meeting Brethren women organized themselves in support of the mission program of the church. An account of the meeting was published in the *Gospel Messenger*:

> At the close of the forenoon session, it was announced that the sisters would meet in the tabernacle to hold a missionary meeting. At one o'clock the tabernacle was well filled, a number of sisters occupying the stand. Several hymns were sung, and prayer was offered by one of the sisters, after which sister Lizzie Miller stated the object of the meeting. She said "An appeal has been made through the *Messenger* by sister Snavely of Urbana, Ohio, to the sisters to help in the missionary work of the church. About one hundred letters have been received, and we are here to open and read these letters." She then nominated sister Ella Brumbaugh to take charge of the meeting. Sister Lizzie Howe was appointed Secretary, and sister Fannie Quinter, Treasurer. Sister Miller then read a number of letters containing words of encouragement and also some money for the work of spreading the gospel. After the reading of the letters, short talks were made by a number of the sisters . . . A collection was now taken up, after which, the Standing Committee coming in, the meeting was dismissed.[9]

Four congregational missionary societies were organized the following year—three in Pennsylvania and one in Illinois. These groups supported home and foreign mission programs and helped care for some of the needs of poor members of their communities. The women of Altoona, Pennsylvania, helped pay the debt on their church property. The Huntingdon, Pennsylvania, society set up a fund "to help worthy girls attend the Huntingdon Normal School."

The denominational Sisters' Mission also intended to continue its work. A call went out through the *Gospel Messenger* for sisters to send offerings again to Annual Meeting. The offering sent to the 1886 meeting was double that of the previous year. Plans for organization of a mission band in every congregation were proposed. These groups were to raise funds for the mission program of the church and to engage in mission education projects.

A paper, however, came to the Annual Meeting asking that there not be separate womens' organizations. Debate on the paper indicated that some thought that the sisters had made mistakes the previous year. Some of the women who spoke during the 1885 meeting were wearing disapproved articles of clothing and improper headdress, it was said. Some also thought that the women had been too vigorous in their organizing efforts. Others felt that the sisters had made an important contribution to the mission cause. S. Z. Sharp asked that the women's sphere in the church not be further restricted:

> If we pass this paper and place those restrictions upon them, we do it most reluctantly, and we feel it in justice to our dear sisters to say something. We have silenced them in the congregation; we have silenced them in the Annual Meeting. That is, they have no longer a voice as they once had . . . We do not allow them to preach the gospel . . . in the name of the church, and they, feeling a desire to do something for the Master, have formed themselves into missionary bands in different places, and endeavored to do something for the Master . . . [If] we pass this paper as it is, we take away from them the last opportunity they have in laboring for the Master, as they seem to think they ought to. Inasmuch as they have no voice in this matter, as they cannot defend themselves, I feel to espouse their cause so much as to say this much on their behalf.[10]

The paper forbidding sisters' mission bands passed. Two papers that came the following year—asking that this decision be amended to encourage the sisters in their work—were not accepted. The work of the sisters was to be under the direction of the male leaders of the church.

Thus it seemed that a system of male dominance was reaffirmed by the church. During the 1891 Annual Meeting, several papers were accepted that reiterated this: women were again denied the privilege of breaking bread with each other and representing their congregations at Annual Meeting. They were told explicitly that they were not installed into church office—including that of deaconness—in their own right but only as "helpmeets" to their husbands. Still, this system continued to be challenged on scriptural grounds. With the coming of the 20th century a more egalitarian system emerged with renewed strength. Acculturation and the influence of the secular women's movement were certainly factors in such a change, but as the following account will indicate, the Brethren also found authorization for change in scripture and their own tradition.

The 20th Century

Women first began to gain a voice in Annual Meeting when the name of Bertha Ryan, a missionary to India, appeared on the delegates list in 1899, the first woman to so appear. Apparently the 1898 decision permitting women to be delegates to district meetings had been interpreted as permitting them to be delegates to Annual Meeting as well. In 1901 there were seven women delegates representing congregations in Indiana, Kansas, and Nebraska. By 1915 of the 42 district delegations 24 included women. The 1913 Annual Meeting had appointed two women to its five-member Dress Committee. As far as is known, these two—Florence H. Myers and Mary Teeter—were the first women to serve on an Annual Meeting committee.

Women and Communion, Continued

The restricted place of women in communion was again questioned. Queries requesting that the privilege of breaking bread and passing the cup be granted to sisters came regularly to Annual Meetings beginning in 1899. A study committee appointed that year "to investigate the Gospel grounds and the expediency of the change" brought a report in 1900 recommending that the bread and cup be distributed to all by the administrator. The vote was deferred for one year, at which time the report was not accepted. The previous practice continued.[11]

About this time claims were again made that the sisters had broken bread for each other in the early days of the church. Drawing on historical material from the library of Abraham Harley Cassel, historian Martin G. Brumbaugh concluded: "Enough has been recorded to show that at the beginning, and at least for fifty-four years, in the early church the sisters were treated exactly like the brethren, and each one passed the cup and broke the communion bread." Brumbaugh gave no documentation for his statement. J. H. Moore claimed that Cassel's materials showed that both the practice of the single mode of feetwashing and breaking of bread by sisters were carried from Germantown to Illinois by a body of Brethren originally under the leadership of Elder Daniel Leatherman, supposedly ordained by Alexander Mack, Sr.

There are presently no documents available from early Brethren history that clearly establish that sisters did break bread. But there is evidence that leaves the question open. In discussing communion in his *Rights and Ordinances* Alexander Mack, Sr., made no reference to different modes of breaking bread for sisters and brothers. In a tract he wrote in 1730 about the Ephrata Community, Mack criticized Beissel's practice of administering the bread and cup himself. The Ephrata chronicle (1786) recorded, in turn, that Beissel disagreed with the Brethren way of breaking the bread "because they were of the mind that all must be equals; and therefore they did not wish to allow any prerogative or privilege to any one person among them."[12]

But if the sisters did break bread and pass the cup in the same way as the brothers in the early days of the church, when and why did this practice change? Perhaps Alexander Mack, Jr., and Christopher Sauer II introduced such a change as they assumed leadership of the Germantown congregation in the mid-18th century. They may have wanted to avoid the disorder they had seen at the Ephrata community when traditional family patterns were changed. A change may have been made in the practice of communion so that the sisters' bread was broken for them to symbolize the headship of man over woman. This was the reason given in the 1857 Annual Meeting. Or perhaps a change was made so that the administrator could be sure that women whose heads were not properly covered would not be able to receive communion, thus assuring their obedience to church authority. These suggestions remain speculative.

Brumbaugh's claim was incorporated into the next query to come to Annual Meeting (Article 5, 1906) asking that the sisters be granted the privilege of breaking the bread and passing the cup. This was a second query from the Grundy County, Iowa, congregation, the first having come in 1899 (Article 1). The author of the Grundy County queries was Julia Gilbert.

She was born in Maryland in 1844 and migrated with her family to Ohio when four years old. Julia was crippled in 1855 by measles and scarlet fever, diseases which took the lives of her brother and sister. She was baptized when fourteen years old and studied scripture from an early age, always concerned that the practice of the church be faithful to the biblical teachings. Eventually, she became involved in what she called the struggle for the sisters to break bread. In 1883 she wrote a letter to the *Gospel Messenger* asking if those who taught that women were subordinate under the law and gospel and therefore should not break bread with each other would please instruct the sisters what to do during feetwashing and the salutation of the holy kiss.

Julia Gilbert brought a query questioning the sisters' privilege of breaking bread to her Ohio congregation council meeting in 1894 and again in 1895; it was voted down both years. Then, after her parents' death in 1896 she moved to Iowa to be with the family of a brother. She brought her query to the council meeting there in 1898; it was sent on to the district and then to the Annual Meeting. When this query was defeated, she again submitted another, the one that came to the 1906 Annual Meeting (along with a separate query from North Dakota). Again, a study committee was appointed by Annual Meeting.

This committee reported in 1909 that, after study, they too found that the administrator should break the bread for all participants, men and women alike. The report was deferred for one year. At the 1910 Annual Meeting, several speakers criticized the report and proposed instead that the sisters be given the same right to break bread enjoyed by the brothers. Julia Gilbert rose to speak (as she had, briefly, during the discussion the year before) on behalf of the sisters from the Grundy County church, thus becoming the first woman known to have spoken during business sessions at Annual Meetings. She began by giving the reason why the query had been brought, pointing to the covenant she and others made at baptism "to live faithful to Christ Jesus until death." In the words read at every communion, she said, Paul commanded: "'Be ye followers of me as also I am of Christ' . . . He followed Christ in breaking the bread, and therefore I think I have the right to ask these delegates to permit the sisters to break bread one to the other."[13] The request was finally granted. Oneness in Christ Jesus ruled out man exercising headship over women during the communion.

Women's Organizations

That same year women organized a permanent Sisters' Aid Society. This organization was a successor to the Sisters' Mission which was forced to disband in 1886. At that time some local organizations had quietly continued their work. Then in 1895 Annual Meeting approved sisters' sewing societies "if the sisters labor in union with the church as expressed in the council, and according to the principles of the Gospel" (Article 6). With this official sanction, women began to organize in congregations across the country. The Sisters' Aid Society of Frederick, Maryland, began publication of a monthly *Missionary Advocate* in 1897. Through its pages they attempted to organize sisters across the denomination to "assist in the Missionary Cause" through fundraising. The paper ceased publication in 1898 at the request of the Standing Committee.[14]

During the 1909 Annual Conference women met in a general Aid Society meeting. They met again in 1910 and organized permanently.

They adopted a constitution, elected officers, and decided to meet annually during Annual Conference to conduct business, worship together, and hear pertinent addresses. By the time of the 1911 Annual Conference there were 119 local societies with a membership of 2,580. They had received over $5,000 for distribution by the General Mission Board. At the 1914 meeting it was stressed that the primary purpose of aid societies was not to raise money but to be "an organization of helpfulness." In 1915 the Aid Society decided to support a specific mission project, a project that would continue for several years. The 1917 Conference recognized the Sisters' Aid Society, at their request, as an official organization of the Church of the Brethren.

In 1928 women decided to study the possibility of organizing a Council of Women's Work to integrate the work of the Sisters' Aid Society, the Mothers and Daughters Association (organized denominationally in 1906 by Catherine Beery Van Dyke), and any other local women's organizations. These organizations came together in 1930 to become the Women's Work program of the Church of the Brethren. By then the Aid Society had grown to nearly 700 local societies. During its 20-year life, it had contributed nearly $1,400,000 to the work of the church. This is a remarkable sum for a period in which few women were employed for wages; most of the money was raised "by the use of needle and by serving meals and lunches." Schools and hospitals for women and girls in India, China, and Nigeria had been constructed with their contributions. (Women's organizations were also established in these countries.) Each society had contributed to meeting local needs as well as supporting home and foreign missions. A 1929 Aid Society report identified the source of "all these deeds of mercy and good-will and love" as "an outward expression of the gratitude in women's hearts for the liberty and equality brought to them by the Lord Jesus . . ."[15]

Women in Ministry

The formal exclusion of women from the preaching ministry of the church was also to come to an end. This came about largely in recognition of the work women were already doing. Following in the tradition of Sarah Righter Major and Mattie Lear, other women began to preach. Bertha Miller Neher began to preach and to do evangelistic work early in the 20th century. She served a year as an interim pastor of the Winona Lake, Indiana, congregation. Bertha Neher was also a teacher, author, and leader in the dress reform program of the church.

Mattie Cunningham (Dolby) was the first woman to appear on a ministerial list of the Church of the Brethren. Born in Indiana, she was baptized at the age of 16 into the church of her parents. She and her brother were the first black students to enroll in Manchester College. After leaving college in 1903, Mattie Cunningham went to Palestine, Arkansas, to establish a Sunday school in the Brethren mission. She felt deep concern for her people: "The history of the Negro is the history of a downtrodden and neglected race. America boasts of her freedom and Christianity, but we, as American Negroes, have known little but to be abused and misled." She believed that educational opportunities needed to be improved as "it has been long since proven that we can be somebody if we only have an opportunity." She asked the Brethren to support the mission with their "luxury money." She was forced by ill health to leave Arkansas in 1906. The Brethren closed the mission one year later.

Mattie Cunningham moved to Southern Ohio and soon married Newton Dolby. They were elected deacons in the Frankfort congregation in 1907; in 1911 she was installed into the ministry. Six children were born to them in the following years, years in which she continued to study the Bible, preach, and teach. Then, because of racial prejudice they were asked in 1924, after a "change in administration," to leave the Brethren congregation in which they were worshiping. She continued her ministry in a Methodist congregation and then in the Church of God.[16]

Queries began coming to Annual Conference asking by what authority some districts were giving women permission to preach. In response, a ministerial statement brought to the Conference in 1922 included a provision for "licensing sisters to preach." A spirited debate followed. Some opposed the recommendation as contrary to scripture and the tradition of the church. Others supported it, pointing to the women who had worked with the Apostle Paul, to Sarah Major, and to the work of women on the mission field. The recommendation passed. For men, licensing was the first step toward ordination to the full ministry; for women it was now possible to be "permanently licensed to preach" but not to be ordained.

After the 1922 decision the number of "licensed sisters" in the ministerial list of the church grew year by year. The ministries of these women were varied. Some preached regularly—on a circuit or in evangelistic meetings. Some served in ministries with their husbands. Others served in home and foreign missions. A few were pastors of congregations but these women faced limitations in their ministry; they were not legally permitted to perform weddings or officially allowed to conduct baptisms or communions. Bertha Cline was one of these pastors. She was a graduate of Bethany Biblical Seminary and had worked for 15 years in home missions before becoming in 1937 a pastor in Oklahoma and Colorado. She was serving the McClave, Colorado, congregation as an interim pastor in 1949 when it petitioned Annual Conference "to allow women equal rights with men in the ministry." This petition was referred by Conference to the General Brotherhood Board, which requested that the following Conference appoint a committee to study this question as part of a larger study of the role of women in the life of the church.

Ruth Shriver, director of Women's Work since 1946, had requested such a study, following the initiative of an ecumenical body. Women's Work had continued the programs of the aid societies and mother-daughter groups. But the National Council under the leadership of Florence Fogelsanger Murphy from 1930 to 1941 was also concerned that women play active roles as lay leaders of the church. Leadership training became an important program of the organization, an emphasis which had been continued by Ruth Shriver.

She served as a member of the study committee on the role of women, appointed by Conference in 1950. The committee brought a report to the 1951 conference but was asked to do further study and report again in 1952. The second report—"The Role of Women in the Life of the Church"—began by affirming the "division of labor which assigns to women a special function in home and family life" as scriptural but also recognized "that experience proves that women can make outstanding contributions in other areas," asserting that this was also "Scriptural and in harmony with the spirit and teaching of the Bible." From a survey it had conducted, the committee concluded that women "do hold a significant place in the life and program" of the church. But it noted that "women to not have representation equal to their numerical strength on the boards and committees of the church." Therefore, it recommended there be "more extensive use of their wisdom and ability."

These sections of the report were accepted without debate. However, the section that recommended that "qualified women be granted equal opportunity with men in the ministry" for "there can be neither male nor female in Christ Jesus" (Gal. 3:28) was debated heatedly. Those who opposed it said there were no scriptural grounds for the ordination of women nor any apostolic precedent. Others claimed that women were to be mothers and not have the responsibility of ministering. Supporters of the recommendation pointed to the leading of the Spirit in bringing about equal opportunity for women in the ministry and for the need of individual women to be able to answer the call of the Spirit. After several hours of debate, a substitute motion was passed that gave a woman who is the pastor of a church "the privileges of the ordained minister to function in the congregation of which she is pastor."

After the authorization for women to preach, some thought women should again be able to serve as deaconesses. During the 19th century the practice had changed so that women served only if their husbands were elected deacons. A 1935 report adopted by Conference deleted the committee's recommendation that women be able to serve in their own capacity. The question was later raised once more. Finally, the 1956 Conference adopted a statement that permitted a woman to serve as deaconess "in her own right;" women were no longer to serve only as "helpmeets." Also, the functions of a deaconess were to be the same as those of a deacon.

The question of the ordination of women was also raised once more. A query came to the 1958 Conference requesting that women be granted "full and unrestricted rights in the ministry." The Standing Committee recommended favorable action on the query, citing the original section on women and ministry in the 1952 report. After a brief debate, the query was passed with less than 15 dissenting votes. Not only could qualified women now be ordained, there were also no longer any official policies limiting the participation of women in the church. The last barrier had been broken.

The Women's Fellowship (the new name for the Women's Work body), noted in 1960 in a handbook for local women's organizations that "today amazing doors of opportunity stand open awaiting the response of women who are willing to serve." Standing Committee membership had been opened to the laity in 1947 and women began representing their districts on the committee in 1949. In 1960 women made up about 7% of its membership. Women had also served on the General Brotherhood Board since its organization in 1947; usually 1 to 3 of its 25 members were women.

Change in Women's Organizations

In 1963 the Women's Fellowship dissolved itself as a national organization. The National Council had been considering such a move since 1954, thinking that the dissolution of a separate women's organization might be necessary for women to be fully integrated into the life of the church. This dissolution was approved by the 1965 Conference. It was noted at that time that 81% of the congregations reported women's organizations, as did all 39 districts. These organizations had "made significant contributions to the life of the church through fellowship, worship, family life activities, study, service projects, sewing activities, and money projects." Yet, women and men were together the church. "To realize this brings us to a new sense of responsibility and a willing acceptance of and participation in the total mission of the church."

Some felt that there were women willing and able to participate in the church but who were not achieving their rightful place or proportional representation within it. Only one woman was on the General Board in the mid-1960s. The ratio of women on the Standing Committee stood at 25%. Women were seldom appointed to Annual Conference study committees. Thus a resolution was brought to the 1970 Conference by Carole Ziegler and Nancy Peters on "Equality for Women," calling the church "to support action to bring women into full participation in the mainstream of American society exercising all the privileges and responsibilities thereof in truly equal partnership with men." It was adopted by the Conference and a committee appointed to study the church's position on women in church and society.

At the 1970 Conference a women's caucus was organized from the work of the two women. In 1971 it nominated Virginia Showalter Fisher for conference moderator, the first time a woman had been nominated. The work of the caucus continued with the publication of a newsletter, *Femailings*, and the appointment of Mary Cline Detrick and Mary Blocher Smeltzer as coordinators. In 1973 about 50 women voted to establish formally a "Womaen's Caucus." A steering committee was organized to carry on its work. The caucus continued to raise awareness of the issues, organize, and act as advocates on behalf of the full participation by women in the church. The caucus was instrumental in securing the appointment of the first woman to serve as a Brethren delegate to the World Council of Churches—Wanda Will Button in 1975—and the establishment of the "Person Awareness" program of the Parish Ministries Commission in 1976—staffed by Beth Glick-Rieman. Under her leadership two women's conferences were held for the denomination, with several hundred women in attendance at each. The Global Women's Project was organized by the 1978 conference, in response to Ruthann Knechel Johansen's call for women to give birth to a new world.[17]

In 1976 a query came to Annual Conference from the Northern Plains District requesting that a committee be elected to study, update, and implement the 1972 paper from the General Board on Equality for Women. The Conference approved the study and a committee of three women and two men was formed. The committee brought a report to the 1977 Conference, which was adopted after the deletion of the recommendations for nominating and balloting procedures to achieve a more equitable representation of women and men on conference-elected boards and committees.

The report as adopted began with the biblical basis for equality of women and men. It affirmed that the intention of creation was a partnership and equality between man and woman and identified an order of patriarchal subordination counter to what God had intended. A new order of "full equality and true partnership of women and men" was said to be envisioned by both Jesus and Paul. The next sections of the paper provided reviews of the historical record and current activity, concluding that "some progress has been made . . . [but] more needs to be done." Recommendations were then put forward to clarify priorities and practices of the church, including "a commitment to the achievement of equality for all its members, male and female" and an affirmation of the importance of the family, "with the nurture and training of children . . . a responsibility of primary importance belonging to both men and women."

Conclusion

Thus an egalitarian system of relationships between women and men was now the official policy of the church. In practice, women continued to find responsibilities that they had never held before. Phyllis Kingery (Ruff) was elected to a five-year term as Annual Conference secretary in 1977, thus becoming the first woman to serve as a conference officer. Ruby Frantz Rhoades became the executive of the World Ministries Commission in 1980, the first woman to serve as an associate general secretary of the General Board. Elaine Sollenberger became the first woman to chair the General Board in 1984. The First International Women's Conference of the Church of the Brethren was held in August, 1985, with nearly 1,000 women and 15 men coming together under the theme "Empowered By Our Birthright."

Yet, representation of women in the ordained ministry and in district and denominational boards and committees is still not proportional to their membership. No woman has been elected moderator, although several have been nominated. Queries and recommendations have been brought calling for a structured ballot to ensure election of women in some positions but none have been accepted by the conferences. Some also suggest that the name of the denomination—the Church of the Brethren—may render women invisible. They ask if it may again be time to consider changing the name to represent more fully the true nature of the church.

In 1985 the church is not of one mind in regard to the use of inclusive language and the adoption of structured ballots. There are a few who still insist that subordination of women is mandated by scripture. As a denomination, however, the Church of the Brethren has committed itself to the achievement of equality for women and men. The coming years offer opportunity for such an achievement.

Notes

1. Donald F. Durnbaugh, ed., *European Origins of the Brethren* (Elgin, IL: 1958; 141–142.
2. Durnbaugh, *European Origins*, (1958), 379.
3. Durnbaugh, *European Origins*, (1958), 389.
4. *Minutes of the Annual Meetings of the Church of the Brethren* (Elgin, IL: 1909), 143. Hereafter, page references to actions of the Annual Meetings will not be cited in the notes. See Pamela Brubaker, *She Hath Done What She Could* (Elgin, IL: 1985), for specific references.
5. Otho Winger, *History of the Church of the Brethren in Indiana* (Elgin, IL: 1917), 302–303.
6. Mary Garber, "Aunt Barbara Yount," *Gospel Messenger* (May 9, 1914): 290.
7. Donald F. Durnbaugh, "She Kept on Preaching," *Messenger* (April, 1975): 18–21.
8. *Report of the Proceedings of the Brethren's Annual Meeting* (1881), 67, hereafter cited as *Full Report*; *Full Report* (1882), 5; *Full Report* (1883), 9.
9. "Notes on the Annual Meeting," *Gospel Messenger* (June 9, 1885): 361–362.
10. *Full Report* (1886), 31.
11. *Full Report* (1901), 47–66.
12. Martin G. Brumbaugh, *A History of the German Baptist Brethren in Europe and America* (Elgin, IL: 1899), 543; *Chronicon Ephratense*, trans. J. Max Hark (Lancaster, PA: 1889), 241.
13. *Full Report* (1909), 12–27; *Full Report* (1910), 101– 114.
14. Mildred Etter Heckert, "*Missionary Advocate*," *The Brethren Encyclopedia* (1983–1984), 855.

15. *Full Report* (1929), 48–51.

16. Mildred Hess Grimley, "Mattie Dolby: No Sound of Trumpet," *Messenger* (January, 1976): 16–20.

17. Mary Blocher Smeltzer, "Womaen's Caucus," *The Brethren Encyclopedia* (1983–1984), 1359.

10

Ecumenical Relations

Edward K. Ziegler

The Church of the Brethren today believes in full cooperation with other churches and participates heartily and responsibly in many cooperative Christian movements. The present stance of the Church of the Brethren toward other churches, however, represents an almost total reversal of its early position.

When the church was founded in Germany in 1708, it was the expression of vigorous protest against many of the practices and beliefs of the mainline churches of that day. Its approach to other churches was polemical and proselyting. Early Brethren history shows that its leaders were often imprisoned and punished in various ways for their bitter attacks upon the state churches and for their insistence upon rebaptizing persons from other churches who were persuaded to join them. In this attitude they were not alone. A spirit of mistrust and divisiveness prevailed. The established churches were intolerant of dissent and of movements toward reform within their own households. There was little irenic spirit displayed either by these churches or by their unwanted and rebellious offspring.

When the Brethren migrated to the American colonies, the more irenic spirit of the Pennsylvania Quakers, who were their hosts, began to permeate the church. While the Brethren and, indeed, most of the Germanic sects, tended to hold themselves aloof from English-speaking groups, there was far more tolerance and interchange of views among religious communities in America than there had been in Europe.

An episode of great significance in Brethren history was its participation in the synods convened by the Moravian leader, Count Nicholas

Ludwig von Zinzendorf.[1] The *Unitas Fratrum* or Moravian Church, known in Germany as the *Brüdergemeine*, was a movement with strong mystical and missionary emphases, growing out of the early Hussite society of Christians. Many of the Moravians, driven by persecution and attracted by the promise of religious freedom, came to the American colonies some years later than did the Brethren.

From the beginning of his association with the Moravians, Count Zinzendorf had a broad ecumenical outlook. He had a vision of the reunification of the various denominations into a federation, a "Congregation of God in the Spirit." He did not hope to establish a monolithic church but rather a union, according to the motto: "In essentials unity, in nonessentials diversity, in all things charity." Zinzendorf believed that the Moravians were uniquely qualified to lead such a movement and that Pennsylvania, with its climate of religious freedom and its multiplicity of German sectarians, would be the ideal place to launch his bold experiment. In 1741 (with the inspiration of Zinzendorf's presence and counsel) Henry Antes, a Reformed layman, sent out a general invitation for a synod to convene in Germantown on New Year's Day, 1742. The purpose of the synod was to confer about the common faith and interests of the churches and to seek ways of closer cooperation. Held at frequent intervals across the next several months, the synods tried earnestly to find grounds of unity and, ultimately, a union of the sects.[2]

Brethren leaders were invited to these synods and attended at least three of them. But alarmed by what they saw as syncretistic tendencies and repelled by the rather high-handed leadership of Count Zinzendorf, the Brethren withdrew. A momentous consequence of this ecumenical contact was the decision of the Brethren to hold their own Great Council in 1742. From this council grew the Annual Conferences of the Brethren, which to the present time constitute the highest governing body of the Church of the Brethren.

For the next 150 years there is little evidence in Brethren history or literature of any interest in ecumenical contacts. They cooperated locally with other groups, it is true, in the use of meetinghouses and cemeteries. They also made common cause with the Mennonites in appealing to state authorities for recognition of their nonresistant stand. However, there was a period in the latter-half of the 19th century when their isolation was interrupted by a series of acrimonious debates with representatives of other denominations, especially Baptists, Disciples, and Lutherans. The published volumes containing the texts of these debates reveal intense polemical spirit and a desire on both sides to show that each competing debater represented the sole repository of divine truth essential to salvation. These debates were typical of the spirit of most denominations just before what may be called the dawn of the ecumenical age.

Early Ecumenical Contacts

It was not until the powerful ferments of the missionary and the Sunday school movements in American Protestantism that the Brethren began to take the first cautious steps toward ecumenism. When the Brethren first sent missionaries to India in 1894, their workers were encouraged to cooperate closely with other missions. From the very beginning they observed the principle of comity. Wherever Brethren foreign missionaries have gone, they have been in the forefront of ecumenical activity. Inevitably their ecumenical experience and spirit have had a profound effect upon the home church. It can be truthfully said that the foreign mission interests in the Church of the Brethren have been the pioneers of ecumenical concern.

Long before the church at large began working with other denominations, their leaders in Christian education enjoyed such contacts. For many years Brethren editors have shared with their colleagues in the planning of the International Sunday School Lessons and other areas of curriculum. In the early days of the Sunday school movement, Brethren were firmly advised not to attend the popular Sunday school conventions. But by 1908 Brethren attended the International Sunday School Convention in Jerusalem and in increasing numbers shared in succeeding international conventions.

In 1916 J. H. B. Williams, then assistant secretary of the denomination's General Mission Board (its most influential administrative unit for many years), wrote to inquire of the Federal Council of Churches of Christ in America (FCC) what steps would be required for the Church of the Brethren to become a member of the council. He apparently believed that the church had moved by then far enough from its earlier separatist position to consider, at least, such membership. About this same time, as the shadows of World War I moved over the world, Brethren, Friends, and Mennonites developed a degree of cooperation and intense dialogue concerning their common problems as peace churches in a time of war.

In 1919, after the war had ended, major Protestant bodies initiated a campaign to capitalize on the growing interest of many Christians in social issues and international problems. They organized a grandiose ecumenical venture called the Interchurch World Movement. Brethren leaders attended the planning conferences, and the denominational boards voted to commit the Church of the Brethren to full participation in the movement. However, upon referring this action to Annual Conference for approval, they found strong resistance and firm disapproval. Conference demanded that the boards withdraw from the movement.

The Church of the Brethren paid in full all its financial commitments to the movement, which soon afterwards collapsed. The Brethren leaders, like others, were caught up in the enthusiasm for a brave new world which characterized the movement, but the mood of the total church was more cautious. While this costly venture into ecumenism may have set back Brethren ecumenicity for 20 years, the church at least had the satisfaction of knowing that the ill-starred movement had had powerful influence for justice in the settling of the famous steel mill strikes of that period and in securing more humane working conditions for the steelworkers.

Conciliar Connections

For nearly 45 years now, the principal Brethren involvement in ecumenical affairs has been through the conciliar movement. In 1936 the Council of Boards of the church appointed M. R. Zigler to represent the Church of the Brethren at the Oxford Conference on Life and Work and the Edinburgh Conference on Faith and Order, both held in the summer of 1937. Encouraged by Zigler's enthusiastic report on the conferences, the Council of Boards then appointed a strong committee to relate the Brethren to these movements. Zigler was appointed as the Brethren representative to to the consultations of world Christian leaders exploring the formation of a World Council of Churches.

During the same period, serious study was being given to the question of Brethren participation in the Federal Council of Churches. In 1938 the Council of Boards voted: 1) that various departments responsible for church program be authorized to cooperate with the corresponding departments of the Federal Council, especially in such areas as peace, temperance, relief, mission, and evangelism; 2) that the Council of Boards authorize an appropriation to the Federal Council from the budgets of the concerned boards; and 3) that the Council of Boards authorize fraternal representation only, at the forthcoming biennial meeting of the Federal Council. M. R. Zigler was appointed to represent the Church of the Brethren.

By 1941 sufficient progress had been made in cooperation and acquaintance with the working of the FCC that the Council of Boards was ready to make a statement recommending full participation of the

Brethren in the Federal and World Council of Churches (in process of formation):

> Since the Church of the Brethren has for a number of years shared partially in the program of the Federal Council of Churches in America by unofficial representation in certain sections of the Council; and since the Conference was officially represented at the World Ecumenical Conferences of Oxford and Edinburg in 1937; and since much progress has been made toward a World Council of Churches in order to give Protestanism a strong voice in many strategic situations which now exist throughout the world; and since the World Council as well as the Federal Council is now actively engaged in peace movements of major proportions and is concerned especially with the problem of the conscientious objector, which has been an important concern of the Church of the Brethren for more than two hundred years; Therefore, the Council of Boards recommends that Annual Conference of 1941 authorize constituent membership both in the World Council of Churches and the Federal Council of Churches of Christ in America and take steps to appoint official representatives to the Councils of these bodies when our membership has been officially approved by the proper authorities.

The statement also asserted that membership would not bind the Brethren to any action of the councils and "in no way compromises its doctrinal position." It demonstrated a desire to "share in the larger fellowship of the Protestant world" and to become a more effective partner in the "great movements for peace and world reconciliation."[3]

The 1941 Annual Conference adopted the recommendation by a large majority vote; it appointed as its official representatives to the Federal Council: Paul H. Bowman, Sr., Rufus D. Bowman, D. W. Kurtz, Edward K. Ziegler, and M. R. Zigler. (Representatives to the World Council of Churches were appointed later.) There were repercussions in the church to this historic action; repeated queries to Annual Conference asked that the Brethren withdraw from the councils. Thorough debates on the membership question took place in 1945, 1968, and 1981; each time full and responsible membership in both councils was reaffirmed with increasingly large majority votes.[4]

When the time came for the First Assembly of the World Council of Churches in 1948, the Church of the Brethren sent their complement of delegates to the historic meeting in Amsterdam. In the meantime, full representation was sent to each meeting of the Federal Council. Brethren became actively involved in the activities of major departments of the FCC. The Brethren were also participating in other interdenominational agencies such as the Foreign Mission Conference, the Home Missions Council, the Stewardship Council, the Student Volunteer

Movement for Foreign Missions, and the International Council of Religious Education. When these and other agencies joined with the Federal Council of Churches in 1950 to form the National Council of Churches of Christ in the USA, the Church of the Brethren from the beginning voted its approval and participated fully in the new council.

Ecumenical Action

Until very recent times the Brethren have not made significant contribution to the theological dialogue in the wider church. The area of greatest competence has been in the fields of peace, social concern and action, relief, and certain specialized aspects of overseas missionary work. During the 1930s and 1940s, the ecumenical contribution was largely shaped by the interests and abilities of the persons selected to represent the church. M. R. Zigler, who during this time was the chief Brethren exponent of ecumenical cooperation and the first Brethren representative to the councils, was not a theologian but a churchman of profound humanitarian concerns. He was always prodding and urging the councils to involve themselves in the quest for world peace and in those activities that would not only bind up the wounds of past wars but prevent future conflicts. These emphases were not only Zigler's personal bias but were inherent in Brethren comprehension of the gospel and its relevance to the modern world. He was strongly supported in his insistence upon these practical issues by the church which sent him and by the colleagues who also represented the Brethren in the conciliar movement.

In his earlier years in conciliar circles, Zigler helped to initiate a strong rural emphasis, primarily through a series of national convocations of the Town and Country Church; these brought together leaders of the rural church movement for many years. After World War II, Zigler spent 10 fruitful years in Europe as head of the church's vast program of relief and rehabilitation and as the Brethren liaison with the World Council's offices in Geneva. He administered a far-reaching program for the Brethren Service Commission, extended the development of the Heifers for Relief program, and also assisted in setting up the World Council's world-wide ministry to refugees and victims of disaster. Zigler's own competence and the role of the Church of the Brethren were recognized in his being given a seat on the powerful Central Committee of the WCC, on which he served from 1955 to 1961.

He continued his deep interest in World Council activities after retirement, attending its world assemblies through the seventh, held at Vancouver, Canada, where he received a standing ovation. During these later years he devoted his energies as well in bringing together the five largest Brethren bodies in informal meetings, initiating a movement to publish a Brethren encyclopedia, and founding the On Earth Peace Assembly. He maintained his keen interest in ecumenical activities until his death in 1985, just two weeks before his 94th birthday. He was nominated for the Nobel Peace prize in 1983.

Norman J. Baugher, executive secretary of the General Board from 1953 to 1968, also served a term on the WCC Central Committee from 1961 until his death in 1968. While the Church of the Brethren is one of the smaller member communions in the World Council of Churches, it takes its membership very seriously, sends a full complement of delegates to all meetings, and has given important leadership to those phases of the council's programs that are consistent with the genius of the Brethren.

Brethren participation in the work of the National Council of Churches has also been vigorous. In proportion to its size, it has supplied an unusually large number of leaders to the NCC. Norman J. Baugher served two terms as vice-president of the council, giving strong leadership in peace and long-range planning. Andrew W. Cordier, long prominent on the United Nations staff and former president of Columbia University, also was a vice-president. Brethren have provided leadership in such departments as peace, worship, evangelism, race relations, and stewardship. Robert W. Neff, general secretary of the Church of the Brethren since 1978, chaired the powerful Presidential Panel of the NCC, which sought to bring a new and more dynamic relationship between the council and its constituent churches.

Church World Service, the NCC department that channels material aid from American churches to the hungry and homeless of the world, owes much to Brethren leadership and initiative. It has also entrusted the administration of its centers for collecting and processing relief materials to the Brethren Service Commission. In recent years these activities and many other social service programs of American churches have been centralized in the facilities of the Brethren Center at New Windsor, Maryland.

Brethren have been responsibly engaged for many years in the conciliar movement in state and local councils of churches. A striking number of lay and professional leaders of these council has been provided by the Church of the Brethren. Such leadership has been especially notable in Connecticut, Indiana, Massachusetts, Pennsylvania, Virginia, Kansas, Arizona, Idaho, and Washington. In most areas where Brethren have congregations, pastors are fully active in local ecumenical activities.

While the Church of the Brethren has not been noted for theological scholarship, in recent years it has provided significant leadership in theological education. Paul M. Robinson and Warren F. Groff, recent presidents of Bethany Theological Seminary, have been respected and innovative leaders in the field. Jesse H. Ziegler served as executive secretary of the Association of Theological Schools; probably the most comprehensive ecumenical organization in North America, it includes virtually all graduate schools of religion, both Roman Catholic and Protestant. Ziegler founded and was the first editor of an influential journal, *Theological Education*, the official organ of the Association. Groff also represented the Church of the Brethren on the Faith and Order Commission of the World Council of Churches.[5]

Ecumenical Involvement Overseas

Mention was made earlier of the significant involvement of Church of the Brethren missionaries in ecumenical work in the foreign countries where they have worked. A brief survey is appropriate here. In India, Brethren missionaries and national leaders have been active in national and regional Christian councils, in literary and translation activities, and in the formation of the Church of North India. This church came into being in 1970 as a merger of Anglican, Baptist, Brethren, Disciples, Methodist, and Presbyterian traditions. The Church of the Brethren in India became an integral part of this important church; the first bishop of the diocese of Gujarat was a Brethren minister, Ishwarlal L. Christachari.

In Nigeria, where the Brethren have had their most spectacular success in building a strong and growing church, they pressed for the formation of a United Church of the Sudan. The *Ekklesiyar 'Yan'uwa a Nigeria* (The Church of the Brethren in Nigeria), plays a leading role in ecumenical activities in Nigeria, including the Theological School of Northern Nigeria. In China, during the years when foreign missions were still permitted, Brethren missionaries and Chinese pastors were prominent leaders in movements toward a united, indigenous Chinese Christian Church. The congregations established and nurtured by the Brethren in Ecuador led in the formation of the United Evangelical Church of Ecuador. In Indonesia, instead of seeking to build a Brethren congregation, Brethren missionaries were seconded to the Church of Indonesia and worked under its direction in the areas of health and theological education.

Probably the most important contribution of the Church of the Brethren to the ecumenical movement overseas was in agricultural missions. Many Brethren missionaries were themselves products of a strong rural and Christian culture, were well trained for working among rural people, and were deeply concerned about the rural millions in the lands where they went. They helped to establish programs of rural church work which were outstandingly relevant to the needs of the people and deeply appreciated by national leaders.

Thus it was that the Rural Missions Cooperating Committee and Agricultural Missions, Incorporated, the major ecumenical clearing house and training agency for rural missions, have had Brethren as leaders. Ira W. Moomaw, a world expert on rural education and the problems of hunger, was for many years the executive director of Agricultural Missions after a distinguished career as a missionary in India. He was followed in this post by another Brethren rural expert, J. Benton Rhoades. Moomaw wrote a number of provocative books about world hunger and rural education. Another Brethren missionary in India, Edward K. Ziegler, wrote in the fields of rural church worship and the training of rural ministers; these books have been widely used in seminaries and rural congregations around the world.[6] The creative and innovative work of Brethren missionaries in Nigeria has been commended by international organizations such as the World Health Organization.

Cooperation on Peace Issues

The outbreak of World War II found the Brethren open and eager for cooperation with others sharing their deep concern for the Christian position regarding war and peace and for the problems of the conscientious objector to war. While this concern was held most deeply by the Friends, the Mennonites, and other Brethren bodies, there was a large sector in other denominations as well who were ready for cooperative planning and effort. E. Raymond Wilson of the Friends, Orie O. Miller of the Mennonites, and M. R. Zigler, along with other leaders of peace action, were able to forge a program for conscientious objectors; they were to serve under church auspices in work "of national importance," acceptable to the US government's Selective Service System. In this endeavor the peace leaders had the support of Gen. Lewis B. Hershey, the chief of Selective Service. The peace churches created the National Service Board for Religious Objectors to organize a Civilian Public Service for the COs. While there was criticism and disillusionment about this program, it was probably the best plan that could then be devised for giving young men opportunities for significant public service, instead of going to prison or compromising their faith by entering "noncombatant" military service.

Brethren have continued to lead in the area of guidance and counsel for COs and the administration of service activities for them. For many years W. Harold Row, executive secretary of the Brethren Service Commission, gave strong leadership in this field, as well as in the whole area of worldwide relief, service, and peace action in the ecumenical movement. An imaginative approach to the problem of world hunger was sparked by Dan West, a Brethren relief worker who administered relief to refugees under the American Friends Service Committee during the unhappy civil war in Spain. He saw the practicality of sending live, bred heifers to countries where there was a shortage of milk and farm animals. This program, initiated by the Brethren, soon became widely ecumenical and has continued to the present day as the Heifer Project International, sending hundreds of thousands of cattle, goats, sheep, swine, and chicks to impoverished people. Brethren have also given capable personnel to CROP (Christian Rural Overseas Program), by which the churches have channeled their contributions of food for world hunger.[7]

Much of what has been described thus far deals with the involvement of the Church of the Brethren in the Life and Work areas of ecumenical concern, where, indeed, the Brethren have had deep interest and some degree of expertise and experience.

Ecumenical Conversations with Brethren

Another area of ecumenical relationships has to do with the conversations carried on to foster closer fellowship with other Christian bodies, which may or may not lead to mergers. It is important now to examine what progress the Church of the Brethren has made in this aspect of ecumenical life. Here the stance of the Brethren is inevitably conditioned by their history and by their perception of the nature of the church. From the beginning of the Brethren movement in Germany, there have been strong separatist tendencies in the church. Since the Church of the Brethren has been moving more into the mainstream of Protestant church life in the past 60 years, there has been a great deal of thoughtful scrutiny of our ecumenical posture.

A matter in which Brethren have a particularly tender conscience is the relationship with the other Brethren bodies rooted in the Schwarzenau experience. In 1881 a very conservative group, the Old German Baptist Brethren, separated from the main body of the church; it has remained an island of social and ecclesiastical conservatism ever since.

In 1882–83 another and larger group, more aggressive and progressive than the main body, also became separate. Across the years this latter group, known simply as the Brethren Church, has become more conservative theologically than the Church of the Brethren.

Nearly 50 years ago the Brethren Church was split by the modernist-fundamentalist controversy, giving birth to a new group now called the Fellowship of Grace Brethren Churches. The Church of the Brethren has hoped and prayed that the unhappy divisions within the Brethren family might somehow be healed. So far as the Old German Baptist Brethren on the one side and the fundamentalist Fellowship of Grace Brethren Churches on the other are concerned, there seems to be little hope of ultimate reunion with the Church of the Brethren. The Dunkard Brethren, who split off from the main body of the church in 1926, also seem likely to remain aloof from any reunion.

With the Brethren Church, however, there is growing rapport and cooperation. For some years there has been a successful combined missionary program in Nigeria; members of the Brethren Church also cooperate with the (Church of the) Brethren Disaster Service and the On Earth Peace Assembly. To maintain and foster this growing relationship, the Church of the Brethren for many years had a Fraternal Relations Committee.[8] Intermittently, friendly talks were carried on with this group, clarifying differences, sharing insights, and exploring avenues of further cooperation.

Although there appears to be little likelihood in the near future of organic reunion of these five Brethren groups, there has been a significant new development of cooperative work among them in the past 12 years. In June, 1973, there took place an historic meeting of 125 members of these groups at the "Tunker House" at Broadway, Virginia. This meeting was arranged by M. R. Zigler, with the support and encouragement of W. Newton and Hazel Long, "just to shake hands." The two-day meeting was so productive of goodwill and shared interest in common history that a whole series of such meetings followed. A meeting of Brethren historians at Bethany Theological Seminary in 1976 stimulated plans to develop a Brethren encyclopedia. In further meetings a corporation was formed to produce this reference work and an editorial board of representatives of all five Brethren bodies was secured. With Donald F. Durnbaugh, professor of church history at Bethany Theological Seminary as editor, the combined effort produced a comprehensive three-volume *Brethren Encyclopedia*, published in 1983–1984. Fred W. Benedict, a printer-historian and lay member of the Old German Baptist Brethren, was made president of the encyclopedia corporation, which plans further publishing projects.[9]

Earlier Ecumenical Conversations with Other Churches

As ecumenical contacts increased in the several denominational program areas, there was greater interest in the Church of the Brethren to hold conversations with other church bodies. The Fraternal Relations Committee, which in 1934 became a permanent committee of the Annual Conference, initiated such conversations or was authorized by the Conference to respond to overtures from other denominations for such talks. As a means of acquainting the total church with the nature and scope of these conversations, the committee has presented to Annual Conference on many occasions fraternal delegates or visitors from the various communions with whom they have been conversing. The committee has also sought to provide resource materials and settings for ecumenical education. When the committee found that its ecumenical contacts called for joint action and program, its concerns were referred to the appropriate board or commission of the church for implementation.

Among the most fruitful and rewarding contacts with other denominations that the Fraternal Relations Committee initiated have been the sustained conversations with others in the Free Church tradition. The many areas of common concern with Mennonites and Friends have led to a series of formal conversations. In 1964 and 1968 conferences where held in which several branches of Brethren, Friends, and Mennonites shared their insights and concerns. One such meeting, held in November, 1968, at New Windsor, Maryland, brought together 60 representatives of 9 groups from this tradition to discuss the rule of the peace churches in today's world. Such consultations are not designed to lead to merger but to provide opportunity for discussing common values and areas of difference in and depth.

Further cementing and deepening of the common heritage and outlook of these groups have taken place in conferences on the Believers' Church. In these conferences Baptists, Disciples, and others in the Free Church line have also been involved. The concepts of the Believers' Church and radical discipleship have provided a strong bond of interest and material for serious ecumenical conversations. An influential group of Brethren theologians and church leaders, probably representing the majority of Church of the Brethren members, believes that the ecumenical future of the Brethren lies in increasingly strong relations within this group of churches. Still conscious of its heritage in the Left Wing of the Reformation and of its roots in the Pietist and Anabaptist traditions, the Church of the Brethren is uncomfortable in movements toward union with churches that do not endorse these concepts.

Among the Mennonite groups, the General Conference Mennonite Church is the one with which Brethren have had the most intimate and practical relationships. From 1945 to 1958, Mennonite Biblical Seminary and Bethany Biblical Seminary shared camps, faculty, and classroom activities in Chicago. This warm cooperation ceased with the Mennonites decided to form the Associated Mennonite Biblical Seminaries with the (Old) Mennonite Church in Elkhart, Indiana, and the Brethren made plans to move Bethany Seminary to a new campus in Oak Brook, a suburb west of Chicago.

Brethren have also carried on ecumenical conversations with several smaller denominations. Among them was the Churches of God in North America, General Eldership. This group, comprising 38,000 members, has a common habitat with the strongest areas of Brethren population and has had many interests and practices in common with the Church of the Brethren. After several years of conversations and a series of grassroots conferences of laymen and pastors of both churches, it was agreed that merger between the two would not be a viable ecumenical direction for either. Conversations have also been held to the present with the Church of God (Anderson, Indiana). The Brethren share some publishing interests with this group. Conversations were also held with the Evangelical Covenant Church of America.

The most intense and serious conversations, leading to many areas of fruitful collaboration, have been carried on for more than 20 years with the American Baptist Churches (formerly the Northern Baptist Convention). Working principles for a possible plan of church union were adopted and studied with great care by local churches and in community or state groups of churches. Thorough study was carried on of all the ecclesiological and theological issues which might draw the denominations together or tend to drive them apart. Areas of greatest divergence are in church polity and the peace issues. Baptists are congregational in church polity, while the Brethren employ a form of representative polity. Baptists support the military chaplaincy, while Brethren are adamantly opposed to this kind of ministry to persons in the armed forces. Theologically, the two churches are similar. In 1969 it was mutually decided not to press for organic union but rather to focus on joint efforts in Christian mission.

An associated relationship between the two denominations was worked out in the early 1970s. In a number of local settings there are now joint Baptist/Brethren congregations. Bethany Theological Seminary and Northern Baptist Theological Seminary, on adjoining campuses in Oak Brook, Illinois, share library facilities, bookstore, and many aspects of theological education. The two denominations work together on architectural services and curriculum resources. For the past several years they have appointed observer-consultants to each other's general boards of administration.

Cooperation with Historic Peace Churches

Cooperation with the various branches of the Mennonite Church has become increasingly active and comprehensive in the last decade. The General Conference Mennonite Church, the (Old) Mennonite Church, and the Brethren in Christ collaborate with the Church of the Brethren in the production of church school curriculum (Foundation Series). Since 1983 these groups have started working on the production of a new hymnal, which will be used by all of them; it is hoped that it can be completed by 1990. Several Brethren biblical scholars are involved in the publication of a new Believers' Church biblical commentary, with sponsorship by the same bodies.

Recently a new era of cooperation with Mennonites has begun in the field of mental health. Since 1946, as an outgrowth of their experience with Civilian Public Service units in mental hospitals, the Mennonites have developed a series of psychiatric centers across the country. They are under the general supervision of Mennonite Mental Health Services (MMHS). In 1984 the Church of the Brethren developed cooperative ownership of several of these centers, beginning with Brook Lane in Maryland. Several church districts now nominate directors for the boards of these centers. The Brethren are also represented on the MMHS board.

In 1976 Brethren, Friends, and Mennonites sponsored a joint movement of peace education and action, New Call to Peacemaking. There have been several important national conferences, building on local and regional events, and notable peace publications. In 1985 the scope of the movement is being enlarged to include peace movements in many other denominations.

Brethren have been involved with these sister churches in two movements in Europe of great ecumenical import. One was a series of conferences sponsored by the Historic Peace Churches and the International Fellowship of Reconciliation, in which their theologians engaged in dialogue with leading theologians from European churches. These gatherings were often called the "Puidoux Conferences," from the location in Switzerland of the first such conference in 1955. Stimulated originally by M. R. Zigler, W. Harold Row, and later by Dale Aukerman, the meetings were characterized as the first serious conversations between the state churches and the Radical Reformation since the 16th century. They were credited with considerable influence on the status of pacifists in several Western European nations.

W. Harold Row and other Brethren also participated actively in the Christian Peace Conferences (CPC), held in Prague since 1958. They are international gatherings of church leaders from East and West, and also from the Third and Fourth Worlds, to discuss issues of peace and disarmament. One meeting of the CPC Working Committee of the conference was held in New Windsor, Maryland. An influential leader in these consultations, before his untimely death in 1978, was the Russian Orthodox leader, Metropolitan Nikodim. The metropolitan was the key figure in the series of theological discussions and church exchanges between the Russian Orthodox Church and the Church of the Brethren, between 1963 and 1971. W. Harold Row was his counterpart among the Brethren.

Consultation on Church Union

The most vigorous debate on ecumenicity within the Church of the Brethren came about through an invitation from the Consultation on Church Union (COCU). In late 1960 Eugene Carson Blake, stated clerk of the United Presbyterian Church, USA, upon the invitation of Bishop James A. Pike, preached a sermon in Grace Cathedral in San Francisco. In the sermon Blake urged the formation of a new united church that would be "truly evangelical, truly catholic, and truly re-formed." Originally addressed to the Protestant Episcopal Church, the United Presbyterian Church, the Methodist Church, and the United Church of Christ, Blake's proposal soon attracted the attention of other denominations; the annual meetings of the consultation since 1962 have included 10 churches as full, participant members. From the beginning, other churches that are not ready for full participation in COCU have been invited and welcomed as observer-consultants. While at first the relationship was more "observer" that "consultant," the churches that have accepted this role have played increasingly important parts in the discussions. Brethren have had observer-consultants at all of the COCU plenary sessions.

In 1965 the Church of the Brethren and some others were asked if they would welcome invitations at that point to become full participants in the consultation. After a year of study and the distribution of much material on the subject, delegates at the Annual Conference in June, 1966, voted by a large majority to continue the observer-consultant status, rather than to seek full membership. This issue deeply stirred and divided the church. The action of Conference declining full membership was interpreted by some as a retreat into narrow sectarianism or as a surrender to resurgent fundamentalism.

On the other hand, the debate clearly showed that the most vocal and persuasive opponents of affiliation with COCU were those who saw the Church of the Brethren hearkening to a different drummer, who saw the Brethren as the champions of the Free or Believers' Church tradition and of radical discipleship. They saw the role of the church not in isolationism but as a strong, if small, voice in the body of the church universal, sustained by a strong church entity, and cooperating fully and trustfully with other Christian groups. (A minority group in the church called the Brethren Revival Fellowship opposes any form of cooperation except with equally conservative groups; this group helped to swell the tide of opposition against the COCU.)

The decision of the Church of the Brethren not to enter fully into COCU membership indicated the desire of the church to maintain a strong peace witness and a quality of radical discipleship that did not seem viable within the shape of the uniting church emerging from the consultation. The option to join COCU, however, is still open. Periodically, there has been further consideration of this issue. The church has maintained a close and direct relationship with the consultation that could, in time, open the way to full participation.

The same 1966 Annual Conference that so decisively rejected the option of full participation in COCU voted to pursue a somewhat different ecumenical direction. The Conference voted to affirm resolute and profound commitment to cooperation with brothers and sisters in Christ through local, state, national, and world councils of churches; it urged Brethren through their local congregations to participate responsibly in all appropriate ecumenical communities. The Conference also voted to explore possible mergers of the Brethren with such churches or groups of churches that are sufficiently similar in doctrine, polity, and mission that merger might be feasible and productive. This conference saw the Church of the Brethren as serving under God as a bridge church, actively seeking to promote cooperation and possible merger with a constellation of churches close to the Brethren in doctrine and polity in order to cooperate in mission.

Restructuring of the Ecumenical Task

Because of the increase in magnitude of the task entrusted to the Fraternal Relations Committee and the changes of direction in the ecumenical movement, the General Board of the church, after two years of study, recommended a new structure for ecumenical concerns. In place of the Fraternal Relations Committee, a new Committee on Interchurch Relations (CIR), accountable to both the Annual Conference and the General Board, was established. This committee has worked closely with the Commission on Christian Unity of the American Baptist Churches and has explored areas of cooperation with other churches and with the National and World Council of Churches. It sends observers to the National Association of Evangelicals, COCU, and to the annual conferences of other Brethren groups.

In 1982 Annual Conference adopted a statement prepared by the CIR at the direction of the General Board, entitled "The Brethren Vision of Unity for the '80s." This foundational statement pointed the direction for all the ecumenical activities of the Church of the Brethren for the years just ahead. It developed a basic scriptural position on the ground of unity as God's gift. This unity does not require compromising belief or demand uniformity. It does commit the church to full accountability to all brothers and sisters in Christ. The statement not only affirms active participation of Brethren in the conciliar movement but envisions the ultimate unity of all God's creation under the lordship of Christ.[10]

The statement commits the Church of the Brethren to: 1) work for full and complete mutual recognition of members and ministers of all families within the larger Christian family; 2) promote involvement in local, national, and international ecumenical worship and service ventures; 3) develop a strong educational program in ecumenicity[11] for all age groups; 4) study ways that interfaith dialogue may lead to a visible expression of God's plan of unity for all of humanity; and 5) share in conversations with others whose aim is the establishment of a communion of communions or a family of families.

Since 1980 the CIR has given an ecumenical award each year to persons in the church who have worked faithfully and consistently in ecumenical activities. The awards have gone to: M. R. Zigler, DeWitt L. Miller, Wanda S. Callahan, Ira W. and Mabel Moomaw, Hazel and Clifford Huffman, and Wanda Will Button. The committee also awards annually an ecumenical scholarship to persons who are pursuing studies or educational programs in ecumenism. Beginning in 1985 this scholarship commemorates Joanne Grossnickle, a worker in the Washington, D.C. office of the Church of the Brethren, who was murdered in 1984.

An exciting new development arose from an invitation from the German Seventh-Day Baptists to members of the Church of the Brethren to participate in love feasts at the historic Ephrata Cloister. This group is the descendant of the Ephrata movement, and thus the successor of the oldest schism. Several members of the CIR and others attended love feasts at Ephrata in 1985 and reported deep spiritual experiences and interest on the part of the representatives of the two groups for continued relations.

After nearly 50 years of careful study, the Faith and Order Commission of the World Council of Churches issued in 1982 a detailed study on "Baptism, Eucharist, and Ministry."[12] All member denominations of the World Council, including the Church of the Brethren, have studied this document and promoted its study in local congregations. The CIR has directed such local studies and will collect the responses in order to prepare the official Brethren reaction.

The committee sees its task as that of guiding the Church of the Brethren at a time when all ecclesiastical structures must meet the test whether they are truly bearing God's mission in and to the world. It accepts the principles that God wills the visibility of the church in the world and that the Church of the Brethren has something unique to share with the whole church of Jesus Christ. Brethren are still searching for ways in which their contribution of God-given insights may best be given.

In the recent past the direction of the ecumenical movement has dramatically changed. Organic union of the churches is no longer seen as its sole important thrust. Ecumenicity must be local if it is to be effective. The most vital ecumenical action occurs when the people of God in each place recognize each other as fellow pilgrims on Christ's way and share in his mission to their local communities and to the world. Ecumenicity means not only the growing unity of Christian churches but also an outlook that embraces the whole of God's creation. Therefore, Christians are increasingly concerned with discovering how, under God, they may express their love and concern for people of all faiths, Christian and non-Christian.

The guiding principles now for Brethren in ecumenical relations are mutuality, collegiality, and accountability to sisters and brothers in Christ.[13] In the years ahead there will certainly be realignments throughout the whole church of Jesus Christ. One important and necessary grouping will be that of churches that hold the Anabaptist, Free Church vision of radical discipleship. Very likely the Church of the Brethren will find its destiny under God in such a group. Whether a group of churches with such a vision can be a part of the great church, which one day may emerge from the Consultation on Church Union, is an open question.

It may well be that a certain amount of pluralism in holy obedience may be necessary for the health and effective mission of the church. What God has given to the Church of the Brethren is important in the world. The concern of the Brethren is that these gifts be used where they can be shared most helpfully. The prayer of the Brethren is the prayer of Jesus Christ—that all his folk be one, one under God, one as God and Christ are one, so that the world may believe in God's mission and turn to God and be saved (John 17:23).

Notes

1. Donald F. Durnbaugh, "Nikolas Ludwig, Count von Zinzendorf," in *The Brethren Encyclopedia* (1983–1984), 1399.
2. Donald F. Durnbaugh, ed., *The Church of the Brethren in Colonial America* (Elgin, IL: 1967), 278–304.
3. *Minutes of the Annual Conferences of the Church of the Brethren, 1923–1944* (Elgin, IL: 1946), 162.
4. *Minutes of the Annual Conferences of the Church of the Brethren, 1945–1964* (Elgin, IL: 1956), 14–19; *Minutes of the Annual Conference of the Church of the Brethren, 1965–1970* (Elgin, IL: 1970), 320–325; *Minutes of the 195th Recorded Annual Conference of the Church of the Brethren . . . 1981* (Elgin, IL: 1981), 254–269.
5. Jesse H. Ziegler, *ATS Through Two Decades* (Vandalia, OH: 1984).
6. J. Benton Rhoades, "Agricultural Missions," in *The Brethren Encyclopedia* (1983–1984), 9; Edward K. Ziegler, *A Book of Worship for Village Churches* (New York: 1939).
7. Donald F. Durnbaugh, ed., *To Serve the Present Age* (Elgin, IL: 1975), Part II: chapters 2, 7, 8.
8. Edward K. Ziegler, "Fraternal Relations," in *The Brethren Encyclopedia* (1983–1984), 510.
9. Donald F. Durnbaugh, "Introduction," in *The Brethren Encyclopedia* (1983–1984), vi–ix.
10. Edward K. Ziegler, "Committee on Interchurch Relations," in *The Brethren Encyclopedia* (1983–1984), 328.
11. As a resource for such study, the committee produced and distributed a book by Fred Swartz, *All in God's Family: Brethren and the Quest for Christian Unity* (1977).
12. *Baptism, Eucharist and Ministry* (Geneva: 1982).

13. This chapter reflects the ecumenical relationships of the Church of the Brethren and does not represent the positions of the other Brethren bodies. Briefly stated, the Brethren Church is a member of the National Association of Evangelicals (NAE); the Fellowship of Grace Brethren Churches, while not a member of the NAE, cooperates with some of its components; the Old German Baptist Brethren and the Dunkard Brethren have no official affiliation with ecumenical bodies, although individual members have as private persons supported some interdenominational relief services. For an overview, see Edward K. Ziegler, "Ecumenism," in *The Brethren Encyclopedia* (1983–1984), 422–423.

11

Brethren Today

Carl F. Bowman

Historically, the Brethren were known as a quiet, plain people of deep religious commitment and high personal integrity. Born of the conviction that faith must be put into practice, they placed great value upon outward obedience to New Testament teachings such as baptism by trine immersion, the Lord's supper, nonresistance, nonswearing of oaths, and nonconformity to the world. Christian unity in the faith was of paramount concern—the church was seen as a holy institution of pious people who, as a unified body, were called to uphold Christ's teachings and the example of the primitive apostolic church. Becoming "Brethren" meant voluntarily leaving behind worldly values and practices, and submitting to the distinctive order of the church. When a member failed in this regard, he or she was confronted according to the guidelines in Matthew 18:15–22.

Today, there is a new breed of Brethren. The Brethren are no longer plain, nor are they quiet. Obedience to a clear and distinct standard of Christian practice is all but forgotten. In fact, the very thought of obedience seems to violate the contemporary Brethren doctrine of freedom of individual conscience. The "ancient and primitive order" of the church has been exchanged for a progressive, forward-looking "disorder" compatible with an era of high technology, large corporations, and fast living. Individualism, variation, and tolerance are now the norms. In short, a new world has produced a new Church of the Brethren, one that has certain threads of continuity with the past but which is perhaps most notable for its discontinuity with old Brethren traditions.

This chapter provides a descriptive profile of the Church of the Brethren today—one that is based *not* on official positions and policies, nor on the views of clergy and church leaders, but on the lives and opinions of the lay members in the 1980s. Who are today's Brethren? How do they live? What do they think and believe? To address these questions, representative information on the national membership was collected in a comprehensive "Brethren Profile Study." Although a national mail survey cannot reveal the power of a sermon, the warmth of a smile, nor the strength of a handshake among Brethren in local congregations, it can provide a systematic overview of the church that is both national in scope and focused upon ordinary church members.

The Brethren Profile Study

In the spring of 1985, with financial support from the Parish Ministries Commission of the Church of the Brethren, the Society for the Scientific Study of Religion, and several anonymous contributors, a representative sample of the entire adult membership[1] of the Church of the Brethren was selected, using established scientific procedures. This sample included 1,411 members from 64 different congregations scattered across the denomination. Seventy percent of those surveyed (990 persons) completed and returned a 16-page questionnaire—a rate of cooperation well above the norm for mass mail surveys of this type. Once collected, the data were compared with existing statistics on the national membership to assure their representativeness.[2]

The questions spanned a variety of topics: religious beliefs and practices, church participation, support for Brethren ordinances, attitudes toward peace and the military, Brethren lifestyles, political opinions, attitudes toward social issues (such as equal rights for women), and, finally, attitudes toward the Church of the Brethren itself. The goal was to provide a general profile of the church, rather than to explore any single topic in great detail.[3] The views of the national sample are often predictable but occasionally surprising. In either case, they reveal new data about the body of believers who call themselves Brethren in the modern era.

Demographic Profile

Preliminary investigation into Brethren membership patterns brings to light two striking facts. First, the Church of the Brethren membership is highly concentrated in the six Mid-Atlantic and upper Midwestern states of Pennsylvania, Virginia, Maryland, West Virginia, Ohio and Indiana.[4] Together, these states account for 79% of the total church membership.[5]

Pie Chart: Membership by State

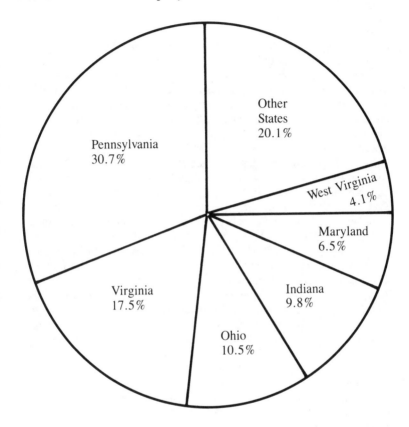

Second, the size of the Church of the Brethren has declined significantly during the past 25 years. Between 1960 and 1983 membership fell by 18%, declining from 200,217 in 1960 to 164,680 members in 1983.[6] This decline occurred during a period when the nation as a whole experienced a 30% *growth* in population. If the size of the church is thought of *relative to* the size of the US population, the Church of the Brethren experienced a 37% loss in membership in 23 years. Of course, these figures must be set in the context of broader trends in American religions. Presbyterians, Methodists, and Episcopalians also experienced marked declines in this period, while more conservative groups (such as Southern Baptists) experienced substantial gains. The Brethren pattern, it is clear, more closely resembles that of mainline Protestantism than that of conservative or fundamentalist groups.

What factors have contributed to the decline in Brethren membership? The *geographic location* of the Brethren and their *average age* are likely factors. Not only do the Brethren live in the slowest growing areas of the USA, the Eastern and Midwestern industrial states, they also live in predominantly rural sections of those states. Brethren Profile data reveal that about one of every five Brethren adults (18%) still lives on a farm. An additional 24% live in open country but not on a farm. These two groups, combined with those who live near but outside of small towns, provide a total of 55% of Brethren who live "in the country." This stands in sharp contrast to the 17% of the total population who live in the same setting. On the other hand, 72% of all Americans nationwide live in or near cities of 50,000 or more residents, whereas only 15% of Brethren live in these urban areas.[7] The pattern is clear—even in today's urban world, the Brethren remain a rural people.

The scarcity of Brethren in and near large cities is cause for concern. It suggests that many younger Brethren may have little opportunity to remain in the church. If their vocations and career aspirations carry them to urban job centers, or to the burgeoning areas of the Sun Belt and the Pacific coast states, young Brethren families may have little, if any, access to an established Brethren congregation. Thus, they are faced with the alternative of establishing a new Church of the Brethren, or, the more likely alternative, of joining an already existing congregation of another denomination.

Given these residence patterns, it is not surprising to find that the Brethren are an aging population. The median age of the Brethren sample is 54 years, with 30% 65 years of age or older. In contrast only 16% of the *adult* US population is 65 years or older.[8] This large block of elderly Brethren is a negative portent for church growth. When a large percentage of any group is elderly, more effort is required to maintain membership at previous levels. The Brethren are no exception. With its large number of elderly members and the church's rural location, Church of the Brethren outreach, retention, and new church development will need to be both vigorous and effective in order to halt the continuing decline in denominational membership.

Socio-Economic Profile

The residential pattern just described might lead one to speculate that the Brethren remain predominantly farmers. This, however, is not the case. Though they continue to *reside* in the country, less than one of

Residence and Age of Brethren Compared with the US Population

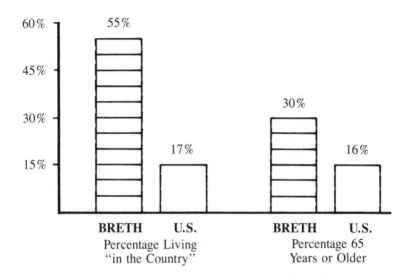

	BRETH	U.S.	BRETH	U.S.
	Percentage Living "in the Country"		Percentage 65 Years or Older	

every ten adult Brethren lists farming as his or her occupation. What is more, if the focus is upon those in the 25 to 54 age grouping, only 3% make a living from farming. This contrasts with the 12% of Brethren aged 55 or older who cite farming as their occupation. Clearly, the trend in 20th century America to abandon the family farm as a way of living has been followed by the Brethren. The Brethren today are a rural people who work primarily in non-farm occupations.

Table 1 compares the percentage of Brethren working in various occupations with the US population at large.[9]

The three most notable vocational contrasts between the Brethren and the national population as a whole are: 1) the high concentration of Brethren in professional occupations; 2) the high concentration of Brethren in farm-related occupations; and 3) the under-representation of Brethren in the service worker category. The Brethren are over-represented among professionals, not because there are large numbers doctors, lawyers, scientists, and engineers but rather because many Brethren are social workers, registered nurses, and most important of all, are *teachers*. Approximately 11% of all Brethren are teachers, the single most common vocation among Brethren today.

Table 1: Occupational Distribution of Church of the Brethren Members and U.S. citizens

Occupation	Brethren	U.S.	
Professional and Technical (Scientists, Engineers, Doctors, Teachers, etc.)	24.5%	15.3%	W H I T E C O L L A R
Managers, Administrators, and Sales Workers (Public & Private)	14.9%	15.4%	
Clerical and Related Occupations (Clerks, Cashiers, Secretaries, Bookkeepers, etc.)	15.6%	19.9%	
Craftsmen, Repairmen and Related Occupations (Carpenters, Electricians, Mechanics, etc.)	11.5%	12.2%	B L U E C O L L A R
Operatives (Machine Operators of Various Kinds, *not* Including Transport Equipment Operators)	10.9%	13.1%	
Transport Equipment Operators & Laborers (Includes Apprentices and Unskilled Laborers, Except for Farm Laborers)	5.2%	6.6%	
Service Workers (Maids, Janitors, Waiters, Cooks, Nursing Aides, Barbers, Day-Care, etc.)	9.6%	15.0%	
Farmers, Farm Managers, & Farm Laborers	7.1%	2.5%	

Brethren have also completed more years of formal schooling than the average American. Only 21% of adult Brethren have not completed high school, as compared with 27% in the nation as a whole. At the opposite end of the educational spectrum, 20% of Brethren have completed a four-year college degree. The comparative figure for the US is 17%. While the differences between Brethren and US educational attainment are small, they follow logically from the prevalence of Brethren in professional occupations and their scarcity in service occupations. In any event, given the 19th century Brethren suspicion of higher education, the fact that one of every five Brethren now has a college degree reflects a notable shift in educational posture.

Even though many of the Brethren surveyed indicated that income is an overly personal matter for investigation, 88% of those who responded supplied the requested information on income. The distribution of Brethren family incomes for 1984, presented in Table 2, depicts the Brethren as predominantly middle-class Americans. Compared with the nation as a whole, there are proportionately fewer Brethren at both extremes of the income scale. This is because 80% of all Brethren fell into the middle income range of $10,000 to $50,000 a year.

Table 2: Annual Family Income, 1984

Annual Family Income	Brethren	U.S.
Less than $10,000	13%	23%
$10,000—$24,999	42%	34%
$25,000—$49,999	38%	31%
$50,000 or More	7%	11%

Religious Participation

Religious participation can be conceptualized on many different levels. Beginning at the personal level, devotional activities such as prayer and Bible study may be viewed in either their individual or small-group expressions. Then, various dimensions of participation in the more structured activities of the local congregation may be observed. Finally, involvement in a national level of denominational-wide programs and activities can be studied. Each of these will be considered briefly in the following discussion.

What are the personal religious habits of the typical member of the Church of the Brethren? First, he or she engages in daily private prayer and says grace before meals on a daily basis. The typical member also reads the Bible about once a week. The level of *individual* religious devotion, therefore, is relatively high. Yet, if the focus is shifted from private devotional expressions to family or group activities, the religious landscape is significantly altered. The typical Brethren member participates in *family* devotional activities once a year or less. What is more, 45% of Brethren today *never* have devotions or worship as a family group. This constitutes a marked departure from the traditional Brethren pattern of worship at the "family altar." Furthermore, 43% of Brethren today *pray* together with family members of friends just once a year (or less), not counting grace before meals. Perhaps the earlier Brethren suspicion that modernity would lead the family away from its devotional responsibilities was not entirely unwarranted. In any event, the Brethren pattern of personal worship and devotion appears to have retreated from the family altar to the chapel of solitary devotion.

At the level of participation in the local congregation, 72% (or almost three of every four Brethren) attend worship services at least once a week, with only 12% of the membership attending less than once a month. This is a much better attendance record than the 33% of Americans nationwide who attend on a weekly basis (or the 49% of Americans who attend less than once a month). But a comparison of the church participation rate of any denomination with that of the society at large will yield a favorable impression for that church.

A more valid comparison is to juxtapose the 72% of the Brethren who attend weekly services with the attendance figures for a similar religious group, the Mennonites. The comprehensive national study of Mennonite church members by Kauffman and Harder reveal that 70% of Mennonites attend worship once a week or more.[10] In this light, Brethren attendance still appears favorable, but no longer unusual. Table 3 compares Church of the Brethren attendance at church services with that of other religious groups.

Table 3: Attendance at Sunday Services for Various Religious Groups[11]

Group Surveyed	% Attending at Least Once a Week	% Attending Less Than Once a Month
Church of the Brethren	72%	12%
Mennonites	70%	3%
Roman Catholic (1963)	70%	14%
Southern Baptist (1963)	59%	7%
Methodist (1963)	23%	21%
All Americans	33%	49%

Two other pieces of information speak to this issue of participation in the local Brethren congregation. First, the typical member comes to the church for some additional meeting or gathering (other than the Sunday morning service) about once a month. Second, when asked how much various persons (or other agents) have shaped their personal outlook on religion and life, Brethren rate their local pastor as a very important influence—more influential, they say, than either friends or relatives.[12] All of these reflect a strong link between the local congregation and the average church member.

How involved is the average Brethren member in the *national* level of denominational programs and events, such as the Annual Conference, the Brethren-related colleges, and Brethren Volunteer Service? The picture is mixed. In spite of the demographic concentration in, or near, states where the conference is periodically held, a majority of Brethren (60%) have *never* attended an Annual Conference. On the other hand, 15% of the membership have served as a delegate to Annual Conference. This would likely compare favorably with comparable data from other denominations.

A little over one-third (35%) of all Brethren who have attended college have gone to a Brethren-related college. However, the preference of Brethren for Brethren colleges is waning, as indicated by the following graph.

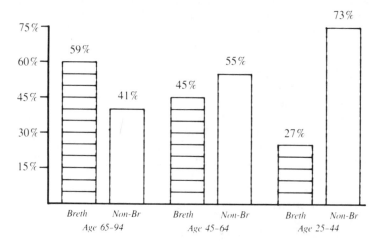

Percent of College Graduates Attending Brethren and Non-Brethren Colleges, by Age of Respondent

This graph suggests that in a period of about 50 years (1920–1970) the percentage of college-bound Brethren going to Brethren-related colleges was cut approximately in half. Only one of four college graduates in the 25–44 year age group has a diploma from a Brethren institution of higher learning.

Two sidelights on Brethren involvement in national programs merit attention: participation in Brethren Volunteer Service (BVS) and support for Brethren periodicals. Four percent of the national sample have participated in Brethren Volunteer Service, a program which requires a total commitment of one or more years of one's adult life. Fifty-two percent of the national membership, on the other hand, receive the *Messenger* in their homes. While this may appear to be low, it is 9% higher than the percentage receiving the second most popular periodical among Brethren, *Reader's Digest*. *Brethren Life and Thought*, a scholarly journal published on behalf of the Brethren with a more select readership, was received by only 2% of the sample. This places it well below *T.V. Guide*, which is received by 21% of the Brethren.

What conclusions can we draw about religious participation in today's Church of the Brethren from the data that has been presented? 1) The extent of the average member's involvement varies depending upon both the level of participation being discussed (personal, congregational, or national) and the specific indicator being considered. 2) Personal religious expressions such as prayer, devotions, and Bible reading appear to be primarily private matters, rather than something that is experienced jointly with family and friends. 3) The tradition of the "family altar," which, according to Ziegler, was "well on the way toward being lost" in 1942,[13] is no longer characteristic of the Brethren. Today only one member of the Brethren in ten engages in family devotions. 4) The individualistic strand of personal religious expression is coupled with a high degree of participation in the local congregation (as measured by attendance at Sunday morning services). 5) Participation in denomination-wide programs and activities is mixed. Forty percent of the general membership have attended an Annual Conference. Support for Brethren-sponsored higher education is waning.[14] Though such matters as subscription to *Messenger* and attitudes toward the national church offices at Elgin fail to indicate an overwhelming identification with the national program, neither do they indicate that support is at a low ebb.

In summary, the Brethren of today are private in their devotional life, active in the local church, and loosely-coupled with the denomination's national program.

Brethren Ordinances

Had it not been for the requirement that all members be baptized by trine immersion, there would never have been a Brethren movement. This outward act of obedience visibly set the Brethren apart from other German Pietists in the early years of the 18th century. Alexander Mack, Sr., wrote that the "true brethren of Christ could never refuse outward water-baptism, because they saw it in their first-born brother, who also commanded them so to do . . ."[15] Early Brethren were admonished to "walk in the doctrine of Jesus, in baptism and other ordinances as he has commanded." The two most basic ordinances are baptism by trine immersion and the love feast.

Yesterday's Brethren set specific guidelines for their doctrines and ordinances, aiming consistently for unity and uniformity of practice across the entire brotherhood. Today, variation is the rule and the idea of obedience to a single religious standard seems puzzling. It was only 27 years ago that the 1958 Annual Conference shed the last vestiges of uniformity by formally approving the acceptance of letters of membership from any Christian denomination, regardless of their mode of baptism. Today, two-thirds of those who come to the Church of the Brethren from other denominations do so without rebaptism. What once would have been considered an act of disobedience to Christ's teachings is now commonplace. Indeed, the person who comes to the church from the outside and requests rebaptism has become something of a rarity.

How far have contemporary Brethren strayed from the earlier Dunker insistence upon *outdoor baptism* (in running water)? Only one-fourth (25%) of the present adult membership joined the church through the traditional outdoor service. Another 58% were baptized indoors, and the remaining 17% of the membership were not baptized in the Church of the Brethren (having joined by transfer of letter.) A look at Brethren of different age groups reveals the magnitude of the transition. Approximately four of every five persons who joined the church before 1920 were baptized outdoors. In contrast, only one of ten members in the younger 25–45 year age group was baptized in this way. Should it be concluded that the practice of outdoor baptism will be abandoned altogether by the more modern Brethren today? Probably not! About 10% of the new members continued to be baptized outdoors, and this figure appears to be holding steady.[16]

As with so many other features of Brethren life, love feast practices have changed with the times. If attendance at love feast is accepted as a measure of its importance to the Brethren, the ordinance now assumes a more marginal position in the liturgical life of the denomination. One-quarter (24%) of the adult membership have not attended at all during the past five years. Attendance is particularly low in the Midwest and on the West coast, where 35% have not attended during the past five years. On the brighter side, 64% of the national membership currently attend love feast at least once a year. Participation is especially high in Pennsylvania, where two-thirds (65%) of the Brethren attend *twice* a year, and only 14% have not attended during the past five years. The accompanying bar graph clearly illustrates the declining support for the love feast as one moves geographically away from the more traditional Pennsylvania Brethren.

Percent of the Brethren Attending Love Feast At Least Once A Year

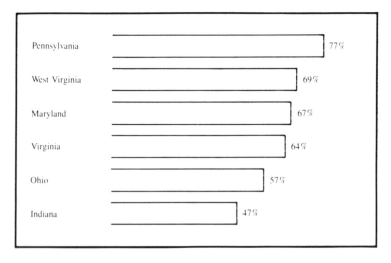

What conclusions can we draw about the support for traditional Brethren ordinances in the 1980s? In spite of the transitions that have occurred, there is still broad support for the love feast and for trine immersion baptism (indoors). About 100,000 Brethren nationwide still attend love feast at least once a year. Yet, compared with the Brethren of an earlier age, the Brethren of today are no longer so *unanimous* in their support for Brethren ordinances. The heavier cape of obedience to a single religious standard has been exchanged for the light frock of toleration by a forward-looking, ecumenically-minded Church of the Brethren. Most within the church breathe a sigh of relief that the former "be dunked or be damned" doctrine has been retired in favor of a more reconciling stance of openness and acceptance of variation.

Peace Position

A theme that has been gradually unfolding as various traits of the Church of the Brethren today are examined is that of individualism and tolerance of variation within the church. This theme is perhaps most pronounced when we consider what has become known as the Brethren "peace position."[17] Looking back as far as the Civil War, we find that Brethren who participated in the military were excommunicated; freedom of conscience was not an issue. By World War II, however, a majority of all young Brethren males participated in regular combatant military service. During this same period, Ziegler's study of three Brethren congregations revealed that approximately 60% of Brethren men believed it wrong to help in any war by fighting.[18] Today, only one-third (34%) of the Brethren agree with the statement that "it is wrong to help in any war by fighting." Of the remaining two-thirds of the denomination's membership, 28% are neutral and 38% *disagree* with this statement. Again is seen the wide diversity of opinion in the church.

Similarly reflecting muted support for the traditional Brethren position of nonparticipation in the military, the data reveal that 32% of Brethren men have, at some time in their lives, served in the armed forces. Additionally, 72% of the Brethren have family members who have served in the military. Probably the most direct single indicator of a personal position against war is the response to this question: "If you were twenty years old and faced with a military draft, what position would you take." One-third of the Brethren today say that they would enroll in regular (combatant) military service. Almost another third (29%) would go into noncombatant military service. The remaining 39% say that they would either go into alternative service (34%), register but refuse service (3%), or refuse to register (1%).

How does this compare with another of the Historic Peace Churches? According to the Mennonite date compiled by Kauffman and Harder, only 5% of the Mennonites would accept regular (combatant) military service. They would be much more likely than members of the Church of the Brethren to avoid the armed services altogether, with 71% of the membership saying they would opt for alternative service. Considering jointly those church members who would accept

214 / Carl F. Bowman

either a combatant or a noncombatant role in the military, the following contrast between the Mennonite and Brethren peace witness emerges:

Response to the question, "If you were twenty years old and faced with a military draft, what position would you take?"

Category	Brethren	Mennonite[19]
Would engage in either combatant or noncombatant military service	61%	18%
Would enter alternative service	34%	80%

Although there still remains a minority of Brethren who would not accept military service of any form, it must be concluded that the *average* Brethren member in the 1980s does not consider participation in the military to be wrong. While Brethren of previous eras who opted for military service were stigmatized and/or "disfellowshiped" by their church communities, today's young Brethren who choose the route of alternative service are as likely, if not *more* likely than those who enlist, to be looked down upon by members of their local Brethren congregation. Despite the fact that official denominational pronouncements against war and the military remain strong, the grass-roots membership provide nothing approaching a consistent peace position in either their attitudes or behavior regarding war and military service.

This treatment of the peace issue has thus far focused primarily upon personal statements of willingness/refusal to participate in the military. What is the Brethren viewpoint on military expenditures and the arms race? First, two-thirds of the Brethren members agree with the statement, "It is important that the United States at least maintain a balance of power with the Soviet Union." In spite of their acceptance of US participation in the arms race, 65% of Brethren today believe that we "are spending too much" on the armed services, armaments, and defense. This compares with 32% of the US population as a whole who feel that too much is spent on arms. Finally, two-thirds (67%) of Brethren today say that they favor a freeze on the production and deployment of nuclear weapons.

In summary, an accurate peace profile of the Church of the Brethren membership in 1985 reveals the following: 1) Brethren believe that the USA is channeling excessive funds into the arms race; 2) Brethren are basically opposed to the production and deployment of nuclear weapons; 3) still, most Brethren believe that it is important for the USA to maintain a balance of power with the Soviet Union; and 4) most Brethren are personally willing to serve in the armed forces, if only in a noncombatant role. Finally, it is interesting to note that nearly seven of every ten Brethren who voted in the 1984 presidential election (69%) voted for Ronald Reagan, a candidate who was renowned for his hard stance on defense and his commitment to increase the military budget. This compares with the 59% of voters nationally who voted for Reagan.

Religious Belief

A general overview of any religious denomination would be incomplete without a profile of that group's religious beliefs. Brethren of previous eras were known for their simple, unquestioning obedience to the gospel. This is what led them to take such firm stands on baptism, the love feast, nonresistance, and other Brethren doctrines. As these have already been touched on in previous sections, the discussion here will focus upon basic Christian beliefs about God and the Bible.

What do Brethren in 1985 believe about God? Nearly nine of ten Brethren (86.5%), when asked to choose among a variety of positions, reported that "I know God exists and I have no doubts about it." This compares with 99% of Southern Baptists, 89% of Mennonites, 81% of Roman Catholics, and 60% of Methodists who respond the same way.[20] Another 9% of the Brethren membership say they *feel* that they believe in God, even though they have occasional doubts, and 3% say that they believe, but not in the traditional image of a personal God. Only 1% of Brethren adopt an agnostic or atheist position when queried about their belief in God.

Regarding belief in the Bible, a little over one-third of Brethren today (35%) believe that the Bible is the "inspired Word of God, not mistaken in its statements and teachings, and is to be taken literally, word for word." This compares with 38% of the general US population who give the same response.[21] However, this "literalist" position is not the predominant view of the Bible among Brethren. A slightly larger number (42%) believe that the Bible is the inspired Word of God *but not always to be taken literally*. Only 1 Brethren in 20 rates the Bible as an "ancient book of legends, history, and moral guidelines recorded by men."

Despite their strong belief that the Bible is the word of God, Brethren read the Bible little more than the average American citizen. Some 17.6% of the Brethren read the Bible daily. This is slightly higher than the most recent national figure of 15%.[22] The typical member of the Church of the Brethren in 1985 reads the Bible about once a week, and almost one-third of the Brethren (30%) read the Bible infrequently—less than once a month. Considering the historic Brethren emphasis upon the New Testament as their only creed and confession of faith, the frequency with which Brethren today read the Bible seems peculiarly average.

In spite of moderate reading of the Bible, the Brethren frequently take the Bible literally in its specific narratives and teachings. For example, in the national debate over "creationism vs. evolution," Brethren take a conservative position, as illustrated in the following chart:

Percentage breakdown of Brethren responses to the question: "Which one of these statements comes closest to describing your feelings about the origin of human life?"

Response	Percent
God created Adam and Eve which was the start of human life.	72%
God began an evolutionary cycle for all living things, including humans, who developed in his own image.	26%
Humans evolved from other animals.	2%

The same propensity toward theological conservatism comes to light in Brethren beliefs about hell and the devil. When asked: "Do you believe in Hell as a place of eternal torment for those who do not believe in Jesus Christ?" no less than 66% of the Brethren answered positively, 19% were uncertain, and only 15% replied in the negative. Two-thirds (67%) of the Brethren responded, "Yes" to the question: "Do you believe the Devil is a personal being who actively directs evil forces and influences people to do wrong?" Only 18% responded "No" to the question. A comparison of these figures with national data for Americans of various religious backgrounds reveals that in their beliefs about creation, the devil, and hell, the Brethren more closely approximate the belief-structure of evangelical and fundamentalist Christians than those of the liberal Protestant mainstream.

Despite this theological conservatism, the pentecostal or charismatic movement has not made much of an impact upon current Brethren. Less than 5% of the general membership report ever having spoken in tongues, while 14% consider themselves to be "charismatic." Moreover, this pentecostal minority is not spread evenly across the denomination, but is largely limited to local pockets of charismatic expression. For example, not a single member reported speaking in tongues in 44 of the 64 local congregations sampled. Further, only 5% of the congregations accounted for more than half (51%) of all who reported tongues-speaking. If one particularly charismatic congregation were to be eliminated from the sample, only 1 of every 37 Brethren members (in the remaining congregations) speaks in tongues.

The analysis of responses by Brethren to doctrinal issues indicates that Brethren are generally conservative in theological position. Their reaction to questions about charismatic expression also allows the conclusion that they are, by and large, conventional.

Lifestyles and Attitudes

Brethren in 1985 are no longer a plain people who refuse to conform to the world about them. In fact, the world about them is brought right into their living rooms—99.4% of current Brethren have at least one television set in their home. Ironically, of the many themes considered in this profile, this is the first to reveal an almost complete uniformity in Brethren practice. Moreover, over half of the Brethren membership (53%) have *more than one* television set in their own home, with 1 of every 25 (4%) having *four* or more functioning sets. On the average, members of the Church of the Brethren spend two-and-one-half hours a day watching television programs, slightly below the national average of three hours a day. The shows they watch span the entire spectrum of television fare. Whatever the image on the screen, the Brethren usually view it in "living color"—92% of Brethren today own a color television set.

What other products of 20th century technology have found a niche in Brethren homes? Almost two-thirds of the Brethren own *two* or more automobiles; 54% own high-fidelity or stereo equipment; half own air-conditioners; and almost half (47%) own microwave ovens. Computer technology is beginning to penetrate Brethren homes, with 10% of Brethren reporting that their family owns a personal computer. The conclusion reached by Ziegler in 1942 is equally true today: "Little resistance has been made to the introduction and use of home conveniences and as a result the Brethren are much like the surrounding culture."[23] The primary difference is that 40 years ago Brethren were installing bathrooms and telephones in their homes; today they are purchasing microwave ovens, computers, and video-recorders.

In regard to the Brethren outlook on moral issues, about half (51%) of the national membership believe that drinking alcohol is "always wrong." This is almost identical with the Mennonite figure of 50% Moreover, Brethren beliefs about alcohol closely parallel their actual behavior; 57% report that they are total abstainers, with the other 43% stating that they use alcohol at least occasionally.[24] Only one-third report that they have never used alcoholic beverages. Extrapolating from Ziegler's data,[25] the percentage of current Brethren who have never had a drink is probably close to what it was at the dawn of the 20th century. However, this does not imply that the rate of abstinence has remained constant throughout the century. On the contrary, the data suggest that there was a period from the 1920s through the 1950s when total abstinence was more prevalent among the membership.

What other things do the Brethren view as being morally wrong? Table 5 lists a variety of items, ranked according to how wrong the Brethren perceive them to be.

Given the church's historic stance against divorce and the use of alcoholic beverages, it is notable that these items rank so low on the list of "immoral" behaviors. Divorce, in particular, seems to have become widely accepted as a reality of 20th century life. More than half (53%) of the Brethren in the sample agree with the statement: "Divorce is preferable to maintaining an unhappy marriage." Only 17% disagree with that statement. This tolerance of divorce for grounds as vague as unhappiness represents a dramatic shift in a denomination that, until 1933, allowed divorced persons to remain in the church only if their spouses had been guilty of adultery.

What percentage of Brethren have actually been divorced or separated? Thirteen percent of those who have been married have gone through such an experience, which translates into one of every eight Brethren who have been married. This is substantially lower than the United States rate of divorce, which is 33% or one of every three who have been married.

Although they are more accepting of divorce than Brethren of previous eras, Brethren today remain highly opposed to what they consider acts of sexual deviance, especially cases of infidelity to the marital bond and instances of homosexuality. While the strong Brethren opposition to homosexuality (Table 5) is very comparable to the attitude of Mennonites, both groups find this behavior more offensive than the public at large (75% of whom say that homosexual behavior is

Table 5: Percentage of Brethren who Consider Various Acts to be "Always wrong"

Activity	Percent who Consider it "Always Wrong"
Smoking Marijuana	92
Extra-Marital Sexual Intercourse	89
Homosexual Relations between Consenting Adults	85
Showing Disrespect to Parents	77
Smoking Cigarettes	71
Premarital Sexual Intercourse	67
Telling a Lie	65
Watching an "X-rated" Movie	62
Drinking Alcohol	51
Abortion	49
Divorce	18
Remarriage After Divorce	14
Marriage of a Christian to a Non-Christian	11
Marriage of a Brethren to a Non-Brethren	1

"always wrong"). Further reflecting their aversion to homosexuality, 70% of Brethren believe that homosexuals should not be allowed to teach in the public schools. For many Brethren today, homosexuality is an emotionally-charged issue on which the Brethren should take a resolute stand of opposition.

The same strong feeling of opposition, however, is not found on abortion. Only 49% of Brethren believe that abortion is "always wrong." An examination of Brethren responses to various questions on abortion reveals mixed sentiment. About equal numbers of Brethren agree (43%) as disagree (39%) with the statement: "A woman should have the right to choose whether or not to have an abortion." Similarly, when asked whether they favor a "ban on all abortions," 44% of Brethren answered "Yes," and 37% "No." While the church seems about evenly split on the issue of whether or not abortion is *always* wrong, a large majority (74%) of Brethren agree it is *usually* wrong.

The question of abortion is both logically and politically linked to the issue of equal rights for women. Where do Brethren stand on women's rights? Two-thirds (64%) of the national sample believe that "though it is not always possible, it is best if the wife stays at home and the husband works to support the family." In spite of this belief, more Brethren favor the Equal Rights Amendment (41%) than oppose it (31%), and three times as many favor the ordination of women (53%) as oppose it (18%). Still, only 49% of Brethren members *disagree* with the idea that "the husband should have the final say in the family's decision making." Again, tremendous diversity is seen in the denomination.

The Brethren tradition of nonconformity to the world obliges reflection upon one final lifestyle question: how do Brethren perceive their place in modern society? What vestiges of simple living remain? The most recent Annual Conference statement on dress (1917), reaffirmed the historic Brethren stance against "the fashions of the age, and extravagance in all manner of living." It advised that the Brethren should wear plain clothing, refrain from wearing neckties, and that women should refrain from wearing jewelry. Today, less than 75 years later, Brethren Profile data show that only one-quarter of the national membership agree with the concept that "Brethren should dress more simply than the average American." Twice as many (48%) Brethren disagree with that statement. What is more, 40% agree that it is appropriate "for Brethren to live the same lifestyle as other Americans." This contrasts with 37% who disagree. Perhaps the most significant finding of all, however, was that 56% of Brethren members responded "Not really" when asked, "Is there any important way in which the Church of the Brethren seems *different* to you from other "mainline" Protestant churches such as the Methodists or Presbyterians?" Only 44% said that the Brethren are different in some important way.

Brethren in the Modern World

Birthday dinners and birthday celebrations are commonplace today in Brethren homes. While this observation appears trite in the 1980s, it was only 100 years ago (1884) that the following query was considered by Annual Meeting:

> Is it right, according to the Gospel . . ., for members to make those birthday dinners or suppers, which are so highly esteemed among the world, and both members and others, joining together in feasting, and perhaps talking about worldly matters . . .?

The answer of the Annual Meeting was: "No, not right, as the principles of the Gospel . . . are almost universally violated."[26] How can something that today appears so innocent have universally violated that generation's gospel? This is the Brethren enigma.

When Brethren in 1985 reflect back upon their 19th century heritage, they do so with a mixture of pride and embarrassment. Some might be said to have a "tourist mentality" with respect to their own religious roots: their past is a thing to be peered at *from a distance*, in wonderment and curiosity, just as tourists in Lancaster County peer at the Amish people from the safe distance of their automobiles. Brethren are baffled that their forebears could ever have been so "closed-minded" in their thinking. Many think of these old Brethren as legalistic, "rule-bound," and even unloving in their treatment of the more worldly members of their community. The "old Brethren" are believed to have been preoccupied with religious minutiae such as bonnets and beards, rather than giving priority to more fundamental matters of the heart.

In this modern era of individualism, it is relatively easy to identify the excesses of the religious heritage, but who can speak for the "old Brethren" and identify current excesses? Were they here to take the pulse of the Church of the Brethren today, they might raise some of the following concerns: If it is true that the old Brethren were too intolerant of individuality, could it not also be true that Brethren today have become too tolerant? If one can err by being overly harsh in applying community standards for Christian living, is it not also possible that one can demand too little? If a church can lose sight of its mission in the world by turning inward toward itself, can it not also lose sight of itself, and its mission, by embracing too much of the world? If the error of the past century was to define the church as being altogether separate from the world, perhaps today's error is to identify the church too much with the world.

Sociologist Steven Tipton has observed that religion in America has undergone a fundamental metamorphosis. Originally authoritarian—stressing obedience to a religious authority known through faith and tradition—American religion has been transformed into a utilitarian expression of the diverse goals of individuals.[27] Stated more simply, religion in the modern world places less emphasis upon individual obedience to authoritative standards of belief and practice and more emphasis upon meeting the personal (and emotional) needs of individuals. Robert Bellah and his colleagues characterize this as a "therapeutic thinning out of belief and practice." They observe that much of mainline Protestant religion is afflicted by a "quasi-therapeutic blandness," meaning that by trying to fill the needs of varieties of people, the church is transformed into an institution that supports everything "in Christian love," and comes to stand for little.[28] Would the old Brethren, with their well-defined standards and obedient community, view the Church of the Brethren today as suffering from religious blandness?

One thing is certain: the Church of the Brethren is less clearly defined today than it was 100 years ago. The price of tolerating diversity among its members has been a certain moral vagueness. While non-Brethren of previous eras may have viewed the Dunkers as a "peculiar people," they also had a clear image of them as an honest, peaceful, nonmaterialistic, humble, and neighborly people. The word *Dunker* brought a focused image to mind. Such is not the case today; if the Brethren Profile data reveal anything, they reveal a portrait of tremendous diversity. There is so much variation among the modern Brethren that it is difficult to think of them in any sharply defined manner.

What is the Brethren mission in the modern world? Is it to reach out to as many diverse individuals as possible, providing them a loving community of support? Or, is it to uphold a prophetic Christian witness to the world? Can both of these be accomplished by a single denomination, or is there an unresolvable tension between the two? Should different denominations fulfill different roles in American religious life—some providing an accepting haven for those immersed in the secular maelstrom of American society and others providing a religious crosswind capable of altering the mainstream currents? If so, where do the Brethren fit into this partitioning of religious roles?

Surely, the Brethren heritage empowers its members, even today, to whisper a prophetic word in society's ear. To whisper of spirituality in an age of rampant consumerism; to speak of community in an age of excessive individualism; to tell of Christian morality in an age of "I'm OK/you're OK"; and to witness to peace in an age of nuclear uncertainty—all of these flow logically from the Brethren heritage.

Of course, the Church of the Brethren cannot (and should not) revive the old choice between obedience and excommunication. To do so would mean shutting out the majority of its members. Brethren today are irreversibly immersed in middle-America, not isolated on frontier farms. Their social environment requires them to place a high value upon individualism and personal decision-making. That is the way American life and work are structured. Yet, the demands of the modern world must not entirely overshadow the "ancient and primitive order" of our heritage. Were this ever to occur, the Brethren as a people who put their faith into practice, might finally fade into memory, even though the Church of the Brethren continues to survive.

Notes

1. The sample was limited to adult members of the Church of the Brethren—persons no longer living at home with their parents. The six smallest districts were excluded from the sampling frame for sampling efficiency. Survey results are generalizable to the 95% of the entire denominational membership which reside in the remaining 18 church districts.
2. For example, Brethren Profile data very closely replicated the national geographic distribution (state by state) of the members of the Church of the Brethren reported in *The Brethren Encyclopedia* (1983–1984), 1465–1478.
3. Further details concerning sampling design, research methodology, research objectives, findings, interpretations, and conclusions are reported in the author's PhD dissertation, in progress at the Department of Sociology, University of Virginia.
4. Sizable groups of Brethren also reside in Illinois, California, Kansas, and Iowa. None of the remaining 40 states has a membership in excess of 3,000.
5. These are data for 1980 taken from *The Brethren Encyclopedia* (1983–1984), 1476.
6. National membership data are taken from the *Yearbook: Church of the Brethren* (Elgin, IL: 1961), 17; *Yearbook: Church of the Brethren* (Elgin, IL: 1984), 306.
7. All US data in this chapter (unless otherwise indicated) are taken from the 1985 General Social Survey of the US population, conducted by the National Opinion Research Center (NORC) of the University of Chicago. Since NORC restricts its sample to US citizens 18 years of age or older, it is directly comparable to the sample in the Brethren Profile, which also excludes children.
8. The percentages of the US population (18 years of age or older) in the 65 years or older age group is taken from 1984 data from the US Bureau of the Census.
9. Percentages represent the cumulative distribution of NORC occupational data (1972–1985).
10. J. Howard Kauffman and Leland Harder, *Anabaptists: Four Centuries Later* (Scottsdale, PA: 1975), 67. The study by Kauffman and

Harder encompasses five, organizationally different, Mennonite groups: the Mennonite Church, the General Conference Mennonite Church, the Mennonite Brethren, the Brethren in Christ Church, and the Evangelical Mennonite Church. All Mennonite data reported in this chapter are aggregated across the five groups. Although there exist marked differences between these Mennonite bodies, such distinctions are beyond the scope of this chapter.

11. A 1963 sample of 3,000 Northern California church members, including Roman Catholics, Southern Baptists, and Methodists, was reported in Rodney Stark and Charles Y. Glock, *American Piety: The Nature of Religious Commitment* (Berkeley: 1968), 86.

12. Rated as influential (in decreasing order of importance) were: 1) the New Testament; 2) immediate family; 3) Brethren pastor; 4) the Old Testament; 5) Brethren friends; 6) Brethren relatives; 7) leaders of the Church of the Brethren; 8) non-Brethren friends; 9) non-Brethren relatives; 10) leaders of other religious groups; 11) Annual Conference decisions; 12) television; 13) local, state, or national political leaders.

13. Jesse H. Ziegler, *The Broken Cup: Three Generations of Dunkers* (Elgin, IL: 1942), 105.

14. This is certainly because of many factors, not least of which would be the cost of a year's education at a Brethren-related college.

15. Alexander Mack, Sr., . . . *Rites and Ordinances of the House of God . . . also Ground Searching Questions . . .* (Ashland, OH: 1939), 89.

16. It is likely that most of those who continue to be baptized outdoors do so for want of an indoor pool or baptistry.

17. Brethren of the 18th and 19th centuries spoke of "defenselessness" or "nonresistance" rather than a "peace position." The former were positions of Christian obedience in a world where the "Kingdom" was distinct from the "world." The latter has greater political overtones, is more of a statement about what governments should be doing in a world to be "Christianized."

18. Ziegler, *Broken Cup* (1942), 118.

19. Responses of "uncertain" were omitted from the computation of percentages for the Mennonite data, in order to increase compatibility with Brethren Profile data; Kauffman and Harder, *Anabaptists* (1975), 133.

20. Glock and Stark, *American Piety* (1968), 28; Kauffman and Harder, *Anabaptists* (1975), 105.

21. Princeton Religious Research Center, *Gallup Report: Religion in America* (1985), 48.

22. *Gallup Report* (1985), 47.
23. Ziegler, *Broken Cup* (1942), 64.
24. On a national basis, 74% of Americans report that they use alcohol, while only 27% report that they are total abstainers.
25. Ziegler, *Broken Cup* (1942), 117, 118.
26. *Revised Minutes of the Annual Meetings of the German Baptist Brethren* (Elgin, IL: 1908), 125.
27. Steven M. Tipton, *Getting Saved from the Sixties* (Berkeley: 1982), 1–14.
28. Robert N. Bellah, Richard Madsen, William M. Sullivan, Ann Swidler, and Steven M. Tipton, *Habits of the Heart: Individualism and Commitment in American Life* (Berkeley: 1985), 237–249.

12

Bibliographical Essay

Donald F. Durnbaugh

Those interested in learning more about the Brethren should turn first to the three volumes of *The Brethren Encyclopedia* (1983–1984). The first two volumes contain about 6,000 articles on all aspects of Brethren history—doctrines, institutions, leading personalities, publications, geographical areas, mission, service outreach, and more—written by hundreds of authors. All of the Brethren bodies are included. The third volume contains charts, statistics, maps, and many lists; the most extensive list contains brief information on every known ordained minister from 1708 to 1980.

Searchers will also find there a long (over 250 pages) bibliography of books and articles about the Brethren; unfortunately it has no subject index. Rather complete listings of Brethren-authored materials are found in *Brethren Life and Thought* (Winter/Spring, 1964), (Spring, 1966)—with a topical index also covering the extensive 1964 list, and (Autumn, 1970). Compilations of theses and dissertations on the Brethren are provided in *Brethren Life and Thought* (Winter, 1958; Autumn, 1970). A related movement is covered in Eugene E. Doll and Anneliese M. Funke, *The Ephrata Cloister: An Annotated Bibliography* (1946), with publications by and about Ephrata.

Many references to the Brethren are found in bibliographies on Pennsylvania and on the Pennsylvania Germans. The most complete are: Emil Meynen, *Bibliography on German Settlements in Colonial North America, Especially on the Pennsylvania Germans and Their Descendants* (1937, repr. 1982), dated but still valuable; Norman B. Wilkinson, *Bibliography of Pennsylvania History,* 2nd ed. (1957), periodically updated; Steven M. Benjamin, *German-American Bibliogra-*

phy for 1979, with Supplements for 1971–1979 (1980), annually updated; Don Heinrich Tolzman, *German-Americana: A Bibliography* (1975). Librarians at the University of Göttingen are currently working on a revision of the classical study by Oswald Seidensticker, *The First Century of German Printing in America, 1728–1830* (1893, repr. 1980).

For the serious student, even the best narrative accounts and analyses cannot replace encounter with the original documents. These are made available in published (and at times translated) form in the following series: Donald F. Durnbaugh, ed., *European Origins of the Brethren* (1958); Donald F. Durnbaugh, ed., *The Brethren in Colonial America* (1967); Roger E. Sappington, *The Brethren in the New Nation* (1976); and Roger E. Sappington, *The Brethren in Industrial America* (1986). A basic source for early Brethren, as well as Ephrata, history, is J. Max Hark, trans., *Chronicon Ephratense: A History of the Community of Seventh Day Baptists at Ephrata, Lancaster County, Penna.* (1889, repr. 1972). See also Eugene E. Doll and Felix Reichmann, eds., *Ephrata As Seen by Contemporaries* (1952). Richard MacMaster and others, eds., *Conscience in Crisis* (1979) contains many documents referring to the Brethren in colonial America.

Useful introductions to Anabaptism are: William R. Estep, *The Anabaptist Story*, rev. ed. (1975) and Walter Klaassen, *Anabaptism: Neither Catholic nor Protestant* (1973). An excellent anthology of source documents is found in Klaassen's *Anabaptism in Outline* (1981). The standard description of Pietism in English is found in two volumes written by F. Ernest Stoeffler: *The Rise of Evangelical Pietism* (1965) and *German Pietism During the Eighteenth Century* (1973). Stoeffler edited *Continental Pietism and Early American Christianity* (1976), which contains a chapter on the Brethren in colonial America by Donald F. Durnbaugh. A useful introduction to Pietism is Dale W. Brown, *Understanding Pietism* (1978). Both Anabaptism and Pietism are included in Donald F. Durnbaugh, *The Believers' Church: The History and Character of Radical Protestantism* (1968; repr. 1985).

There is no adequate general history of the Brethren movement. Floyd E. Mallott, *Studies in Brethren History* (1954, repr. 1980), focuses on some aspects of the history. Albert T. Ronk, *History of the Brethren Church* (1968), gives general coverage of the shared Brethren history until 1881 from the "Progressive Brethren" viewpoint, and then the story of the Brethren Church; it replaces the classic older work by Henry R. Holsinger, *History of the Tunkers and the Brethren Church* (1901, repr. 1962), by the founder of the Brethren church. Homer A. Kent, Sr., *Conquering Frontiers* (1972), follows the same pattern as Ronk, from the viewpoint of the Grace Brethren. John M. Kimmel, *Chronicles of the Brethren* (1951), provides concise information in chronicle form, following the history of the Old German Baptist Brethren since 1881.

The pioneer history, *A History of the German Baptist Brethren in Europe and America* (1899, repr. 1907, 1961, 1971), by Martin G. Brumbaugh, covers basically the 18th century and is now outdated. A contemporary, Julius F. Sachse, published a richly-illustrated, two-volume history, *German Sectarians of Pennsylvania: 1708-1742; 1742-1800* (1899-1900); long considered the standard work, it has been criticized by scholars for its imaginative interpretations. The capstone of earlier Brethren historical writing is the bicentennial volume edited by D. L. Miller, *Two Centuries of the Church of the Brethren* (1908).

Anecdotal history was published by Freeman Ankrum, *Sidelights on Brethren History* (1962), H. Austin Cooper, *Two Centuries of Brothersvalley Church of the Brethren* (1962), and Rolland Flory, *Lest We Forget and Tales of Yesteryear* (1973-1978), five volumes. Some writing has been for educational purposes. Emmert F. Bittinger, *Heritage and Promise*, rev. ed. (1983), is a study guide. Virginia S. Fisher, *The Brethren Story*, rev. ed. (1974), was written for young people, as were the older works by J. E. Miller, *The Story of Our Church*, rev. ed. (1957) and C. Ernest Davis, *Our Church* (1923). Otho Winger, *History and Doctrine of the Church of the Brethren* (1919), has a textbook format.

Rich sources for understanding Brethren heritage are found in histories published by many districts of the Church of the Brethren. The first was by Southern Illinois (1907), the most elaborate by Eastern Pennsylvania (1915, repr. 1922, 1967, 1971, 1977), the most recent by Middle Pennsylvania (1980). Three were written by Roger E. Sappington—Idaho/Western Montana (1966), the Carolinas (1971), and Virginia (1973). Grace Brethren in Southern Ohio published a history in 1975; a comparable volume for the Old German Baptist Brethren is *"Roots by the River"* (1974) by Marcus Miller. In addition to district histories which typically contain congregational sketches, many congregations have published anniversary pamphlets, booklets, and books on their own. The most extensive is that of Roland L. Howe on the First Church of Philadelphia (1943).

Monographs and biographies also contain valuable historical information of general interest. Among these (in chronological order) are: George N. Falkenstein, *The German Baptist Brethren or Dunkers* (1900); John D. Flory, *Literary Activity of the German Baptist Brethren in the Eighteenth Century* (1908); Gladdys E. Muir, *Settlement of the Brethren on the Pacific Slope* (1939); Donald F. Durnbaugh, "Brethren Beginnings," PhD thesis, University of Pennsylvania (1960); Esther F. Rupel, "An Investigation of the . . . Prescribed Dress Worn by Members of the Church of the Brethren," PhD thesis, University of Minnesota (1971); David B. Eller, "The Brethren in the Western Ohio Valley, 1790–1850," PhD thesis, Miami (OH) University (1976); James H. Lehman, *The Old Brethren* (1976), on the decade of the 1840s; William G. Willoughby, *Counting the Cost: The Life of Alexander Mack, 1679–1735* (1979); and Stephen L. Longenecker, *The Christopher Sauers: Courageous Printers . . .* (1981).

Several dissertations have been written on Brethren theology. The most comprehensive is Dale R. Stoffer, "The Background and Development of Thought and Practice in the German Baptist Brethren (Dunkers) and the Brethren (Progressive) Churches," Fuller Theological Seminary (1980). See also William G. Willoughby, "The Beliefs of the Early Brethren," Boston University (1951); C. David Ensign, "Radical German Pietism, c. 1675–c. 1760," Boston University (1955); and Herbert W. Hogan, "The Intellectual Impact of the 20th Century on the Church of the Brethren," Claremont Graduate School (1958).

The pioneer Brethren theology was by Peter Nead, *Theological Writings on Various Subjects* (1850, repr. 1866, 1950). Of the later writings, one of the most widely used was Robert H. Miller, Sr., *The Doctrine of the Brethren Defended* (1876, repr. 1899, 1907). Other popular books were J. H. Moore, *The New Testament Doctrines* (1914); D. W. Kurtz, *An Outline of the Fundamental Doctrines of the Faith*, rev. ed. (1914); D. W. Kurtz, S. S. Blough, and C. C. Ellis, *Studies in Doctrine and Devotion* (1919); Edward Frantz, *Basic Belief* (1934); Warren W. Slabaugh, *The Role of the Servant* (1954); and William M. Beahm, *Studies in Christian Belief* (1958).

In the Brethren Church, the leading studies in theology (including the ordinances) were: C. F. Yoder, *God's Means of Grace* (1908); James M. Tombaugh, *Some Fundamental Christian Doctrines* (1919); J. Allen Miller, *Christian Doctrine* (1946); and Joseph R. Shultz, *Soul of the Symbols* (1966). The leading theologians among the Grace Brethren were Louis Baumann and Alva McClain. Baumann's *The Faith Once For All Delivered Unto the Saints* (1908) went through many editions. McClain's major work was *The Greatness of the Kingdom* (1959). The other Brethren bodies produced some doctrinal tracts but no extensive studies of doctrine.

Sociologists have found the Brethren movement an interesting subject. The earliest study was *The Dunkers: A Sociological Interpretation* (1906, repr. 1972), by John L. Gillin, a leader in the Brethren Church who went on to become a well-known scholar in the field. Some of the later studies were: Frederick D. Dove, *Cultural Changes in the Church of the Brethren* (1932); Jesse H. Ziegler, *The Broken Cup* (1942); Robert F. Eshelman, "A Study of Changes in the Value Patterns in the Church of the Brethren," PhD thesis, Cornell University (1948); Emmert F. Bittinger, "The Church-Family Relationship in the Church of the Brethren Across Two Centuries," MA thesis, University of Maryland (1951); Robert B. Blair, "Modernization and Subgroup Formation in a Religious Organization," PhD thesis, Northwestern University (1974); and Carl F. Bowman, "Cultural Transformation Among the Brethren: 1850 to the Present," PhD thesis in progress, University of Virginia.

The Brethren position of peace and nonresistance was studied by social scientists. These include: Don Royer, "The Acculturation Process and the Peace Doctrine of the Church of the Brethren . . .," PhD thesis, University of Chicago (1955); Lorell Weiss, "Socio-Psychological Factors in the Pacifism of the Church of the Brethren During the Second World War," PhD thesis, University of California (1957); and Ronald C. Arnett, "A Dialogical Interpretation of Interpersonal Conflict Viewed from the Nonviolent Peacemaking Tradition," PhD thesis, Ohio State University (1978), published in revised form as *Dwell in Peace: Applying Nonviolence to Everyday Relationships* (1980).

Rufus D. Bowman, *The Church of the Brethren and War* (1944, repr. 1971) is the most complete study. An updated interpretation is Dale W. Brown, *Biblical Pacifism* (1986), a revision of *Brethren and Pacifism* (1970). There is important historical information on the Brethren in the detailed histories by Peter Brock, *Pacifism in Europe* (1972) and *Pacifism in the United States* (1968). The work of Brethren Civilian Public Service is described in Leslie Eisan, *Pathways of Peace* (1948). The theological basis of Brethren pacifism is included in Donald F. Durnbaugh, ed., *On Earth Peace* (1978), with discussions between the Historic Peace Churches and European churches.

Roger E. Sappington's study, *Brethren Social Policy* (1961), a condensation of his PhD thesis (1959), gives the most complete history of Brethren Service activity. It may be supplemented by memoirs of participants in BSC programs—Donald F. Durnbaugh, ed., *To Serve the Present Age* (1975); a description of a major BSC center—Kenneth I.

Morse, *New Windsor Center* (1979); and a booklet—Lorell Weiss, *Ten Years of Brethren Service* (1952).

The mission program of the Church of the Brethren was earlier written about extensively. Important books are: Galen B. Royer, *Thirty-Three Years of Missions in the Church of the Brethren* (1913) and Elgin S. Moyer, *Missions in the Church of the Brethren*. The individual "mission fields" were described in many publications. A recent booklet on Church of the Brethren missions by B. Merle Crouse, *Bread Upon the Waters* (1976), is revised from a chapter in *The Church of the Brethren: Past and Present* (1971). A general study of Brethren Church missions is Albert T. Ronk, *History of Brethren Missionary Movements* (1971).

Higher education has drawn much interest. The first comprehensive study was S. Z. Sharp, *The Educational History of the Church of the Brethren* (1923). Dissertations on Brethren education were produced by John S. Noffsinger (Columbia University, 1925), Tobias F. Henry (University of Pittsburgh, 1938), Auburn A. Boyers (University of Pittsburgh, 1969), and Robert V. Hanle (University of Pennsylvania, 1974). A book prepared as the basis for a study conference is James H. Lehman, *Beyond Anything Foreseen: A Study of the History of Higher Education in the Church of the Brethren* (1976). Brethren-related colleges have also published anniversary volumes.

In recent years there has been increased study of Brethren worship and hymnody. An overview is provided in Kenneth I. Morse, *Move in Our Midst* (1977). Nevin Fisher wrote *The History of Brethren Hymnbooks* (1950); it is updated on German-language hymns and hymnals by Hedda T. Durnbaugh, *The German Hymnody of the Brethren, 1720–1903* (1986). Donald R. Hinks, *Brethren Hymn Books and Hymnals: 1720–1884* (1986) is a detailed bibliographical study of ca. 150 Brethren hymnbooks and their publishing history.

Many biographies have been written about Brethren personalities. They are listed in the citations appended to articles in *The Brethren Encyclopedia*. A Brethren "Who's Who" was compiled by Elgin S. Moyer; although never published, it was used as the basis for many encyclopedia articles. Books that contain numbers of biographies are (in chronological order): D. L. Miller and Galen B. Royer, *Some Who Led* (1912); W. Arthur Cable and Homer F. Sanger, *Educational Blue Book and Directory of the Church of the Brethren* (1923); John S. Flory, *Builders of the Church of the Brethren* (1925); J. H. Moore, *Some Brethren Pathfinders* (1929); Mary Garber, *Brethren Story Caravan* (1950); *Brethren Builders in Our Century* (1952); Mary Garber and others, *Brethren Trail Blazers* (1960); Inez Long, *Faces Among the*

Faithful (1962), on women. Biographies of missionaries were published in booklets by the Brethren Church, Church of the Brethren, and Grace Brethren.

Statistical analyses of the Brethren are contained in *The Brethren Encyclopedia* (1983–1984), 1465–1478. The pioneer gleaning was done by the Baptist pastor/historian Morgan Edwards in his *Materials Towards a History of American Baptists Both British and German* (1770ff.) Because of Brethren disinclination to gather such statistics, it was not until the late 19th century that a collection of such data was published. This was Howard Miller, *Record of the Faithful* (1882), which also contains information on the date of congregational foundings and names of ministerial leaders. With the beginning of the publication of almanacs by Brethren publishers, lists and addresses of ministers became available. After 1911, membership and other statistics began to be included. In the early 20th century, the almanacs were replaced by yearbooks, which provide the most complete statistical records for the Brethren Church, Church of the Brethren, and Fellowship of Grace Brethren Churches. Private individuals publish directories (with statistics) for the Old German Baptist Brethren. The Dunkard Brethren have no such separately published data but include lists of congregations and ministers (without tabulation of membership) in their church periodical.

A still incompletely explored source of Brethren history is the denominational periodical. Beginning with the *Gospel Visitor* (1851) and extending to the present day, these periodicals provide virtually complete information on personalities, teachings, attitudes, and development. Their use is hampered by several factors: 1) some are scarce and hardly accessible; 2) some are deteriorating physically and can barely be used; and 3) there is no full name and subject index. The last point has one exception: a computer printout by author, title, and subject for articles in *The Vindicator*. The production of a comprehensive index to Brethren periodicals is an urgent research priority.

The current denominational periodicals (all issued monthly) are: *Bible Monitor* (Dunkard Brethren); *Brethren Evangelist* (Brethren Church): *Brethren Missionary Herald* (Grace Brethren): *Messenger* (Church of the Brethren); and *Vindicator* (Old German Baptist Brethren). In addition, *Brethren Life and Thought* (1955ff.) is published quarterly in the interests of the Church of the Brethren and *Old Order Notes* (1978ff.) is issued on an irregular basis in the interests of the Old German Baptist Brethren. The Fellowship of Brethren Genealogists publishes a quarterly *Newsletter* (1969ff.); *Mennonite Family History* (1982ff.) includes a regular section on Brethren families. An earlier journal edited by Floyd E. Mallott, *Schwarzenau* (1939–1942), contains many historical articles.

The primary sources for questions of doctrine and practice for all five Brethren bodies are the collections of printed minutes. These are available, in most cases, both in separate annual form and cumulative collections; titles of published minutes may be found in *The Brethren Encyclopedia*. The first compilation was made by Henry Kurtz: *The Brethren's Encyclopedia* (1867).

Relatively complete collections of books, periodicals, and records on Brethren history are found in the libraries of colleges and seminaries related to or sponsored by Brethren denominations. These include: Ashland College and Theological Library (Ashland, OH); Bethany Theological Seminary (Oak Brook, IL); Bridgewater College (Bridgewater, VA); Elizabethtown College (Elizabethtown, PA); Grace College and Theological Seminary (Winona Lake, IN); Juniata College (Huntingdon, PA); Manchester College (North Manchester, IN); McPherson College (McPherson, KS);; and the University of La Verne (La Verne, CA). The most complete collection is found in the (Church of the) Brethren Historical Library and Archives (Elgin, IL); research materials and photographs collected in the course of creating *The Brethren Encyclopedia* are also deposited there. The BHLA pursues an active acquisition policy, collecting retrospective as well as new materials. It also houses the most complete genealogical data presently available.

Index of Persons, Places, and Subjects